DRIFTING ON A READ

SUNY series, INTERRUPTIONS:
Border Testimony(ies) and Critical Discourse/s
Henry A. Giroux, Editor

DRIFTING ON A READ

Jazz as a Model for Writing

MICHAEL JARRETT

STATE UNIVERSITY OF NEW YORK PRESS

Published by
State University of New York Press, Albany

© 1999 State University of New York

For information, address State University of New York
Press, State University Plaza, Albany, N.Y., 12246

Production by E. Moore
Marketing by Anne Valentine

Library of Congress Cataloging-in-Publication Data

Jarrett, Michael, 1953–
    Drifting on a read : jazz as a model for writing / Michael
Jarrett.
        p.   cm. — (SUNY series, interruptions — border
testimony(ies) and critical discourse(s)
    Includes bibliographical references and index.
    ISBN 0-7914-4097-4 (hc. : alk. paper). — ISBN 0-7914-4098-2 (pbk.
: alk. paper)
        1. Written communication. 2. Jazz—History and criticism.
3. Popular culture. 4. Criticism. I. Title. II. Series:
Interruptions.
ML3849.J39 1999
781.65'11—dc21   98-11823
                                                      ·   CIP
                                                               MN

10 9 8 7 6 5 4 3 2 1

For
Pam and the Chattanooga Public Library

Contents

Preface

He suddenly became aware that the weird, drowsy throb of the African song and dance had been swinging drowsily in his brain for an unknown lapse of time.
                              —George Washington Cable (96)

Music is an oversimplification of the situation we actually are in.
                              —John Cage (149)

Because his every note is a response to prior texts, reinforcing or challenging established ways of playing, the jazz musician shares a special kinship with the critical theorist. Both proceed by elaborating or palimpsestically "writing over" that which is already composed. Both push interpretation until it becomes invention. That said, I encourage readers to conceive of this book as a literary analog of jazz: My story and critical orientation serve me in much the same way that autobiography and a jazz tradition serve the jazz musician. If that makes sense, then I can readily explain the purpose and structure of the study that follows. It begins with a warmup, a cadenza that introduces main concerns. Blame Paul Gonsalves, John Coltrane, and Sonny Rollins for its length. Next follow four chapters—four choruses actually—that first exposit and, then, play on the *tropes* or signifiers of connotation that characterize jazz for our culture.

The tropes of jazz—I label them *satura*, obbligato, rhapsody, and *charivari*—mark jazz as it enters symbolic discourse. Or more simply, the tropes of jazz bring jazz into language. They are monster metaphors. They enable jazzography, which is to say all writing that finds a referent or inspiration in jazz. Because the tropes of jazz grant music a voice—and organize it on a highly abstract level—they enable us to recognize jazz as a music with meaning. More importantly, these tropes are useful for both exegesis and grammatology. That is to say, they function (1) *hermeneutically*, as pedagogical tools or ways of *writing about* jazz, and (2) *heuretically*, as tools for invention or *writing with* jazz. The tropes of jazzography provide jazz with an explanation, but they provide invention with a methodology.

Heuretics—anything but a common word—prompts a varied set of connotations: eureka, heurestics, heretics, hieratic, heretics, and, yes, diuretics. It represents the flow of theory, ideas, and writing. "It is based," Krin Gabbard tells me, "on the Greek verb *heuriskein*, 'to find out,' 'to discover,' 'to invent.'" *Heureka* literally means, "I have found [it]." By the Middle Ages, heuretics and hermeneutics (a term used to designate absolutely any interpretive grid) were vocabulary words for theologians. But while hermeneutics migrated to the humanities early on—legitimating the study of texts and providing scholars with methodologies of reading—heuretics remained largely an art practice until the coming of postmodernism. The term itself did not enter critical discourse until Gregory Ulmer introduced it in *Teletheory* and developed it in *Heuretics*. In both of these books, Ulmer observes that vanguard artists have routinely employed theory generatively. They've taken what, for critics, would function as a means to interpretation and turned it into a template for invention. For example, recall André Breton's use of psychoanalytic theory as suggestive of ways to make surrealist art. Or consider Sergei Eisenstein. From Marxism, he created (or at least defended) a radical, montage style of film editing.

Poststructuralist literary theory, on the other hand, is beginning to shift the teacher-student relationship and to learn from vanguard art. Or consider that, while the philosophical legacy of poststructuralism remains a topic of controversy, its "artistic" import is indisputable. Derrida, Barthes, Deleuze, Serres, and others not only changed the direction of critical theory, they altered its *look*. To scholars, who diligently tell their charges that form is as important as or that it is indistinguishable from content, this should matter. Generally, though, it hasn't. Most of the scholarly writing done in English and comparative literature departments still looks like text trying hard to be philosophy, political science, sociology, or psychology—anything but art. Additionally, while most of the texts required in contemporary literature courses are beautiful, their beauty is only occasionally the focus of study. Students enroll in courses confident that, for example, *Madame Bovary* is on the reading list because it is somehow great art. They leave having discovered that Flaubert's novel is psychology or social criticism by other means.

The catch is, this urge to politicize and demythologize is a good thing. There's no reason to reverse what has become "normal science" in the humanities. Doing so would be naïve and wrongheaded—counterproductive to the goals of a liberal education. But the question arises: How might the contemporary humanities classroom take into account the artistic strategies of texts, actually learn invention from art, without forsaking interpretation and critique? Poststructuralist theory recommends turning objects of study into tutor texts. Several American scholars have applied this lesson to their own work with great success. Off the top of my head, I can think of Hugh Kenner, Ihab Hassan, Rachel DuPlessis, Greil Marcus, and Avital Ronell. There is, however, a group of theorists associated with the University of Florida in Gainesville that constitutes something of a School of Heuretics. I consider myself part of this group, which includes Gregory Ulmer, Robert Ray, Craig Saper, Camilla Griggers, Jon McKenzie, Eric Faden, and Christian Keathley.

Oriented toward the pleasures of theory and the love of jazz, *Drifting on a Read* is designed to show how one might employ popular culture—actually representations of popular culture—as a means to invention and innovation. But it does not abandon philosophical critique (identified with the Yale School and deconstruction) or cultural critique (identified with the University of Birmingham Centre for Contemporary Cultural Studies and the Center for 20th Century Studies at the University of Wisconsin). While it may be presumptuous of critical theory to speak knowingly about music, it is perfectly logical for theory to analyze the end product of musicology and ethnomusicology. That product, after all, is not music, but language. Thus, I am confident that theory has much to teach jazzography (about hermeneutics). I am, however, equally convinced that jazz—inseparable from its representations—has much to teach theory (about heuretics). Modernists, especially in Harlem and Paris, were onto these lessons years ago. They heard jazz as a paradigm for *writing with texts*, a model for pushing interpretation until it becomes invention. Their experiments in heuretics—interrupted by the Holocaust and World War II—have been taken up again by poststructuralists. This study suggests ways to further develop experimental writing by once again bringing the inventive practices of jazz into theory and cultural studies classrooms.

～～

In this most secular of ages it is somehow fitting that acknowledgments take the form of prayers, as Derrida would remind us, always already heard and answered. In every case, they are benedictions posing as invocations. Written after books are complete, they nevertheless stand at their beginnings; their placement, in the liturgy of the Book, represents a call to personal muses that will be summarily answered. Here, then, are the names that are, to me, magical. First is Pam, my wife. She's interested in theory sometimes, and in jazz seldom. Her love is mysterious and motivational. Next are our sons, Adam, Nat, and Ian. Then, there's Gregory Ulmer. When I was a grad student at the University of Florida, he directed my dissertation (a very different version of what ultimately became this book). He continues to support my writing. Finally, there's a host of inspirational figures I'd like to recognize: Richard and Yvonne Jarrett, Krin Gabbard, Robert Ray, Michael and Lori Fagien, Jon Michael Spencer, Will Garrett-Petts, Randy Rutsky, Anthony DeCurtis, Karen Smythe, Jed Rasula, Craig Kleinman, Byron Borger, Jay Jackson and Dan Missildine, Bruce Carnevale, Iko's Records (Paul, Dave, Jack, Todd, and Cindy), Eric Whiteside, Marc Weidenbaum, Jackson Griffith, Gary Collison, John Madden, Meredith Rousseau, Linda Kline, my colleagues at Penn State York, and at SUNY Press Priscilla Ross, Jennie Doling, and Anne Valentine. Fred Haag initiated the design that became this book's cover, making concrete my vague specification that it needed to look like a design Reid Miles might have created for a beginner's level music book.

The financial support of the Pennsylvania State University made it possible for me to write this book. Portions of it have appeared in *American Literary History, South Atlantic Quarterly, Strategies, Essays on Canadian Writing, Black Sacred Music, LIT, Integrating Visual and Verbal Literacies* (Inkshed Publications), *Pulse!,* and *Jazziz.* A version of the signature experiment that concludes chapter 2 was published in *Text Book: An Introduction to Literary Language* (St. Martin's). I am grateful for the permission to reprint.

Acknowledgments

Vance Bourjaily. "In and Out of Storyville: Jazz and Fiction." Used by permission of the author.

Sterling A. Brown. "Cabaret." From *The Collected Poems of Sterling A. Brown*. Copyright © 1991 by HarperCollins Publishers. Used by permission of Harper Collins Publishers.

Duke Ellington. "Music Is My Mistress." From *Music Is My Mistress*. © 1971 by Doubleday, a division of Bantam Doubleday Dell Publishing Group, Inc. Used by permission of Doubleday.

Bernard Gendron. "Jamming at Le Boeuf: Jazz and the Paris Avant-Garde." *Discourse*. Reprinted with the permission of the author.

Thomas Lewis. "Reference and Dissemination: Althusser after Derrida." *Diacritics*. © 1983 by The Johns Hopkins University Press. Reprinted with the permission of The Johns Hopkins University Press.

William Matthews. "Bmp Bmp." From *The Jazz Poetry Anthology*. Used by permission of the author's family.

Bill Milkowski. "Eno." © 1983 by *Down Beat*. Reprinted with the permission of Down Beat.

"Muscadine Jam" reprinted by permission of Grosset & Dunlap, Inc. from *Southern Cooking* by S. R. Dull. © 1941 by Mrs. S. R. Dull, copyright © 1968 by Grosset & Dunlap, Inc.

From *Coming through Slaughter* by Michael Ondaatje. © 1976 by Michael Ondaatje. Reprinted by permission of W. W. Norton & Company, Inc.

Craig Owens. "The Allegorical Impulse: Toward a Theory of Postmodernism." © 1980 by October. Reprinted with the permission of the author's family.

Jon Pareles. "It's Got a Beat and You Can Surrender to It." *The New York Times.* © 1993 by The New York Times Co. Reprinted by permission.

Gunther Schuller. From *Early Jazz: Its Roots and Musical Development.* © 1968 by Oxford University Press. Used by permission of Oxford University Press, Inc.

R. J. Smith. "Dixie Fried: Jim Dickinson's Memphis Productions." Copyright © 1992 by The Village Voice. Reprinted with the permission of The Village Voice.

Michael Zwerin. "Sax and the Man." Used by permission of the author.

∾∾∾

Cadenza:
Jazz as a Model for Writing

*"I mean, I'll have a lot of studying to do, and I'll have to
study everything, but, I mean, I want to play with—jazz
musicians."*

—James Baldwin (189)

*Couldn't I try. . . . Naturally, it wouldn't be a question of
a tune . . . but couldn't I, in another medium? . . . It
would have to be a book: I don't know how to do anything else.*

—Jean-Paul Sartre (178)

Warming up a Riff

Everyone must know this anecdote. A socialite asked Louis
Armstrong to define jazz. He replied, "Lady, if you gotta ask what
it is, you'll never know."

No other story that brings or, rather, that refuses to bring jazz
into language has attained wider currency. Within the realm of jazz
discourse, it is endlessly repeated and evoked. It enjoys the status
of proverb, imparting a simple but profound truth: Jazz defies cir-
cumscription. And it resists inscription, foiling those who would
encode it as words, as images on TV and movie screens, or as
graphic notations on musical scores. Jazz even thwarts those who
attempt to capture it on magnetic tape. (As cognoscenti are apt to
remind us, recordings only indicate a faint trace of what jazz giants
actually sounded like.) In short, jazz is paradoxically represented as
music that inevitably eludes representation. It needs no apologist,
says Louis Armstrong. It prefers to speak for itself—thank you.

Or as Elvis Costello once said in a remark now widely quoted,

1

"Writing about music is like dancing about architecture. It's a really stupid thing to want to do" (qtd. in Goodwin, 1). Costello's wit is notoriously barbed, which ensures that interviews with him are always thoroughly enjoyable. But his sentiments, echoing and extending Armstrong's, are diametrically opposed to mine. First, as a side point, I'd jump at the chance to see dancing about architecture. Second, writing about music is hardly any more problematic than writing about any other subject.

Nevertheless, this book isn't, strictly speaking, "writing about music." It's not an attempt to describe what jazz is. Its subject is *jazzography*: what people say jazz is. It shifts the focus of study from music to representations of music, although I readily admit that jazz and its representations are ultimately inseparable. Just as jazzography (a neologism referring to all writing about jazz) relies on jazz for its existence, jazz is shaped and sustained by texts that bring it into language. Certainly, these texts include the instructions of a master improviser to a neophyte, recordings and radio transmissions, and charts or arrangements for bands. But they also include musicological and ethnomusicological studies as well as television programs, movies, and literary works. I plan to pay special attention to this latter group of texts.

In this respect, *Drifting on a Read* resembles Hayden White's *Metahistory* and Edward Said's *Orientalism*. Like the authors of these books, I theorize a group of texts that constitutes a body of knowledge. My attention is thus directed toward "style, figures of speech, setting, narrative devices, historical and social circumstances, *not* the correctness of the representation nor its fidelity to some great original" (Said, 21). White's work characterizes the central historical texts of the nineteenth century as "*formalizations* of poetic insights," and it elaborates a schema that systematically graphs how these insights became rhetorical tropes and, eventually, plots, arguments, and ideologies of history (xii). Said's work regards Orientalism as "a *distribution* of geopolitical awareness into aesthetic, scholarly, economic, sociological, historical, and philological texts, . . . an *elaboration* not only of a basic geographical distinction . . . but also of a whole series of 'interests'" (12). My conceptualization of jazzography follows the lead of these two scholars, but my emphasis differs from theirs. White foregrounds the logic of consciousness: how historical thinkers chose conceptual, rhetorical strategies for explaining and representing data (x). Said foregrounds the logic of ideology: how "intellectual, aesthetic, scholarly, and cultural energies" make an imperialist tradition (15). I foreground writing, the "logic" of the signifier: how the discourse of jazz models or projects jazz music to this culture by granting jazz a voice and organizing it on a highly abstract level.

So we begin with this basic question: When people refuse to let jazz "speak for itself"—when they knowingly violate interdictions forbidding representation—what do they say? Answered simply, they say that jazz is a topic worth arguing about. While detractors may dispute its value (Theodor Adorno is infamous on this account), no one questions the cultural significance of jazz. It provided modernism with a soundtrack, and the United States with a popular art form and a coveted export. It shaped the music of this country (jazz/blues and country/ballads form the double helix of American popular music), and it affected the world's music in a manner analogous to Hollywood's effect on world cinema. Today, there are jazz bands in virtually every country, and the methodology of jazz, like the methodology of Hollywood (continuity editing), has been assimilated by musics as dissimilar as the Argentinean tango and South African mbaqanga.

Good enough. Because jazz is important, its representations are also worthy of study. But what have people said that jazz is? As one might expect, arguments regarding the essential characteristics of the music abound, but nobody has constructed a definition that satisfies everybody. That's hardly surprising. Still, on one primary point there's consensus. Jazz is always understood as dependent on improvisation. It is music that drifts on a read. It starts with what is given and spins off new melodies, rhythms, and harmonies. That's the main reason modernists—especially artists associated with surrealism and the Harlem Renaissance—found it attractive. That's also why it later found favor with Beats in the '50s and black radicals in the '60s. All of these groups heard jazz as "authentic," redolent of some essence, but they also believed that it posed an alternative to "classical" ways of thinking, writing, and producing art. Jazz has historically modeled generalizable strategies for invention, strategies we might characterize collectively as *tropes*.

Out of the Tropics

The word "trope" refers to "turns" or "tricks" of language, but it's also a musical term that, used loosely, signifies "any interpolation of text, music, or both into a liturgical chant" (Randel, 523). As readers might recall, most medievalists hold that it was from tropes—specifically, the *Quem quaeritis* texts—that medieval drama developed. David Bevington writes:

> According to a ninth-century monk from St. Gall named
> Notker Babulus, "tropes" had begun as wordless musical
> sequences with which the singers in the choir would embell-
> ish the vowel sounds of certain important words in the ser-
> vice. One such word, for example, was the *alleluia* in the
> introit (opening processional chant) of the Easter mass. Babu-
> lus reports that musical tropes of this sort had become so elab-
> orate in the ninth century that words were added to make the
> sequences easier to memorize. (21–22)

On the most basic level, tropes were amplifications of holy texts:
the liturgy and the scriptures. As signifiers of excess, they marked
a fissure or a potential weak spot in the Church's hegemony. Taken
collectively, tropes tended toward glossolalia or plurality. They
allowed—some might say they encouraged—the rhetorical figure of
catachresis (literally "misuse"), "the manifestly absurd metaphor
designed to inspire ironic second thoughts about the nature of the
thing characterized or the inadequacy of the characterization itself"
(White, 37). Just as surely as the Protestant Reformation did (in
1517 Luther affixed his 95 theses to the Schlosskirche at Wittenberg), tropes opened up the possibility of aberrant readings. They
implied that scripture was not a closed book. It was subject to interpretation. It could be added to, commented on, in short, endlessly
glossed. The Bible, playwright Alfred Jarry later claimed, "can be
made to 'mean all things equivocally'" (qtd. in Shattuck, 241). And
still later, expanding on this notion, Walter Benjamin wrote: "Any
person, object, any relationship can mean absolutely anything else"
(1977:175). Troping, it turns out, is a condition of language. It
makes communication simultaneously possible—and impossible.
This observation is the basis for deconstruction's doctrine of textuality.

> The traditional or common-sense meaning of a text, then, has
> no more exclusive claim to be the *true* meaning than any
> other that can be found in the same words. All interpretations
> are on a par, are equivalent. (Shattuck, 241)

As a means to invention within the liturgy, troping "flourished from the 10th through the 12th centuries" (Randel, 524).
Then, the implications of what we might call "tropological promis-
cuity" or "the logic of embellishment" began to grate upon the
Church Fathers and, finally, proved too much to bear. At the Coun-

cil of Trent (1545–63), the culmination of the Counter-Reformation, the church considered abolishing "all music in the service other than plainsong" and ended up suppressing "all but four tropes and sequences" (121). This regulation, an affirmation of promised renewals and reforms, helped seal the triumph of the Papacy over "those Catholics who wished for conciliation with the Protestants" (Livingstone, 133). In effect, it served notice: Catholics don't trope.

But jazzmen do. If classical music is the Roman Catholic Church, then Louis Armstrong is Martin Luther. The music he championed, jazz, is always represented as an art form devoted to following the Law of the Trope. It is conceptualized as a more-or-less conscious deployment of iterability, the possibility of endlessly reconfiguring musical materials. Put historically, the development of classical music is conventionally understood as dependent upon writing, especially the ideographic inscriptions of standard notation. Jazz is represented as alien to the order of notation. It arose in orality, was shunned by literate culture, and flourished in electronic culture. What is essential to jazz is, as I have already mentioned, traditionally regarded as untranscribable. But think again. Jazz is commonly understood as a generative method for making music from music. It is a metamusic devoted to the systematic exploration of the conditions that give rise to inscription. More verb than noun, jazz has been regarded for years as a paradigm of invention (Mackey, 1992:52).

Jazz and poststructuralist theory share a generally unexplored kinship. They both signal a shift from *reading as referendum* (the work of interpretation) to *writing as troping* (the play of invention). Or stated even more hyperbolically, learning the methods of classical music demands that one learn to *reread* (what has already been written). Learning the methods of jazz demands that one learn to *read perversely* (the already written). Rereading is the essence of careful scholarship; perverse or aberrant reading is the essence of creativity, a skill that our educational institutions have, for the most part, neglected to teach. Most students know how to reread poorly, how to read aberrantly not at all.

Making Pops Talk

Let's return to where we started—back to Louis Armstrong's exchange with the socialite. I want to stage an experiment. What might result if I, on paper, treated this mythic anecdote as jazz musicians treat the products of Tin Pan Alley? Instead of assuming

FIGURE 1.1
Louis Armstrong (courtesy of Columbia/Legacy Records)

that it speaks for itself, that its meaning is self-evident, what if I ran
changes on its surfaces? What if I read it perversely? Perhaps the
trick is to emulate tenor saxophonist Paul Gonsalves, who at the
1956 Newport Festival prompted mass hysteria when he soloed for
twenty-seven choruses. A poststructuralist with a horn, he
employed "Diminuendo and Crescendo in Blue," a relatively simple blues, as text. To him, the piece meant nothing absolutely.

Therefore, it could—at least theoretically—mean absolutely anything. It provided an occasion for invention because it implied the ceaseless play of signification. So without further ado, we look again (and again) at Armstrong's terse reply to an anonymous socialite's query. *One-two / One-two-three-four*:

1. Armstrong the Zen Master (*"If you must, ask; you'll never know"*). To this Armstrong, speculation—merely entertaining the *need* to ask what jazz is—precludes knowing. Or·try another scenario. Let's imagine we asked the (long-deceased) trumpet master why he responded to the lady's question as he did. His answer might take the form of an infinite regress, a *mise en abyme* of his initial response: something like, "If you gotta ask why I said what I said, then you'll never know—that is, either why I said what I did or why I didn't say what I can't and still won't." Maybe, though, he'd smile upon us and bless us with a completely straight answer; in which case aren't we still left wondering, not about the point of this new statement, for let's pretend that it is "completely straight," but about its relationship to the earlier utterance? By what law or logic could he (or we) substitute or clarify one statement with another? Cf. John Cage, *Diary: How to improve the World (You will only make Matters worse)* (eight compact discs, Wergo).

2. Armstrong the Phenomenologist (*"I can't deal it; you gotta feel it"*). Jazz has no existence except in the "coordinates of pure consciousness" (Holman, 329). Thus it is of the order of experiencing (examining *phenomena*), not the order of knowing (inspecting *noumena*). Armstrong fears that the act of verbalizing jazz will alter (one's consciousness of) jazz. Or to borrow Lawrence Grossberg's phrase: "too much intellectual legitimation will redefine the possibilities of its effectiveness; it will become increasingly a meaningful form to be interpreted rather than a popular form to be felt on one's body and to be lived passionately and emotionally" (Grossberg, 79). Cf. Hans-Georg Gadamer, *Truth and Method*.

3. Armstrong the Saussurean (*"I'm jazz, and you're not"*). Asking "What is jazz?" can only be answered by delineating what we do *not* mean by the sign *"jazz."* "Jazz" is defined not by knowing *it*, and all that it involves, but through an awareness of all that is excluded in constructing the set *jazz*, that is, in the relational difference between the set of signs the particular sign *"jazz"* includes and the set of signs it excludes (that is, everything from acoustic phenomena to styles of clothes). The socialite who asks Armstrong

to define jazz cannot know jazz; she is, by definition, one of the "signs," one of the absences, that structures jazz. Cf. Ferdinand de Saussure, *Course in General Linguistics*.

4. Armstrong the Metaphysical Poet (*"Had we but world enough, and time,/This coyness, Lady, were no crime"*). Given the obscene etymology—or the well-known connotations—of the word "jazz," the socialite's question becomes a euphemism for asking: "What is fucking?" But what can be said of Armstrong's answer? Ask a coy question, you get a coy answer? Sure, but is it brazenly flirtatious or strategically evasive? Is it the opening move in a (copulative) sexual game or a sly admission? Armstrong doesn't need the woman. He has a horn. And keep this in mind: The jazzman's musical play, like the writing "games" of poststructuralists, is routinely criticized as self-indulgent, as a variety of masturbation. Armstrong denies nothing. His response is a steady-rolling forward look to imminent pleasure. Cf. Alan P. Merriam and Fradley H. Garner, "Jazz—The Word."

5. Armstrong the Modernist (*"Lady, maybe Ezra Pound said it best when he noticed that 'definition always moves away from the simple things' a man knows perfectly well; 'it recedes into an unknown region, that is a region of remoter and progressively remoter abstraction'"*—19). Jazz isn't a commodity. You don't acquire it then exchange it as if it were a Persian rug. It's a tradition. "If you want it you must obtain it by great labour. It involves, in the first place, the historical sense . . . and the historical sense involves a perception, not only of the pastness of the past, but of its presence" (Eliot, 38). The proper method for understanding a jazz solo is the method of science, "'which is the method of poetry,' as distinct from that of 'philosophic discussion'" (Pound, 20). You examine the solo firsthand by comparing it with other solos. Cf. Ezra Pound, *ABC of Reading*.

6. Armstrong the Structuralist (*"Excuse me, are you some kind of android?"*). In his Overture to *The Raw and the Cooked*, Claude Lévi-Strauss echoes Armstrong. He declares that music is "the only language with the contradictory attributes of being at once intelligible and untranslatable" (Lévi-Strauss, 1969:18). It cannot be "the object of linguistic discourse, when its peculiar quality is to express what can be said in no other way" (31). Hence, we notice that the discourse of music abounds with examples of catachresis: synaesthesia ("blue note," "hot jazz," "sweet jazz," and "hard bop") and oxymorons ("musical sign" and "sound object"). Still, couldn't one side with Stéphane Mallarmé? He claimed:

"Mystery is said to be Music's domain. But the written word also lays claim to it" (Mallarmé, 32). Ultimately, aren't all languages, in the broadest sense of the word, intelligible and untranslatable? And isn't translation both an impossibility and a precondition of language, whether one is mapping painting onto linguistic discourse, English onto Chinese, or the thoughts in my brain onto the printed words of this page? "No," says Lévi-Strauss, and he, too, calls upon a French poet to help make his point. Charles Baudelaire, Lévi-Strauss recalls, once made the profound remark that while each listener reacts to a given work in his own particular way, it is nevertheless noticeable that "music arouses similar ideas in different brains." If this is true, then the intelligibility of music is hardly an effect produced by intersemiotic mapping. Music, like myth, appeals to mental structures that we all have in common (26). Both music and mythology, Lévi-Strauss maintains, are natural systems, automatically intelligible, because they are expressions of the *a priori* conditions that make communication possible. They are originary languages. Everyone understands them (for they constitute the conditions for understanding); no one can translate them. Or stated differently, "when the mind [individual or corporate] is left to commune with itself and no longer has to come to terms with objects, it is in a sense reduced to imitating itself as object" (10). The product of such self-reflexive objectification is music (individually produced) or mythology (socially produced). Therefore, we understand music and mythology because these isomorphic, original languages mimic—actually model—the structures of the human mind. This is why Lévi-Strauss can declare, "music has its being in me, and I listen to myself through it" (17). Demonstrate the logical operations that govern music and mythology, and you reveal the pattern of basic and universal laws that govern human beings. This is, in effect, the overarching goal of structuralism. Cf. Jacques Derrida, *Of Grammatology.*

7. Armstrong the Deconstructer (*"What it [jazz] is is a question of what is is"*). If we presume to ask the question "What is jazz?" we have already assumed the validity of, and the possibility of a recoverable answer to, the recursive question, "What is *is*?" That is, we have already linked our inquiry to a preestablished conception of negativity (nonbeing) as absence and hence cast our lot with the certainty of reappropriating being (in some form of truth) as presence. Thus it is that the initial (characteristically Western metaphysical) question of *is*ness assumes too much: namely, that jazz *is*, and that it is a system—a tradition or construct—that we

can know from a position outside this system (outside textuality). Armstrong's statement—which cunningly and parasitically mimes the operations of a metaphysics of presence—defers representation of being and, thereby, conjures both the absence and the imminent return of mimesis, the (im)possibility of representing jazz. It exemplifies a politics of indirection (through a ruse, it teases out ontological presuppositions), and it deconstructs jazz (as a transcendental signified) by suggesting that it is a textual effect generated by and conceived as a refusal to define: since, ultimately, nondefinition—structurally indistinguishable from definition—sets in motion what we might call "being effects" by predicating a fundamental gap between words and things. Cf. Paul de Man, "The Rhetoric of Blindness," in *Blindness and Insight: Essays in the Rhetoric of Contemporary Criticism*.

8. Armstrong the Ironic Historian (*"I can't tell you, because you can't believe a word I say"*). Building on the work of modern theorists such as Claude Lévi-Strauss and Roman Jakobson, Hayden White contends that a historical text results when data are linguistically expressed—given voice or imaged—by employing one of four basic tropes: metaphor, metonymy, synecdoche, and irony. The Armstrong anecdote provides a limit case of historicizing in the ironic mode, in that it refers to, but at the same time summarily refuses to define or sanction, an accepted body of knowledge about jazz. It is "'sentimental' (in Schiller's sense of 'self-conscious')" or artificial, pointing to the "capacity of language to obscure more than it clarifies in any act of verbal figuration" (White, 31, 37). In other words, through the rhetorical figure of *aporia* (literally "doubt"), Armstrong brings jazz, albeit fleetingly, into language and imbues it with an ironic voice that tacitly alludes to an inarticulable body of knowledge and an ever-receding epistemology, all for the express purpose of warranting an authoritative, but highly problematic, withdrawal from historical discourse. Cf. Hayden White, *Metahistory*.

9. Armstrong the Home-Spun Philosopher (*"Ask a silly question, you get a smart answer"*). Abraham Lincoln, if we trust material given in "The Query," a short play written by Woody Allen, was once asked, "Mr. President, how long must a man's legs be?" He replied, "Long enough to reach the ground" (113–21). The witty rejoinder, which subordinates logic to common sense, always takes aesthetic not moral deficiency as its satiric target. Repeated (and it always is), it gains recognition as a proverb and gives up its status as the exclusive product of a single consciousness. Proverbs express the

doxa. For the materialist, they are products of ideology; for the metaphysician, utterances of truth. Therefore, elevating (or lowering) Louis Armstrong's rejoinder to the level of proverb paradoxically reduces (or raises) its author to one—and not even the first—in a series visiting an "already-written" topic. Repetition retrospectively transforms Armstrong into a metonym: the collective, anonymous voice of jazz (Barthes, 1974:18). Cf. Horace, *Satires.*

10. Armstrong the Feminist (*"Lady, if you're a woman, why do you ask me?"*). In her study of the discourse of film music, Carol Flinn observes a widespread "tendency to align music in general with the feminine" (57–58). Indeed, music is traditionally characterized as "irrational," "unrepresentable," "largely unknowable and mysterious." It metaphorically inhabits a female body. For example, novelist Fatima Shaik, in *The Mayor of New Orleans*, has her character, Walter, declare, "Music and love is both women and truth is too" (10). She thus reiterates Nietzsche's formula: "Truth is a woman." Duke Ellington, on the other hand, is more psychoanalytic in his orientation. He imagines the drum as a woman: "its form a womb, its skin a maidenhead" (Ellington in Morton, 12). In a poem from his autobiography, *Music Is My Mistress*, he writes:

> Music is a beautiful woman in her prime,
> Music is a scrubwoman, clearing away the dirt and grime,
> Music is a girl child
> Simple, sweet and beaming,
> A thousand years old,
> Cold as sleet, and scheming. (Ellington, 39–40)

Granted, this stanza is awful, enough to make one glad that, as a rule, Ellington resisted the Muse of poetry, but it is also helpful, because it reveals the context of Armstrong's remark. In fact, the point of the remark becomes gender (sexual difference) as the social context for musical reception. By subtly but effectively revealing the questioning woman as a transvestite (she does not know "naturally" what she should), it exposes the gender codes that structure jazz. Then again, is Armstrong the woman? Tradition, of course, says otherwise (he was called "Pops," though he never fathered biological children). Nonetheless, in this anecdote, he occupies the position and plays out the role of music-as-woman. Cf. Honoré de Balzac, *Sarrasine.*

11. Armstrong the Castraphobe (*"If you gotta ax, I gotta go"*). The lady lacks what Armstrong has: knowledge, a trumpet, a penis.

And "she's gotta have it." That's hardly surprising. "If it is true," writes Krin Gabbard, "that no one ever possesses the phallus of the father—the first phallus that anyone desires—then all of us, male and female alike, are castrated. The trumpet can then be conceptualized as a compensatory, even hysterical mechanism to ward off castration" (1992b:45). Speculate further and what do we get? "Armstrong [who never knew his biological father] regularly used his trumpet to express phallic masculinity along with a great deal of the sexual innuendo that was already an essential element of jazz performance" (44). He undoubtedly perceived the lady—a stand-in for what? woman? white people? the ruling class? the culture industry?—as a potential threat, an agent of emasculation. Cf. Krin Gabbard, "Signifyin(g) the Phallus: *Mo' Better Blues* and Representations of the Jazz Trumpet."

   12. Armstrong the Itinerant Musician (*"Just whom or what do you think I am?"*). Coming from the most sanguine of entertainers, one detractors accused of obsequiousness (charged with playing the role of Uncle Tom), Armstrong's rejoinder seems uncharacteristically curt. It fractures his received image, sounds like something Miles Davis would say. And that forces a choice. Do we recoup or revise our Armstrong? (A) Maybe we should dismiss his comment altogether and, thus, restore his image to its former plenitude. We're reading too much into an innocent remark. Probably, Armstrong was clowning around. (*"Old Louis, he a good boy, massa. Shucks, he jus playin' witcha."*) Or, perhaps, he was frustrated: his lip was cracked and hurting, he missed New Orleans, he needed some marijuana, he had smoked some marijuana, and so on. (B) Then again, maybe our picture of Armstrong needs adjusting. We have two options. First, we could synthesize a "new" Armstrong by revising our "old" image to accommodate new information. Or second, we could reverse the received view of Armstrong: peel back *persona* from real man, dismiss the shuck-and-jiver and affirm a sly, old fox. (A third option, to live with a radically divided Armstrong, is to live without a picture.) In their net result, then, the strategies of recouping and revising share one aim: the construction of a unified subjectivity to control disruptive textual effects, that is, dissemination. Pursuing Armstrong's irretrievable motivations becomes the raison d'être for speculation (about the text's "outside"), holding forth the promise of locating meaning but, paradoxically, proliferating meanings. And the remark comes to signify nothing except the infinitely explorable conditions that could have prompted its utterance. Cf. Irvin Ehrenpreis, "Per-

sonae," in *Restoration and Eighteenth-Century Literature: Essays in Honor of Alan Dugald McKillop.*

13. Armstrong the Lacanian (*"Jazz exists for the Gaze"*). Insofar as jazz appears in jazz (and I am well aware of my scopocentrism), it appears not so much in what gets played or even in what is left unplayed, but in hesitations, the unsettling interruptions, and the possibilities that, according to Craig Saper, "open onto a void or an impasse" (1991:51). This is what I (Jarrett) find so arresting (J'arrête)—simultaneously menacing and stimulating—in Armstrong's cadenza to "West End Blues" and in the anecdote associated with him. They don't model Jacques Lacan's notion of the gaze; they don't entangle themselves in a project of demystification. Rather, they model creation through the gaze. Their nervousness—the flutter of missing intentions—makes me stumble; it "unsettles empiricism and sets in motion the (re)appearance of gaps, fadings, and flickerings in . . . perception and understanding" (43). Cf. Craig Saper, "A Nervous Theory: The Troubling Gaze of Psychoanalysis in Media Studies."

14. Armstrong the African American (*"Hey white girl, whatcha doing uptown?"*). In a radio interview broadcast on National Public Radio, Ice-T told *Fresh Air*'s Terry Gross, "Rap music is black music that's being sent back and forth to us in the ghetto. White America picked up the phone and listened to it, and said, 'Ah, how can they talk like this!' This is just how we talk. Put the phone down. . . . White America just won't understand it, but I'm just going to have to say, 'It's a black thing.'" Substitute "jazz" for "rap" and "play" for "talk," and the gangsta rapper becomes little more than the fulfillment of the promise latent in every note Pops blew. Cf. Greg Tate, *Flyboy in the Buttermilk: Essays on Contemporary America.*

15. Armstrong the Marxist (*"Them that ask have got to go"*). Seizing upon the term "socialite" might not be the only way to find Marx—and class struggle—in the Armstrong anecdote, but it is certainly the fastest way to accrue hermeneutic capital from the exchange of lady and jazzman. In resisting the ruling class—its attempts to alienate him from the meaning of his labor—Armstrong models the revolutionary act and, paradoxically, defines jazz. It is musical liberation, freedom: interesting not because it represents consensus, a common unified ethos, but because it is the accumulated record of passionate conflicts. It represents achievement *out* of conflict, not a sublime rising above (Greenblatt, in Begley, 1993:36). Cf. LeRoi Jones, *Blues People: Negro Music in White America.*

16. Armstrong the Hipster (*"Sorry, the only way I could have answered you was if you didn't ask"*). Armstrong's response to the lady is, in effect, a pronouncement: "You're so square (and baby, I do care)." Because it conveniently divides the world into asymmetrical halves—those who do not know what jazz is and those who no longer ask—it implies a jazz version of Calvinism where the elect automatically know the truth, and the preterits are damned to try and figure out things for themselves—but without asking. Or perhaps more kindly, the lady presents Armstrong with an impossible task. Her question is so elemental—so outside the world of jazz—that it bars Armstrong from the only discourse he knows: a vocabulary fully capable of addressing the lady's question but not in words she can understand. Therefore, he stands before her mute. The body of knowledge that differentiates him from the larger culture, marking him as a prominent member of a subculture, has also decisively cut him off. He has purchased identity at the expense of communication. Cf. William Shakespeare, *King Lear*.

17. Armstrong the Ethnomusicologist (*"Hey, don't you listen to records or the radio?"*). For the sake of his music, Armstrong lays claim to this double enigma: one can neither represent jazz in words, nor in symbolic-graphic form on a score. Jazz is incommensurate with standard methods of graphic representation: translation or mapping capture only that which is common to both it and notation. That which is specific to jazz eludes translation. Unlike classical music, which began in orality (for example, with the early plainchant of monks) but came to share a reciprocal relationship with notation (literacy), jazz arose in orality (for example, with the field hollers of slaves) but developed in the modern world of "secondary orality." It is a consequence of electronics: as imbricated with radio and phonography as classical music is with writing and printing. An ethnomusicology of jazz might, therefore, begin with Armstrong's rejection of analytico-rational explanation—adequate for the study of art during the Gutenberg era (literacy)—and explore ways of writing in the Edison era (that is, writing with electronic culture). It could also profit by politicizing (critically reexamining) that notion of musical literacy. Cf. Gregory Ulmer, *Teletheory: Grammatology in the Age of Video* and *Heuretics: The Logic of Invention*.

And so on, and so on. This speculative cadenza is designed to introduce a variety of motifs explored in subsequent chapters, but it is also calculated to teach a lesson about writing. The lesson—

what we might call the law of signification—states that any attempt to delineate what a text means (to circumscribe its set of possibilities) will always obtain the opposite effect. Rereading—the push and shove of interpretation—opens up the text. Jazz musicians and poststructuralists, rather than working against this law, seek to exploit it as a means of invention.

Still, it's probable that plenty of people must wonder: Is drifting on a read—or at least the sort of troping that characterizes poststructuralist experiments with language—worth doing? Should such play be encouraged, or should it be discouraged as an extreme case of scholarship become self-indulgent and pretentious? Does the jazz method—troping—have any practical lessons to teach writing and thinking? Obviously, I believe so.

However much it may seem like a *tour de force* of flashy theorizing (signifying nothing), the preceding experiment was not created *ex nihilo*. It follows well-established methods of aberrant or perverse reading, methods that can be generalized for critical/theoretical writing. Notice, for example, that all of the towering geniuses of jazz, no matter how unique their styles, patterned inventive ways of playing that countless others adopted and employed. My performance—which recalls Sonny Stitt more than Charlie Parker—was jazz-derived. It was learned. My intention, in the pages that follow, is to show readers how to transfer jazz strategies of perverse—no, make that creative—reading to the realm of scholarship and the cultural-studies classroom. I want to demonstrate that the tropes organizing jazz and jazzography (identified through interpretation or hermeneutics) are also useful for grammatological invention (what I call heuretics). But there is a problem. Inventive techniques that are *de rigueur* ("normal science") among jazz musicians are often discouraged among scholars. They are banished to the realm of poetics, to the creative-writing classroom. I believe that the techniques of troping should be disseminated. My bet is that they could revitalize and popularize writing in the humanities.

Instead of assuming that music and language are different expressions of similar conditions (the formalism espoused by T. S. Eliot) or isomorphic systems that can be grasped through some especially sufficient metadiscourse (the structuralism exemplified by Claude Lévi-Strauss), this study of jazzography suggests that debates over referentiality can be displaced by a model of textual production that imagines language and music as the play of several tropes (grammatology). The reason for this shift of theoretical orientation is not metaphysical—"to get things right this time"—but pragmatic. Although I am not afraid of "getting things right," generating what we might call "truth effects" (the flip side of "understanding effects"), my goal here is less to explain than to stage a demonstration of applied grammatology oriented toward the pleasures of theory. I want to show readers how to turn (or trope) an art form into a paradigm for creative invention. Jazz as it is represented by jazzography will serve as a test case. My goals, therefore, are pedagogical. My interests are far more personal. I want to write about jazzography because I love jazz and think that it has much to offer critical theory.

Thriving on a Riff

Outside of institutional sites—schools, churches, courts, and the media—where "trained" exegetes make sense of things for us, we are seldom bothered by hermeneutical anxiety. Even if we believe otherwise, we tend to behave as if things simply mean what they mean (which, in effect, means that we have just internalized what "trained" exegetes have taught us). That's why my elaborate explication of an oft-repeated anecdote about Louis Armstrong might strike many as, at best, parodic (scholarship become academic camp), or at worst, pedantic (scholarship become academic kitsch). First, the labor of exposition imbues the story with value: treats it as a means of teasing out a whole world of ideologically assigned suppositions. Exposition exposes assumptions about what does and does not merit attention (*"It isn't a line by Pope or Keats! It's Louis Armstrong talking, for crying out loud, not Schoenberg!"*). And second, exposition violates a widely held but tacit interdiction that forbids speculation. It undercuts the assurance that things are exactly what they seem to be, and it thus opposes any notion of a "correct" or "definitive" interpretation (*"Pops—Mr. Louis Armstrong to you—meant just what he said! Asking what he could have meant is crazy, almost as wrongheaded as somebody asking what jazz means"*). "The meanings I find in a sign," writes semiotician John Fiske, "derive from the ideology within which the sign and I exist: by finding these meanings I define myself in relation to the ideology and in relation to my society" (151). Or as Fredric Jameson puts it:

> we never really confront a text immediately, in all its freshness as a thing-in-itself. Rather, texts come before us as

always-already-read; we apprehend them through sedimented layers of previous interpretations, or—if the text is brand-new—through the sedimented reading habits and categories developed by those inherited interpretive traditions. (9)

I picture jazz as the musical dissemination of four monster metaphors: *satura*, obbligato, rhapsody, and *charivari*. They are the images that organize jazzography, allowing us to recognize jazz as music (and as a music with particular meanings). As readers have already seen, I call monster metaphors "tropes," but they also go by other names. Robert Ray calls them "constitutive words" (1988:163). The Situationists favored "grammologues" and "magical floating words" (Hugo Ball, in Marcus, 221). Roland Barthes assigned them the term "symbolic codes." He understood these words as the linguistic equivalent of radioactive isotopes: codes that bundle together contradictory connotations. Early in his career, Barthes emphasized the cultural labor directed toward governing the connotations of such codes. This governance, he theorized, constructs ideology. Explication is, therefore, always potentially threatening to power structures because, by exposing the polysemy or plurality that underlies culturally manufactured codes, it reveals that

> denotation [truth, objectivity, the law] is not the first meaning, but pretends to be so; under this illusion, it is ultimately no more than the *last* of the connotations (the one which seems both to establish and to close the reading), the superior myth by which the text pretends to return to the nature of language, to language as nature. (1974:9)

In subordinating denotation to connotation, in reintroducing meanings that were banished for the sake of insuring univocality (banished ineffectually, because plurality cannot be sent "outside" ideology), Barthes effectively transformed the goal of literary criticism and theory. He substituted a model of textual production for the classic model of representation (4–7). Or let me put it this way. Barthes, who as far as I know cared nothing for jazz, redefined the scholar's role as remarkably like that of the jazz musician. Toward the end of his life, he didn't interpret texts so much as bootstrap off them: employing "primary" works to create texts of his own.

Barthes first made a name for himself when he forsook "the path of the object," which studies the "objective" structures of texts, for "the path of the subject," which foregrounds the interpretive categories or codes through which we read and receive texts (Jameson, 9). In the middle of his career, however, Barthes seemed weary or suspicious of this latter path. Its goal turned out to be completely consistent with the overarching goal of traditional humanistic pedagogy: increase ideological sensitivity by spreading (disseminating and popularizing) myths of demythification. "[D]enunciation, demystification (or demythification)," Barthes wrote, "has itself become discourse, stock of phrases, catechistic declaration" (1977b:166). The challenge, therefore, wasn't how to deconstruct culturally manufactured codes (that's done by laying bare the rhetorical-philosophical means by which institutions exclude connotations in order to achieve closure and hegemony). No, the challenge is to employ deconstruction as but a necessary step on the way to constructing new myths. At the end of his career, the time of *Roland Barthes* (1977) and *A Lover's Discourse: Fragments* (1978), Barthes was writing texts that, while not abandoning demystification as a vital pedagogical effect, experimented with the possibilities of employing the suppressed connotations of culturally endorsed codes as paradigms for new modes of composition.

This is what draws Barthes and Jacques Derrida together. In addition to formulating a history of writing ("logocentrism") and a theory of writing ("grammatology"), they consistently pushed toward application: the development of alternatives to mimesis, hermeneutics, and critique. Most scholars interested in Barthes, Derrida, and other postmodern textualists have elucidated their historical-philosophical agenda. Gregory Ulmer has focused on and developed their compositional program. He calls it *heuretics* and identifies it with the avant-garde's use of theory as a "generative" device (Ulmer, 1991:3). For example, risking oversimplification for the sake of clarification, we might notice that Sophocles told a story about Oedipus (he produced a mimetic or realistic effect). Freud interpreted this story (he produced a hermeneutic or truth effect). Feminism critiqued it (producing a political or ideological effect). And surrealist André Breton—extrapolating from Freud's theories—used it to make poetry (he produced a heuretic or inventive effect). If contemporary scholarship wishes to renew itself, loosen the burden of interpretation and critique, Ulmer suggests that it might reverse the direction of conventional scholarship: assume a position of ignorance (play student instead of teacher) and apply art strategies, such as Breton's, to the writing of theory. My work heeds this suggestion. It starts with the observation that Breton and other surrealists heard jazz as an artistic validation of the generative potential of psychoanalytic insights. Jazz was psychoanalysis by other means. It had already accomplished in music what the surrealists wanted to do in other mediums. My aims are similar to theirs. Without forsaking representation, explanation, and critique as rhetorical effects, I want to use the four tropes of jazz as a way to bootstrap theory, to learn heuretics from jazz.

Composting

Bedouin Hornbook, Nathaniel Mackey's epistolary novel, suggests an entry point for such a project. In one of its scenes the protagonist—known simply as N.—wakes from a dream and writes to his correspondent, the Angel of Dust:

> I awoke to the even more radical realization that it's not enough that a composer skillfully cover his tracks, that he erase the echo of "imposition" composition can't help but be haunted by. In a certain sense, I realized, to do so only makes matters worse. The question I was left with, of course, was: What can one do to outmaneuver the inertia both of what one knows and of what one feels or presumes to feel? There must be some way, I'm convinced, to invest in the ever so slight suggestion of "compost" I continue to get from the word compose. (1986:78–79)

N. is a founding member of a musical collective known as the Mystic Horn Society, an aggregation redolent of the Sun Ra Arkestra and the Art Ensemble of Chicago. His aesthetic, like the music of another one of this novel's characters, manifests a "somewhat French-inflected sense of African drumming" (144). His insight—that one might invest in the barely motivated relationship connecting "compost" and "compose"—results from a conjunction of jazz and critical theory. It amounts to a central clue in solving the grammatological problem: How to divert interpretation (rereading) into invention (aberrant readings)?

Although N. writes that he hasn't quite figured out how to realize his insight, he also declares that he's actively working toward a solution. He's spending a lot of time listening to *Coltrane Live at the Village Vanguard Again!* and he admits that he has probably assumed the goal John Coltrane stated in the album's liner notes. N., like the famous tenor saxophonist, is "trying to work out a kind of writing that will allow for more plasticity, more viability, more room for improvisation in the statement of the melody itself" (79). What N. hears in Coltrane's improvisations is the sound of songs composting. Or rather, he smells shit. Composters, both those who play music and those who write theory, *maneuver* their basic materials into a kind of textual heap from which other texts can grow (manure is, by the way, etymologically linked to the Old French *maneuvre*, to work with the hands, cultivate). "Hence *decomposition* is here contrary to *destruction*" (Barthes, 1977a:63). Decomposters are saprophytes; they regenerate by feeding "off the decay of tradition" (Ulmer, 1983:106).

Composting, like deconstruction, is the discourse equivalent of reversing the direction of sublation (the lifting up of the "sensible" into the conceptual). For example, when N. detects the ever-so-slight whiff of "compost" in the word "compose," he has, in fact, begun the work of returning composition, a master trope of Western thought, to the bodily image (or alloseme) from which the concept (or philosopheme) grew. What distinguishes composting from deconstructing, then, is mainly a matter of connotation. Composting is a way to picture in one word both aspects of grammatology. Put specifically, I compost jazzography into its tropes, first, for exegetical reasons. They provide tools for explaining or *writing about jazz* (tropes used pedagogically, as a means to create effects of demystification, correspond most directly to popular conceptions of deconstruction). But composting can also support research. The tropes of jazz provide tools for invention, for *writing with jazz* (tropes used heuretically, as a means to create new myths for problem solving, draw attention to a neglected side of grammatology) (Ray, 1988:163). As pedagogical tools, jazz tropes teach us a lesson about the discourse of jazz; as heuretical tools, these tropes suggest methods for writing creative theory.

For the Record

The following four chapters are similarly structured. All except chapter 1 have six sections. They start with an extended definition, introducing a trope that structures jazz. Then, they provide a list of recordings, a ninety–minute soundtrack for illustrating or, better, for potentially making audible and material the jazz trope under discussion. The third section of all chapters is devoted to exposition; tropes are employed as ways to open up the discourse of jazz. Next, there are sections that describe paradigmatic texts that have employed tropes heuretically, sections that propose writing assignments, and, finally, sections that carry out experiments in writing with jazz. These experiments—the core of this book—are designed to demonstrate that jazz methods are useful for thinking and writing.

One introductory matter, however, remains unaddressed. How does one go about identifying the tropes of jazz or, for that matter, the tropes that compose any discourse? I started by reading texts that jazzography, as much as it can be considered an institution, endorsed— regarded as seminal. I took note of the recurring metaphors that picture jazz. Next, by reconceiving these metaphors as metonyms—elements of larger sets of images—I sought to imagine (and name) the smallest number of sets that could possibly organize the recurring images used to represent jazz. These sets (or metaphorical domains) are the tropes of jazz. Every one appears in the first paragraph of the preface to Gunther Schuller's *Early Jazz: Its Roots and Musical Development*. This passage, actually the book's entire preface, serves my design in much the same way that the chord changes to George Gershwin's "I've Got Rhythm" served beboppers, or Balzac's *Sarrasine* served Barthes in *S/Z*. It is a point of departure, a palimpsest for writing over, and a tutor text. Schuller writes:

> Although there is no dearth of books on jazz, very few of them have attempted to deal with the music itself in anything more than general descriptive or impressionistic terms. The majority of books have concentrated on the legendry of jazz, and over the years a body of writing has accumulated which is little more than an amalgam of well-meaning amateur criticism and fascinated opinion. That this was allowed to pass for scholarship and serious analysis is attributable not only to the humble, socially "unacceptable" origin of jazz, but also to the widely held notion that a music improvised by self-taught, often musically illiterate musicians did not warrant genuine musicological research. Despite the fact that many "serious" composers and performers had indicated their high regard for jazz as early as the 1920s, the academic credentials of jazz were hardly sufficient to produce a serious interest in the analysis of its techniques and actual musical content. (vii)

This passage is central to the concerns of both Schuller and me. It initiates a succinct *diachronic* history of jazzology (nonfiction writing about jazz), and it registers the author's attitude towards that history. Additionally, it presents a *synchronic* representation of jazzology. Schuller—former president of the New England Conservatory of Music, artistic director at the Berkshire Music Center at Tanglewood, the French horn player on Miles Davis's *The Birth of the Cool*, and winner of the 1994 Pulitzer Prize for "Of Reminiscences and Reflections"—accuses the majority of books on jazz of some very specific mistakes. His reasons are obvious. They're a rhetorical necessity. To distinguish his work—to set it apart from the pack—Schuller must simultaneously perpetuate and repudiate a critical tradition. He therefore positions his own work within a critical field, situating it at the end of a historical-intellectual lineage. His rhetoric attributes an extraordinary, albeit negative, unity to a diverse group of writings. It conceptualizes early jazz scholarship as a legacy of lack, assigning images of paucity to past texts but filling in this poverty with a barely tacit promise of imminent plenitude. The science of jazzology—what Schuller calls "serious analysis"—has come to transcend (supplement or cast out) the merely rhetorical—the deficiencies of "general descriptive or impressionistic" texts.

As it turns out, the "negative" images Schuller uses to organize and disparage jazz writing are, in slightly disguised form, exactly the same images that he will use to represent jazz. Early jazzology is a hodgepodge or amalgam of various strains (the *satura* trope). It's tangential to—an embellishment of—the music itself (the obbligato trope). It's a counterfeit—remarkably, one authorized or at least allowed to pass as genuine (the trope of rhapsody). But as to status, jazzology is something of a pariah (the *charivari* trope).

Because they uncover rhetorical blindness, my comments here and in the following pages could be misconstrued as an attack on Schuller's text and, more generally, on much jazzography. That would be a mistake. This book should be taken as a literary theorist's attempt to understand how jazzography succeeds—how it comes to count as truth—not as a gleeful exercise in exposing how it inevitably fails or is stalled by contradictions. The fact is, jazzography (which, of course, includes my own writing) is riddled with contradictions. It has blind spots. Strange as it may seem, though, contradiction and blindness have never been barriers to writing, to the rhetorical creation of truth effects. Far from it. As structuralism has repeatedly shown, contradiction motivates discovery and invention, and as poststructuralism is fond of pointing out, blindness enables insight. The semiotic conditions that would undo writing (for example, the impossibility of establishing a stable context that can secure interpretation) also make writing possible (iterability, the mobility of the sign, allows us to form words and sentences). Which is to say, I have not singled out the preface to *Early Jazz* because I figured that it would make an easy target. Still, I do not claim disinterest. I chose this text because it exemplifies the contradictions that animate (enable and defeat) jazzography and because it evidences a level of scholarship that books on jazz have consistently sought to achieve, but have seldom attained.

❧

ONE

Satura:
Filé (under) Gumbo

Tropology: The Art of Mixing

Never a meal passes without music, and the dessert course is never scanted. . . . For they are much inclined to think that no kind of pleasure is forbidden, provided harm does not come of it.
—Sir Thomas More (48)

Satura, the Latin term from which we derive the English word "satire," literally means "mixed dish," "farrago," "hodgepodge," or "medley." Originally employed as an adjective meaning "full" in the phrase *satura lanx* ("full plate"), it referred to a platter of mixed fruits—a fruit cocktail or ambrosia—offered to the gods (Gresham, 10–19). It was associated with copiousness (having *more*), with the worship of Saturn, and the celebration of the Saturnalia.

Saturn (Kronos) has a real appetite. When his son, Jupiter, was an infant, he tried to eat him. Sublimating, he invented agriculture. In the earth, Saturn's influence produces lead (saturnism means lead poisoning); in mankind, the blues or melancholia (the temperament most frequently associated with Muses and scholars); in history, he promotes disastrous events ("fatal accidents, pestilence, treacheries, and ill luck in general"). "In Dante his sphere is the Heaven of contemplatives. He is connected with sickness and old age" and with our contemporary picture of a scythe-in-hand Father

Time. The most terrible of the seven gods/planets/influences, "he . . . is sometimes called The Greater Infortune, *Infortuna Major*" (C. S. Lewis, 105, 172–73). Nevertheless, Saturn's reign was the Golden Age, from which people sprang and to which they will ultimately return (Adams, 95–96).

The Saturnalia both commemorated and anticipated the Golden Age as a time when, as Lucian of Samosata put it, "every man's table was spread automatically" and "rivers ran wine and milk and honey" (Lucian, in Adams, 101). Celebrated toward the end of December, it was a weeklong carnival during which everybody "got real gone for a change." Everything was topsy-turvy. Kids ditched school, soldiers stopped all "peacekeeping" missions, and traffic cops wrote no speeding tickets; social hierarchies were inverted, distinctions of rank abolished, and gifts were exchanged— wax tapers, clay dolls, and, presumably, rare 78s. Saturnalia was the Garden of Eden without snakes, the New Jerusalem without apocalypse, communism without burcaucracy (or tyrants such as John of Leyden, Josef Stalin, and David Koresh), a three-ring circus without elephant turds, and Mardi Gras without indigestion and hangovers. It was Utopia (a Greek word coined by Sir Thomas More, "'utopia' is compounded from Greek *ou* and *topos*, meaning 'no place,'" but it also puns on *eutopos* or "good place"; its Latin equivalent, *Nusquama*, means "nowhere" or, better, "nowhere"—3). Oh yeah, and everybody wore suits made of gold lamé.

Secularized and generalized as a trope or grammalogue (an image one *writes with*), *satura* received literary expression in a number of encyclopedic works: Apuleius's *Golden Ass*, Rabelais's *Gargantua and Pantagruel*, Robert Burton's *The Anatomy of Melancholy*, Sterne's *Tristram Shandy*, James Joyce's *Ulysses*, and Thomas Pynchon's *Gravity's Rainbow*. But it was Petronius's proto-novel, *Satyricon*, that first completely utilized the term as a generative device or trope for writing. The title of this book, William Arrowsmith notes, suggests a pun on both *satura*, a potpourri of "mixed subjects in a variety of styles," and *saturika*, a literary piece "concerned with satyrs, which is to say, lecherous, randy" (Arrowsmith, vii). Thus, it announces the method and content of the text that follows. Petronius, who was Nero's social chairman, projected theme onto form. His book, especially in its now-fragmented form, was itself a *satura*. He not only wrote about food and lecherous boys, he arranged his literary materials in a manner resembling a smorgasbord. The classic example is Trimalchio's banquet (ch. 5), but even in the novel's first chapter, Petronius associates literary composition with food preparation. He accuses rhetoricians of concocting "great sticky honeyballs of phrases, every sentence looking as though it had been plopped and rolled in poppyseed and sesame." He, therefore, charges them with *his* most glaring "crime," abandoning substance for style. "By reducing everything to sound," the rhetoricians had concocted a "bloated puffpaste of pretty drivel whose only real purpose is the pleasure of punning and the thrill of ambiguity" (Petronius, 21–22).

Marcus Terentius Varro (116–27 B.C.) contributes another gastronomic association to *satura*. He states that it may have been an alternate term for a kind of stuffing ("farcimen," from which "farce" is derived). We should also observe that the title of his own *Saturae Menippeae*—about 150 works named after Menippus of Gadara (340–270 B.C.)—meant "satiric medleys in the Cynic manner of Menippus" (Van Rooy, 56). Or finally, consider two more examples of this term. Another logophage, Juvenal, in Satire I, refers to "the mixed mash [or 'farrago'] of my verse" (68). And according to Gilbert Highet, when Quintus Ennius (239–169 B.C.), the originator of Roman satire, took the term *saturae* for the title of his four books of miscellaneous poems, "he meant not only that they were a mixed dish of simple coarse ingredients, but that they grew out of an improvised jollification which was (although devoid of plot) dramatic" (Highet, 233).

In the modern age, one name given for writing (composting) with the trope of *satura* is collage. A French word that literally means "pasting," collage "is also a slang expression for two people living (pasted) together—that is to say, an illicit sexual union"; its past participle, *collé*, means "faked" or "pretended" (Perloff, 51). We might assume that all of these meanings resonated for Picasso when, in 1912, he grafted onto what was essentially a Cubist painting "a piece of oil cloth printed to look like chair caning" and, thereby, created his first collage. This mixed-media work, *Still Life with Chair Caning*, provides a short seminar on the theory and practice of what we might call "saturetic writing": using the trope of *satura* as a means to invention (heuretics), not interpretation (hermeneutics). First, it models an alternative to the ancient Platonic formula that understands painting as mimesis, as ultimately a representation of something real. It suggests that representation is always a collage effect, generated not by suturing, quotation, or appropriation (or by any other "positive" phenomenon), but by displacements that prompt what Craig Saper calls kinetic, flickering, or nervous contexts of reception (1991:44, 42). Or put more succinctly, representation depends on gaps. Additionally, *Still Life with Chair Caning* recommends an artistic strategy. It serves notice that fecundity lies in the artistic equivalent of miscegenation: mixing signs from different orders of signification; the intercourse of "identity categories" (Brown, 8).

Listening: Hybrids for C90

America may not be a melting pot, but our only original art form, jazz, is the stew to which so much of the world wants to add its local spices.
—Allen Barra (72)

It's conceivable that everything anyone needs to know about jazz-as-*satura* is offered on the recordings of Jelly Roll Morton. *Jelly Roll Morton 1923/24* (Milestone) and *The Jelly Roll Morton Centennial: His Complete Victor Recordings: 1926–30; 1939* (Bluebird) are historically significant. They're to jazz what Picasso is to modern art. But *The Library of Congress Recordings, Vols. 1–4* (Rounder), made by Alan Lomax late in Morton's career (1938), grant real insight into jazz methods. Morton plays piano, sings, and tells (frequently obscene) yarns. He casually presents himself as a mythic figure, the inventor of jazz. He comes off as a collage artist, a master of appropriation and transformation (adding a "Spanish Tinge" to blues is a famous example of his compositional strategy).

At this late date, however, many people will have difficulty hearing Morton's music and most of the jazz that followed his as a *satura* of styles. I am therefore recommending a number of explicitly syncretistic recordings. None of these tunes sounds *pure*. Their power derives from mixing jazz styles and strategies with other types of music.

While somewhat representative of the variety of jazz hybrids available, this list has absolutely no aspirations to completeness. Rather, it aims for utility. Like the lists found in other chapters, it is programmed for a ninety–minute cassette. Plus, it's road tested. I'm certain that it sounds good in a Buick. But I'm also reasonably sure that most readers will not feel the slightest inclination to follow my lead and compile such a tape. That's okay, too. The list should work as text, as imaginary cassette. Finally, two points of information: (1) unless otherwise indicated, all dates on this and other lists refer to year of recording, not year of release; (2) all titles have been issued on compact disc, though that is no assurance that they remain in print.

Side I

01. Les Misérables Brass Band (1989) "Precious Lord, Hold My Hand," *Manic Traditions*, Northeastern/Popular Arts.   12:44

    Thomas Dorsey, who wrote "Precious Lord," is to gospel music what Louis Armstrong is to jazz. He shifted the responsibility of church music-making from the congregation (relying on folk/oral forms) to talented singers (reading sheet music).

02. Toshiko Akiyoshi/Lew Tabackin (1975) "Children in the Temple Ground," *Toshiko Akiyoshi/Lew Tabackin Big Band*, Novus.   5:30

    Akiyoshi weaves together personal style (a unique blend of traditional Japanese music and Bud-Powell-inspired bebop) with professional technique (an Ellingtonian ability to voice sections and encourage soloists such as her woodwind-playing husband, Lew Tabackin).

03. Machito and His Afro-Cuban Orchestra featuring Flip Phillips (1949) "Tanga," *The Original Mambo Kings—An Introduction to Afro-Cubop Anthology*, Verve.   5:10

    This anthology could have been the soundtrack to Orson Welles's Touch of Evil. It's that steamy.

04. Django Reinhardt (1937) "Minor Swing," *Djangology, Vol. 3*, EMI France.   3:15

    This gypsy guitarist owed much to black music, but he repaid everything he borrowed—with interest. His solos—blazing runs, bent notes, and clusters—are breathtaking and unmistakably his own invention.

05. Don Byron (1992) "Seder Dance," *Don Byron Plays the Music of Mickey Katz*, Elektra Nonesuch.   2:14

    Katz is to 1950s popular music what the 2,000–year-old man is to comedy; which makes Byron the Billy Crystal of contemporary clarinet players.

06. Robin Holcomb (1990) "This poem is in memory of!"
    Robin Holcomb, Elektra Musician.　　　　　　　2:57

    As big-city music, jazz rarely gets a visit from its country cousins; that's why Holcomb (who, in addition to composing, plays piano and sings) is such a marvel. Her allegiance to Monk and other boppers hasn't tempered an endearing Appalachian accent or an affection for rock and folk music.

07. Jim Pepper (1983) "Witchi Tia To," *Comin' and Goin'*,
    Rykodisc.　　　　　　　　　　　　　　　　　8:19

    There's grandeur in this meeting of jazz and Native American themes—Pepper was a Kaw Indian—because it never strays from the cadences of dance.

08. John Zorn (1984–85) "The Big Gundown," *The Big Gundown*, Elektra Nonesuch/Icon.　　　　　　　7:17

    Listening to Zorn and his co-conspirators manipulate the music of Ennio Morricone is an experience akin to watching a hot-shot twelve-year-old wrestle a video game.

09. Trilok Gurtu (1987–88) "Shobharock," *Usfret*, CMP.　7:35

    "Shobharock," the disc's opening track, is named after guest vocalist Shobha Gurtu—the leader's mother and the "Queen of the Thumri." It pairs classical Indian singing with a propulsive beat: a kind of Bodhisattva brew or raga jazz.

Total playing time 45:01

Side II

01. Charles Mingus (1957) "Ysabel's Table Dance,"
    Tijuana Moods, Bluebird.　　　　　　　　　10:24

    Expansive, informed by a Rabelaisian wit and a Gargantuan appetite, Mingus's music sprawls.

02. Dudu Pukwana (1973) "Baloyi," *In the Townships*,
    Earthworks/Caroline.　　　　　　　　　　　5:18

    A highly developed form of marabi—a jazz style forged in sheebeens or illegal bars when rural South Africans, lured by industry and coerced by apartheid, migrated to the townships and blended their music with the imported sounds of hard bop.

03. Maleem Mahmoud Ghania with Pharoah Sanders (1994) "Moussa Berkiyo/Koubaliy Beriah La'Foh," *The Trance of Seven Colors*, Axiom.   4:34

    Pairs Coltrane's greatest disciple with the Master Musicians of Joujouka, Morocco.

04. Wayne Shorter (1974), "From the Lonely Afternoons," *Native Dancer*, Columbia.   3:13

    During the fusion years, jazz and Brazilian music renewed their acquaintance; here saxophonist Wayne Shorter converses with falsettist Milton Nascimento.

05. Kip Hanrahan (1982–83), "What Is This Dance, Anyway?" *Desire Develops an Edge*, American Clavé.   3:40

    Horns and guitars couple with Jack Bruce on a bed of Afro-Cuban drums.

06. Rahsaan Roland Kirk (1969), "I Say a Little Prayer," *Does Your House Have Lions: The Rahsaan Roland Kirk Anthology*, Rhino.   7:55

    Going where no jazzman has gone before, Captain Kirk punches a bright hole in the boundary separating experimental and popular music.

07. John Surman (1981), "Kentish Hunting (Lady Margaret's Air)," *The Amazing Adventures of Simon Simon*, ECM.   2:56

    Draws upon Celtic folk-song and electronic music.

08. Mike Westbrook (1986) *Westbrook—Rossini*, hat ART.   7:07

    In Westbrook, one of the most significant orchestrators (lone arrangers) in jazz, Rossini found a lover not a victimizer.

Total playing time 45:07

Archeology: What's Cooking with Jazzography?

> *That grand wild sound of bop floated from beer parlors; it mixed medleys with every kind of cowboy and boogie-woogie in the American night.*
>
> —*Jack Kerouac (72)*

The sound filled the beige chamber with a muted deso-
lation. A fuzzy, hybrid tone, an acoustical alloy.
                                        —*Josef Skvorecky (144)*

Back to the Fertile-Crescent City

The founding image of jazz is the *satura*, the figure of mixing.
It structures every account of the music's origination and generation. I will not attempt to substantiate this claim fully, but I do
want to provide several illustrations of this trope at work in the discourse of jazz. For example, Mark Gridley states that jazz "is the
result of a gradual blending of several musical cultures" (56), and
Winthrop Sargeant argues that jazz and spirituals "represent a
fusion of musical idioms in which both White and 'African' contributions play indispensable roles" (211). Leonard Feather, who is
even more specific about the ingredients composing jazz, writes:

> The music we recognize today as jazz is a synthesis drawn
> originally from six principal sources: rhythms from West
> Africa; harmonic structure from European classical music;
> melodic and harmonic qualities from nineteenth-century
> American folk music; religious music; work songs; and min-
> strel shows. (24)

"It seems in retrospect almost inevitable," concludes Gunther
Schuller, "that America, the great ethnic melting pot, would pro-
create a music compounded of African rhythmic, formal, sonoric,
and expressive elements and European rhythmic and harmonic
practices" (3). Inevitable indeed. Jazz functioned as an agent of ideology. It repeated, on an aesthetic level, myths of identity-through-
integration. It naturalized and helped shape a social regime, state
apparatus, or, more kindly, values we hold dear. Simply put, America enlisted jazz as one of its metaphors.

Jazz, like the city of New Orleans, finds a metaphor in gumbo;
it is an emblem—a New World repetition—of the *satura*. And while
this metaphor may strike some readers as nothing more than a
commonplace of "nonscientific" writing about music (a "literary"
image, an "angle" for journalism, or an example of musicology trying to be friendly), everyone must admit that music is regularly
transubstantiated as food, through an aural/oral displacement. Gus-
tatory images abound in all types of musical description, from
"platters" to "tasty tunes" and musicians with "chops." They are

not, however, restricted to the realm of music, or even to the realm of art. Gustation dominates Western philosophy. Its metaphors structure our understanding of both the pleasures of assimilation and the necessity of judgment. For instance, when we speak of a person's native "tongue," we refer to the language that designates membership within a particular group. And in the words "taste" and "consumption" we hear an implication of both aesthetics and ethics (Ulmer, 1985:53–56). Deconstruction—a term now in disfavor but, nevertheless, an essential strategy for thinking—reverses this process of elevating "sensible" metaphors (allosemes) as concepts (philosophemes): a process Hegel called *Aufhebung*. It digests the founding metaphors of Western metaphysics and, from its decomposed fragments (the excluded *morceau*), writes. . . .

Although my goal in this section on the archeology of the *satura* is social history not philosophy, my investigation of writing about jazz follows strategies associated with Derrida's deconstructive method. It begins by noticing that *satura* is the metaphor structuring both our picture of jazz and our picture of jazzography, and it proceeds by tracing effects of this conceptualization. I ask, What are the consequences of employing the image of *satura* as a means of writing *about* jazz? In the fourth section of this chapter, which takes the theory of John Cage's *Silence* and the practice of Michael Ondaatje's *Coming through Slaughter* as paradigmatic, I explore writing *with* the trope of *satura*.

The Amalgam

Gumbo requires okra. In fact, the Tshiluba (Bantu) word for okra is *ki-ngumbo*. What else gets added is pretty much up to the whims of the cook. I typically work variations on a recipe clipped from an old issue of *Southern Living*. Its ingredients include chicken, smoked sausage, and bacon, onions and peppers, corn, tomatoes, and spices. But when my budget allows, I have also added seafood: crawfish or shrimp, crab meat, and oysters. The goal in cooking is to blend flavors without destroying the distinct identities of various ingredients, or stated more theoretically, taste is an effect of spacing, maintaining a measure of difference. Boil gumbo too long, and you get a slimy mush: homogeny at the expense of alterity.

Generalizing further, we observe: In addition to metaphorizing jazz as musical gumbo—an artful *conglomeration* of diverse elements—jazzographers have also pictured it as an amalgam. Look again at the above descriptions of jazz. They imagine it as a *conflu-ence* of diverse elements—the result of blending, fusion, or synthe-sis. The amalgam is to gumbo what compounds are to mixtures. Thus, the amalgam solves a problem for jazz. It forges an identity for the music, casts it as a body, ostensibly diverse but essentially unified. Gumbo, because of its tendency to carnivalesque inclu-siveness and its reluctance to annul difference, threatens to col-lapse jazz/nonjazz distinctions. What can't be tossed in the pot? What isn't jazz? The amalgam, on the other hand, admits and then, through the motions of integration, summarily suppresses diver-sity. By effacing alterity it achieves homogeny.

Really, though, isn't scrutinizing the logic of this metaphor a trivial enterprise? Absolutely, it is trivial, and we should never for-get (or forgive) that. For example, at least one writer, Gunther Schuller in his preface to *Early Jazz*, has pictured nonfiction jaz-zography as "a body of writing . . . which is little more than an amalgam of well-meaning amateur criticism and fascinated opin-ion." Probably, he gave little thought to this image conveniently welding together a multifarious body of texts. And probably he did not notice or did not care that, in his haste to focus on "techniques and actual musical content" of jazz, he pictures jazz writing through exactly the same image—one of those "general descriptive or impressionistic terms"—that others used to picture jazz (Schuller, vii). "And yet," to quote Denis Hollier, "who would be able to say, precisely, concerning a metaphor, where and when it *starts*—or stops?" (Hollier, 3). Once a metaphor starts rolling—once a tenor (from the French *tenere*, to hold) finds a vehicle—who can hold it back? What prevents us from making something of the amalgam, taking the vehicle that structures jazzography out for a spin? Maybe we'll find out how such an activity came to be regarded as trivial.

What follows is a brief account of nonfiction writing about jazz. It is necessarily incomplete—for reasons that smack of "kettle logic." First, a complete history of jazzography needs to be written, but it merits a substantial volume of its own (and demands a researcher with skills—for example, a measure of patience—that I lack). Second, to summon a dead horse that I will not flog, the notion of a "complete history" is philosophically vexed; all histo-ries are necessarily incomplete. And third, completeness isn't my goal anyway. But it is, to some extent, my object of study. I want to develop an argument already broached. The amalgam, a trope bring-ing jazz into language, admits diversity as a means to completeness, unification, or closure. It reverses the direction of the *satura*. The amalgam incorporates; the *satura* disseminates.

Notice again how the amalgam works for Schuller. It not only provides him with a picture of nonfiction jazzography. It implies a plot, a history. The logic of the amalgam motivates the discourse of jazz, moves it teleologically toward completeness, toward a purity of essence: the "genuine musicological research" of Schuller's own work. Gene Santoro, in a perceptive review of *The Swing Era* (Oxford UP, 1989), the massive second volume of Schuller's history of jazz, makes a similar point. He provides a historical-cultural context for Schuller's larger, perhaps unconscious, agenda, and he notices a pattern that typifies most jazzography. Santoro links Schuller's work with "the tradition of the anatomy, that ancient methodology that's bequeathed us pleasurable texts from Aristotle and Lucretius through Rabelais and Burton to Joyce and Proust and even Pynchon" (188). But as Santoro also observes, Schuller exhibits no desire to do for jazz what Burton did for melancholy. He does not write *saturas*; his texts are not gumbos. Rather, Schuller strives for synthetic grandeur. He amalgamates. His "evolutionary tropes and organic metaphors . . . stem directly from the Hegelian tradition that informs his work." They are productive, but they are not without cost. They lift his research above "the simpleminded Mount Rushmore model most music critics seem to use to understand the development of sounds" and, thus, impart an epic sweep to the unfolding story of jazz (191). But they also blind Schuller. Like his predecessors, he does not realize that his science (grounded on the "positivist's insistence on irreducible facts"—186) is shaped and is, perhaps, a consequence of the images he employs and suppresses. He does not see that the amalgam (or the pot that holds the gumbo) allows us to conceptualize jazz and jazzography.

From the Top

The first survey of jazzography, Roger Pryor Dodge's "Consider the Critics," appeared in Frederic Ramsey and Charles Smith's *Jazzmen* (1939). It is neither organized around proper names (the Mount Rushmore model), nor is it, as Ramsey and Smith claim in their introduction, a "careful résumé of the critical attitude which developed along with jazz" (xi). Instead, it is a thinly veiled polemic. Dodge works off basic oppositions that organized jazz listeners in his day. His survey is a pretext for challenging "premature white-collar meddling": the process that replaces "primitive impro-

visation" with "symphonic jazz" (Dodge, 301). What's most arresting about this essay, though, is the sense of déjà vu that it evokes.
Jazz lovers know Dodge's argument. We inherited it, not as a matter of continuing debate, but as a matter of received truth. "The
pattern of rhetorical shifts in inter-war jazz commentary is," as
Simon Frith detects,

> familiar from later responses to rock and roll: the initial treat-
> ment of the music as primitive and gimmicky, its survival
> depending on rapid assimilation into tried and tested forms of
> "good" music; the later appreciation that such "commercial-
> ization" is precisely what saps the sounds of their distinctive
> energy and truth. (1988:57–58)

Insofar as rhetorical shifts in the discourse of popular music gauge
attendant shifts in audience response to popular music, Dodge's
disapproval of "commercialized" jazz amounts to both an alignment and a demarcation. He isn't just making a valid point. He's
competing for allies, rallying troops to determine what will and
will not finally count as jazz. By organizing jazzography through a
commercial/authentic opposition, Dodge contributes to a process
that will seal the definition of jazz, and to a history that will
inevitably conclude and perfectly coincide with his own vision.

Put metaphorically, if jazz is musical gumbo, a *satura*, then
jazzography is its self-appointed taster. Before World War II, it des-
ignated two flavors of jazz. They were conventionally labeled "hot"
jazz and "sweet" or commercial jazz, but they were never represented more perfectly than in the wonderfully ambiguous title to
the first musicological study of jazz. *Jazz: Hot and Hybrid* (1938),
by Winthrop Sargeant, distinguishes and, by connotation, ranks the
"two general types of jazz." Additionally, it evokes the image of a
jazz trope in transfer: a metaphor turning from gumbo (*Jazz: Hot 'n'
Hybrid*) to the amalgam (*Jazz: The Hot Hybrid*) to imminent purity
(*Jazz: The Hot vs. The Hybrid*). Which is to say, read as a poetic
image, Sargeant's title repeats the rhetorical shifts of interwar jazz
commentary identified by Frith.

Cayenne Pepper and Penny Candy

Like all practicing modernists, Sargeant regarded the critic's
task as judgment and the critic's method as positivism (embodied
in musicological analysis). His vocation was to separate the gold of

art from the dross of commerce, which, within the realm of jazzography, meant distinguishing hot from sweet jazz. "The former," Sargeant writes,

> is more purely Negroid, more purely improvisatory, and comparatively independent of composed "tunes." The latter is the dance and amusement music of the American people as a whole. The tunes on which it is based issue from Tin Pan Alley, the center of the popular song-publishing industry. These tunes are, some of them, purely Anglo-Celtic or Central European in character, some of them pseudo-Negroid. (54)

Substitute "Black" for "Negroid" and this citation could pass for one written by LeRoi Jones in the mid-1960s. As it stands, it repeats the terms that had defined debate about jazz for as long as twenty years (since 1919, when Robert Goffin, a Belgian attorney and an expert on Apollinaire, praised jazz for its appeal to "the senses"— Frith, 1988:58). Redolent of reviews written by John Hammond and Spike Hughes for Britain's *Melody Maker* in the early '30s, Sargeant's comments completely reverse the opinions of Henry Osgood, author of *So This Is Jazz* (1926). The first American to write a book on the subject, Osgood pushed for the "rapid assimilation [of jazz] into tried and tested forms of 'good' music." He cheered on Paul Whiteman's efforts to turn "folk" music into "art," adopting, even developing, what Frith calls "the jazz-progress-from-jungle-to-ballroom line" (57).

Osgood's critical position, which was regularly repeated in the '20s and '30s, served two purposes. First, it connected jazz with highbrow art. Osgood aligned himself with that host of modern composers and conductors who sang praises to jazz: Aaron Copland, Ernst Ansermet, Igor Stravinsky, George Gershwin, Edward Burlingame Hill, Constant Lambert, Darius Milhaud, and Virgil Thompson. Next, Osgood's critical position defended jazz against numerous opponents. Schuller summarizes their discourse of panic:

> [T]here was an avalanche of derogatory articles and pamphlets by popular writers who fantasized relentlessly over the pernicious influence of jazz on music and morals. Moreover, the statements of many jazz musicians themselves in the early years of jazz encouraged others to treat the subject lightly. (vii)

The first of these two sentences scans quickly and easily. It corresponds to the first rhetorical phase of interwar jazz commentary: "the initial treatment of the music as primitive and gimmicky." We have grown accustomed to the phenomenon it describes. A subculture scandalizes a larger culture by expressing forbidden contents (consciousness of racial, sexual, or class difference) in forbidden forms (Hebdige, 1979:91). The second sentence, however, frustrates easy reading. Written from an ideal vantage point—where one can hear musicians frustrating the Will of Music—it also refers to very specific historical information.

Press Agent's Dream

Schuller dubs it "a press agent's dream come true," but the Original Dixieland Jazz Band (ODJB) was a musicologist's nightmare. The first jazz band to cut a record (1917), the ODJB defined the prerequisites of fame within electronic culture, embracing what Freddie Keppard and the Original Creole Band feared. Early in 1916, the Victor Phonograph Company had offered Keppard, a New Orleans trumpeter, a recording contract. He reportedly thought it over and said, "Nothin' doin', boys. We won't put our stuff on records for everybody to steal" (Russell and Smith, 22). While Keppard seemed unaware of the long-term consequences of his evasive maneuver, he was fully cognizant of the disseminative implications of electronic media. The ODJB, however, was more than cognizant; its members were prepared to exploit opportunities afforded by the paradigm shift from orality to electronics.

The ODJB treated musicianship as merely one component in the fabrication of a marketable image. It played the media with the panache of Alfred Jarry and the brilliant effrontery of later stars such as Elvis Presley, Bob Dylan, John Lennon, Johnny Rotten, Madonna, Ice-T and, more recently, Noel Gallagher. For instance, in a scene that foreshadowed similar events in the Sex Pistols saga, Columbia Records rushed to record the ODJB, but upon hearing its "uncouth and raucous" test pressing, promptly dropped the band (McDonough, 10). Victor immediately issued a contract, took the ODJB into a recording studio, and cut "Livery Stable Blues." It outsold records by Sousa and Caruso. Or witness the media-ready provocations of the ODJB's members. Trombonist Edward B. Edwards, "who read music and was well-trained on his instrument," told reporters, "Jazz, I think, means jumble"; it is "the untuneful harmony of rhythm" (*Ragtime Review*, in Schuller, 176).

Nick LaRocca, the band's leader and cornet player, in describing "how jazz works," said, "I cut the material, [clarinetist Larry] Shields puts on the lace, and Edwards sews it up" (177). Another time, "in a widely published interview," he called jazz "revolution in 4–4 time," and after ODJB pianist Henry Ragas died of alcoholism—"a strenuous round of parties and engagements" had "undermined his health"—LaRocca recalled, "I don't know how many pianists we tried before we found one who couldn't read music" (Russell and Smith, 51). Surveying the band's damage ("contributions" is hardly the word), Schuller writes:

> The career of the ODJB was both as fantastic and as typical as any that jazz has had to offer. Its story features the inevitable high points: the gradual grouping together of basically self-taught musicians, their sudden catapulting to world-wide fame, their equally sudden demise, and, in between, the million dollar law suits over copyrights and the petty jealousies, alcoholism, premature deaths, and all the rest. (176)

Musicologist's Nightmare

At this juncture, we would do well to notice a rhetorical pattern. It functions as a metonym for a larger pattern operating across musicology. Schuller acknowledges that the ODJB's claim to musical illiteracy greatly contributed to the effect that its "playing was *ipso facto* freshly improvised and inspired during each performance," perpetrating "the myth of total anarchy." But he makes this observation with an eye toward establishing a clear distinction between music—"a purely acoustical factual record"—and "extra-musical factors." He declares, "The ODJB . . . did not actually improvise." Its "recordings show without exception exact repetitions of choruses and a great deal of memorization"; "these choruses were set and rehearsed, and they were unchanged for years" (180). Schuller works to demythologize. He seeks to drive a wedge between "rhetoric" (what one claims to be the case) and "dialectic" (what, arguably, is the case) and, more specifically, between language about music and language about music makers.

Schuller's assumptions contrast sharply with those of Dick Hebdige in *Subculture: The Meaning of Style* (1979). In this study of youth subcultures in postwar Britain, Hebdige postulates the musical object (for example, "White Riot") and the musical subject (for example, the Clash) as thoroughly imbricated effects of ideology. A semiologist, his approach is one version of ethnology. Schuller, on the other hand, evokes the musical subject in order to deny it admittance to his study of musical objects. Undoubtedly, he believes that musicology is not ethnology (semiotics, ethnomusicology, anthropology, sociology, critical musicology, and such). What he fails to recognize, though, isn't an ethnological thesis about music and culture (he would probably concede that), but a theory of musicology. It goes like this: The rhetorical operation of evoking, barring, and subsequently (unconsciously or surreptitiously) inviting back the social dimension of music is sufficient to generate the science of musicology; the construct "musical object" is an effect of musicological discourse.

One could, of course, continue in this deconstructive mode, play out what would surely count as both musicological heresy and critical dogma. But this type of writing has become about as useful as a recording featuring bebop interpretations of the Elton John songbook. Which is to say, deconstruction—a close reading of a text's (im)possibility—requires tremendous ability, but it has been done so frequently and so well that it is no longer interesting and probably not needed. Today, we need only invoke deconstructive theory. To write it out is to craft academic kitsch.

That said, I still want to invoke one more theory about the relationship between Schuller and the ODJB: between musicology and music. Again, we turn to Hebdige. He demonstrates that a fractured social order is repaired when the "offending" subculture is "incorporated as a diverting spectacle within the dominant mythology from which it in part emanates" (Hebdige, 96). Schuller unwittingly assists such a mending or recuperative process in at least two ways. First, by undercutting myths that the ODJB cultivated, he separates musical subject (Nick LaRocca) and musical object ("Livery Stable Blues"), designating the former as subversive, the latter as neutral. This allows him to dismiss the antijazz rhetoric that surrounded the band as pure fantasy "over the pernicious influence of jazz on music and morals." More importantly, it provides him with an object of study conveniently shaped for analytical methods. Second, by employing the rational-analytical methods of musicology, Schuller manages or controls the potentially disruptive effects of electronic technology. For example, he knows full well that the fame of the ODJB depended on phonograph records and that, as an industry, recording represented a paradigm shift on the order of the Gutenberg revolution. After all, Schuller's own work registers this shift. While histories of "classical" music depend on scores,

Schuller depends on recordings (and scores transcribed from recordings). He is interested primarily in performance and only secondarily in compositions. Histories of "classical" music reverse this relationship (Schuller, x). But as surely as Schuller's work registers the shift from print to electronics, it also magically resolves disruptions brought about by this shift. Musicologists, apparently, do not study recordings or scores. They study music *through* these media. In this way they at once rely on technology—it gives rise to their object of study—and deny the full range of its consequences.

When We Boil It Down

It should now be evident: A rhetorical figure that we can designate as "boiling down" traverses jazzography. It motivates musicology devoted to the study of jazz—especially in attempts to concentrate on music and music alone—and it motivates the discourse of those who discovered in jazz a metaphor of modernism, an emblem of America. This discourse, writes MacDonald Smith Moore, "emanated primarily from two sources: domestic white critics with impeccable old-line Protestant credentials, and foreign observers caught up in the romance of America as a symbol of cultural freedom" (Moore, 92).

Catholics

Just as they drew Picasso to African masks, catholic tastes and a passion for the exotic drew European composers, conductors, and critics to jazz. Igor Stravinsky's *Histoire du Soldat* (1918) and Darius Milhaud's *La création du monde* (1923) incorporated "early jazz into modernist compositional practice" (Gendron, 3). And Swiss conductor Ernst-Alexandre Ansermet (1919) wrote glowingly of Sidney Bechet. But these figures were, in the final analysis, high-art tourists in the realm of popular culture. It was French critic Hugues Panassié who found in jazz a dwelling place and a vocation. Of his literary debut, *Le Jazz Hot* (1934), Whitney Balliett writes: "Aside from the erratic *Aux Frontières du Jazz*, brought out two years before by the Belgian Robert Goffin, it was the first book of jazz criticism, and it put jazz on the map in Europe and in its own country—an English translation was published here in 1936 as *Hot Jazz*—where the music had been ignored or misunderstood its forty-year life" (1986:3). Josef Skvorecky has the protagonist of his novel, *The Bass Saxophone*, liken *Le Jazz Hot* to the "Book of Mormon written in the language of angels" (121).

Panassié strikes an exceptional figure in jazzography. In addition to writing over a dozen books, he organized four recording sessions for RCA Victor in 1938 that helped precipitate a revival of traditional New Orleans jazz. He was an ardent spokesman for jazz primitivism, and he was the nemesis of beboppers (self-conscious modernists). Bebop, Panassié declares in *Guide to Jazz* (1956), a book published one year after Charlie Parker's death, is a "form of music distinct from jazz" (Panassié, in Balliett, 1986:4). "In music primitive man generally has greater talent than civilized man. An excess of culture atrophies inspiration" (Panassié, in Gioia, 1988:29). Panassié may be the Jean-Jacques Rousseau of jazz criticism, but he was, first and foremost, an authenticist. His writings aimed to restrict the usage of the word "jazz": to stop it from referring to just any sort of "syncopated dance music with Afro-American influences" (Gendron, 13). Or stated differently, Panassié may have finally lost his battle with bebop—that is, with the modernist future of jazz—but he and other early-jazz boosters (for example, Robert Goffin, Wilder Hobson, Frederic Ramsey, and Charles Edward Smith) won another, and probably more decisive, victory. They boldly answered the question, "What is jazz?" In doing so, they gave jazz a past: a history (or canon) that necessarily excised much of what had been previously called "jazz." It is no wonder, then, that Panassié joined forces with Charles Delaunay—the only child of the geometric-futurist painters Sonia Delaunay-Terk and Robert Delaunay—and founded *Jazz Hot* ("now the world's oldest pure jazz magazine"—Balliett, 1986:4–7). The two shared both an aesthetic and an agenda. Delaunay wrote *Hot Discography* (1936), the first reference guide to recorded jazz and, thus, laid out the boundaries of jazz.

Protestants

MacDonald Smith Moore's *Yankee Blues: Musical Culture and American Identity* (1985) demonstrates that musical discourse between World War I and II provided a language for debating issues of American identity (Moore, 2). Here is a summary of its argument. In the 1920s, Yankee composers and critics (for example, Charles Ives, Daniel Gregory Mason, and Henry Adams), feeling "increasingly isolated from the sources of political and economic power," found it difficult to extol Emersonian values (individualism and progressivism) as special interest groups repeatedly appropriated "the symbolism of redemptive America" for their own purposes. These groups seemed to picture themselves as modern Pilgrims on new missions to the wilderness, while their opponents became ever more convinced that Yankee ideals were being misused and that such misuse fed a materialistic society. Consequently, these old-line "Protestant" composers and critics "sought to reestablish their vision of an essentialist American faith: one that would delineate not merely a horizontal democratic order but a vertical order of transcendental values" (6). To this end, they "managed to link music in the United States with issues of American identity" (3). "[M]usic criticism became a primary locus of national cultural conflict" (2).

"Through metaphors of musical valuation," Moore writes, "Americans struggled to define and rank the key symbolic groups in American society of the twentieth century: Yankees, Negroes, and Jews" (3). "Writers of all backgrounds attributed a sensual culture to Negroes and a spiritual culture to Yankees." Jews, emblematized as both "coarse and sensual" and "neither black nor white," were understood as terms of mediation—"rootless middlemen . . . who combined in an ethos of consumption capitalism the bewildering intellectuality of technology and the preference for immediate gratification" (170).

Jazz, Moore explains, came to be read as expressive of the paradoxical temper of modern America: "its egoistic fragmentation of community, its materialism, its fascination with modernism in general and with avant-gardism in particular" (66). It was championed by "white rebels" or "foreign observers" who drew on "romantic racialism" and "affirmed the artistic, spiritual, and national value of sensualism" (68). And it was damned by those who saw it standing "for the basest form of musical romanticism, the devolutionary forces of sensual blackness" and, paradoxically, "the antimusic of robots and riveting machines, the technology of urban civilization" (82, 108). Critics attributed the popularity of jazz among whites, "not to Negroes, deemed too dull to exploit their own essential characteristics, but to an intermediate symbolic group, the Jews." "[T]he religious metaphor of Jew-as-horned-Devil was replaced gradually by the racial metaphor of Jew-as-Oriental," a merchant "trading on the base sensuality attributed to Negroes and the Anglo-Saxon, spiritual tradition associated with Yankees" (170, 71).

The Yankee vision of "redemptive culture" perished during World War II, and jazzography, at least temporarily, ceased to function as an open forum for cultural debate. Its discourse shifted from criticism to analysis as it began to appropriate the methods of musicology for the study of jazz. Many factors affected this methodological shift, but none were so great as the increasing complexity of jazz and the advent of rock and roll. Advanced improvisations (Louis Armstrong), arrangements (Fletcher Henderson), and compositions (Duke Ellington) had made jazz not only "worthy" of, but susceptible to, "the tools of theoretical analysis." They created conditions that enabled Sargeant to publish *Jazz: Hot and Hybrid* in 1938, and as jazz developed further, they later allowed André Hodeir to tighten the "analytical screws" once again. In 1956, "taking full advantage of the perspective provided by the innovations of Charlie Parker and the whole modern jazz movement," Hodeir published *Jazz: Its Evolution and Essence.*" This study, according to Schuller, was the first to meet the standards Sargeant had set (viii).

Thus, the institutionalization of jazz as an art music, as the purview of scholars both professional and amateur, coincided with the popularization of rock and roll. The year 1956 was Elvis Presley's *annus mirabilis*. It was also a time when pontifications about jazz the sort of contentious rhetoric associated with jazz critics from Henry Osgood to Hugues Panassié—came to appear ridiculous, hopelessly anachronistic.

This claim finds a perfect illustration in a scene from *Jailhouse Rock* (1957). Vince Everett (Elvis Presley), an ex-con and would-be recording star, accompanies his manager to a cocktail party where the conversation turns to the "dissonance" and "altered chords" of Dave Brubeck, Paul Desmond, and Lennie Tristano. A socialite declares, "Some day, they'll make the cycle and get back to pure old Dixieland. I say atonality is just a passing phase in jazz music." She then asks, "What do you think Mr. Everett?" He replies, "Lady, I don't know what the hell you're talking about." Disgusted, Vince exits the party. However much it's a caricature—satirizing both the suburban audience for "modern-jazz" and the insolent rocker—the scene still works. It's funny for being schematic. It emblematizes the cultural shift announced by rock and roll, the ascendancy of youth culture, as well as the conditions that made this ascent possible. Elvis does more than refuse generational and cultural continuity. He lays claim to a title once reserved for jazz fans (and early bands, such as the ODJB). He is a philistine, while jazz fans have become nothing if not respectable. They sit (in living rooms and clubs); Elvis dances (beside his swimming pool and on TV).

In musicology and the close, text-based readings of New Criticism, jazzography located an analytical language sufficient for the complexities of bebop and successive postwar jazz styles, and appropriate for its dwindling, specialist and intellectual, audience. This discourse found full expression in the pages of *The Jazz Review* (1958–61), a magazine co-edited by Nat Hentoff and Martin Williams, and featuring contributions by Gunther Schuller. But its influence far exceeded the boundaries of that publication. It still dominates jazzography (much as semiotics dominates film studies), directly shaping the writings of Gary Giddins (*The Village Voice*), Francis Davis (*The Atlantic*), Richard Cook and Brian Morton (*Penguin Guide to Jazz*), and indirectly affecting criticism appearing in *Down Beat, Jazziz, Cadence, Coda, The Wire, Jazz Times*, and other specialty magazines.

But postwar jazzography also took another form that, ironically, resurrected earlier dreams of "redemptive culture." As the popularity of jazz declined, when huge numbers of white kids followed after rock and roll, its status among African Americans rose. Jazz became a source of black intellectual pride. Moore describes how this shift in audience and, correspondingly, in the connotative value of jazz affected its discourse:

> As the ideological rationales for "Black Power" peaked in the late 1960s, jazz served increasingly as the cherished touchstone of self-worth for Negro intellectuals. No longer just entertainment, jazz was believed to express specifically Afro-American values. In the black aesthetic of identity, jazz possessed a uniquely organic beauty which drew inspiration from the sensual warmth—"soul"—of the Negro spirit. Black redemptive culture came full circle; some black writers, including Harold Cruse, voiced antiwhite and occasionally anti-Semitic racism. Still trapped by their opposition and by the metaphors of the old racial stereotypes, in pain and anger they acted out roles drawn from the music drama of the 1920s. (171)

For two examples of jazzography shaped by the dream of "black redemptive culture," we might consider LeRoi Jones's *Blues People* (1963) and Ortiz Walton's *Music: Black, White and Blue* (1972). Jones reads "black" music as an index (or, as he calls it, "an analogy") of American history. It reveals "something about the essential nature of the Negro's existence in this country . . . as well as something about the essential nature of this country, that is, society as a whole" (1963:x). Walton's book amplifies Jones's thesis. It is less a history of black music than "a sociological study of its development, its use and misuse." It states, "[E]ven though a deliberate plan was executed to deprive Blacks of their African culture . . . what persevered and developed were the *essential qualities* of the African world view, a view concerned with metaphysical rather than purely physical interrelationships" (2).

Whether they were creative interventions—examples of radical catachresis or synaesthesia (*black* music?)—or just ideological interpretations of the most naïve sort, the writings of Jones, Walton, and others informed by a "black aesthetic of identity" had tremendous implications for jazzography. Their emphasis on "verifiable emotional referents and experiential categories of Afro-American culture" repoliticized jazz discourse (affecting it much as feminism affected film studies). Explicitly, the black aesthetic argued that the cultural codes that made normative judgments possible were, by definition, inaccessible to white writers whose criticism never ceased to be informed by racialism (Baker, 1984:74–78). Implicitly, it questioned the musicological methods endorsed by white jazzographers, revealing that so called "objective analysis" always functioned as "criticism" (raising and resolving issues of meaning and value). The discourse of positivistic methodology always belies an attempt to block connotations that would destabilize its hegemony.

Paradigm: A Lesson from Ondaatje's *Coming through Slaughter*

Notes is good enough for you people, but us likes a mixtery.
            —Anonymous ex-slave (in Mackey, 1986:39)

Listening to Buddy Bolden

Probably, Michael Ondaatje doesn't label the jazz tendency to mix "the *satura* trope." After all, when artists describe what they do, they typically use the name of their idiom. For example, jazz musicians "play jazz," or they "just play" (Bailey, xii). Ondaatje writes.

His 1976 novel, *Coming through Slaughter* (*CTS*), is about Buddy Bolden, the first mythic figure of jazz, "the first to play the hard jazz and blues for dancing" (Louis Jones, in Ondaatje, 5). In simplest terms, it's a docu-novel or collage narrative. Ondaatje treats the legend of Buddy Bolden the way he imagines Bolden's band treated songs: as departure points. For example, in one of the novel's many internal monologues, Ondaatje has Bolden describe the musical function of valve trombonist Willy Cornish. He was the one, muses Bolden, "who played the same note the same way every time who was our frame our diving board that we leapt off, the one we sacrificed so he could remain the overlooked metronome." Cornish was "the only one able to read music." "[H]e brought us new music from the north that we perverted cheerfully into our own style" (112).

Unlike Donald Marquis (whose book, *In Search of Buddy Bolden: First Man of Jazz*, appeared two years after *CTS*), Ondaatje doesn't seek to recover a referential Bolden—to erase the apocrypha patched onto the figure of the Jazzman. His text is not, strictly speaking, mimetic of history; it subordinates factual accuracy to "the truth of fiction" (4). Neither is it interpretive (except as an aftereffect). Ondaatje doesn't lift up Bolden as symbol or allegory, or read him hermeneutically. And he doesn't critique him as a power-fully evocative and resonant icon, designating and disseminating a culturally significant myth. Bolden offers no universal or private truths. Rather, Ondaatje uses the legendary cornet player (that is, the cornet player of legend) as a way to make something new, as a means to organize the release of information.

In the remaining pages of this chapter, I want to sketch out a recipe for a type of academic writing that would treat its object of study as Ondaatje treated Bolden (and as Bolden treated the "new music" Cornish brought from up North). I intend to do this by, in effect, reversing the direction of conventional scholarship. Instead of teaching—showing readers what I have shown *CTS* about itself—I take a position of ignorance (sublimate the role of teacher to the role of student). I assume that the artistic strategies employed in *CTS* speak directly to a theoretical practice that—while not abandoning representation, explanation, and critique as rhetorical effects—would concern itself, first of all, with invention. In other words, I seize *CTS* as a tutor text for heuretics. Perhaps, what I have really done, though, is assume the mantle of Pierre Menard, author of the *Quixote*, and Louis Borges's exemplary postmodernist scholar. For, like him, I have lost interest in writing about my tutor text (though that activity too much occupies me). I want to learn how to write *CTS*, that is to say, learn how to write scholarship with it. To be, in some way, Ondaatje, to think in his brain and body, however, seems less arduous to me—and, consequently, less interesting—than to continue being myself. I would like to possess *CTS* by reaching for the compositional principle that generated it and, then, compose texts of my own by employing this principle (Borges, 48–49).

I, therefore, ask: What did Bolden teach Ondaatje? What is the compositional principle that enabled *CTS*? The short answer is, Bolden taught Ondaatje how jazz is made. He showed him a recipe for *satura*. But what might this mean? Dude Botley offers an explanation which Ondaatje quotes in *CTS* (it's part of a monologue that originally appeared in Martin Williams's *Jazz Masters of New Orleans*). One night, about eight o'clock, Botley followed Bolden up New Orleans's Canal Street and saw him enter a barber shop through its back door. Knowing that this was Bolden's former place of employment made Botley more curious than alarmed. He surreptitiously watched Bolden through the window of the darkened shop, and when he saw him sit in a chair and, then, heard him playing cornet very quietly, he moved closer. This is what Botley said he heard:

> Thought I knew his blues before, and the hymns at funerals, but what he is playing now is real strange and I listen careful for he's playing something that sounds like both. I cannot make out the tune and then I catch on. He's mixing them up. He's playing the blues and the hymn sadder than the blues and then the blues sadder than the hymn. That is the first time I ever heard hymns and blues cooked up together. (80–81)

The *satura* trope, again—and in a myth accounting for the genesis of jazz. Although Bolden never made a recording, his innovation of mixing secular and sacred music—cooking up God's music and the Devil's music in one pot of gumbo—repeats itself in every jazz performance. We know jazz, write and read it, through the *satura*. *CTS*, however, not only employs this trope as an image for explaining (as all who represent jazz must do). It exploits the *satura* as a paradigm for writing, as a set of instructions for composing (composting).

Mystory

CTS mixes and then condenses into one account information from three levels of discourse: *popular* (folklore or the myths of popular culture), *professional* (expert or disciplinary knowledge), and *personal* (autobiography). It is representative of an emerging experimental genre that Gregory Ulmer has named "mystory"

(1989a:209). And it is comparable to making jazz, since in both activities the idiomatic (one's private discourse) joins with the institutional (the recognized "grammar" of one's discipline) in order to rewrite (or in Brecht's term "refunction") an object of study. For the jazz musician, this means projecting one's inimitable "sound" onto the "grammar" of jazz (for example, the blues) in order to recompose a Tin Pan Alley song or "standard." For the writer, mystory provides an alternative to what Barthes calls "*reading*," a pleasureless activity that has become "nothing more than a *referendum*" (1974:4).

Mystory responds to the blues, to the melancholia traditionally associated with the "artistic temperament" and the influence of Saturn. By requiring its writer to perform a myth he or she lives by—but to address this myth through the discourse of personal experience and to disrupt it through formal experimentation—mystory functions as both story and critique. For example, in Bolden's image—the popularized picture of the jazzman as well as the literal photograph reproduced on the title page of *CTS*—Ondaatje recognizes himself. He writes:

> The photograph moves and becomes a mirror. When I read he stood in front of mirrors and attacked himself, there was the shock of memory. For I had done that. . . . Defiling people we did not wish to be. (Ondaatje, 133)

Emotion, what Roland Barthes (in *Camera Lucida*) labels the *punctum* or sting of recognition, guides Ondaatje to a myth (an enabling or, perhaps, disabling story/ideology) that composes his identity. As a mystory, *CTS* externalizes or stages this psychological process of identification; it serves its author in much the same way that Brecht's "learning plays" were intended to educate actors (Ulmer, 1989a:210)—or as playing the blues prompts an affective shift in jazz musicians: from alienated thought to carnivalesque thinking. The following three sections, corresponding to three levels of discourse, develop the lesson in heuretics or mystory writing taught by *CTS*. The fourth and final section of this chapter proposes an assignment, carried out in the experiments that close subsequent chapters.

Popular Dimension: The Story

Mystory begins with a writer appropriating a "figure become mythical . . . as a ready-made organizing device," using it as if it were "a kind of index, or a mnemonic system": "*inventio and memoria*" (Ulmer, 1991:7). For Ondaatje, in *CTS*, this mythic figure or popular icon is, of course, Buddy Bolden. Ondaatje has said that he was drawn to this image not because of "nation," "colour," or "age," but through a "cryptic newspaper reference": "Buddy Bolden who became a legend when he went berserk in a parade" (Witten, in Barbour, 100; Ondaatje, 134). Granted, this fragment refers to a particular story (one which Ondaatje came to research and write in *CTS*), but more importantly, it evokes a popular story about the high cost of fame. The Buddy Bolden myth is the flip side of the Louis Armstrong myth. It is, to evoke a metaphor I shall soon clarify, a hologram of jazz; shattered, it transubstantiates over and over again in the tragic tales of Bunny Berigan, Bix Beiderbecke, Fats Waller, Charlie Parker, Serge Chaloff, Bud Powell, Fats Navarro, Thelonious Monk, Billie Holiday, Albert Ayler, and others. It is also the Kurt Cobain story. It evokes recognition and response from Ondaatje not only because he has often heard this particularly cruel inversion of the Horatio Alger myth, but because he has internalized it so thoroughly. The newspaper reference—a minimal anecdote—articulates a highly compressed cultural myth or metanarrative integral to Ondaatje's identity formation.

The archetype of the Crescent-City tale of the self-destructive artist lies in romanticism, but the most direct antecedent of the story told by *CTS* is Dorothy Baker's *Young Man with a Horn* (1938). The first novel to employ a jazz musician as protagonist, it relates the story of Rick Martin, a trumpet player modeled after Bix Beiderbecke. Martin is, to borrow a phrase Norman Mailer would later coin, a "White Negro" (Huck Finn with a horn). But the psychodrama that drives him also drives Ondaatje's Bolden. Martin, writes Richard Albert, is "an artist who must struggle with his own aspirations to be the greatest as he seeks to promote his individuality" (3). He fails (except in the 1950 film version of the novel), and Baker tells why.

> Our man is, I hate to say it, an artist, burdened with that difficult baggage, the soul of an artist. But he hasn't got the thing that should go with it—and which I suppose seldom does—the ability to keep the body in check while the spirit goes on being what it must be. And he goes to pieces, but not in any small way. He does it so thoroughly that he kills himself doing it. (1938:6)

FIGURE 1.2
Charlie Parker (photo courtesy of Billy Vera)

In his survey of jazz fiction, Vance Bourjaily labels the plot shaping *Young Man with a Horn* "The Story," and he declares that it "is used, with variations, in more than half the jazz stories" he can call to mind. An "Anti-Story Story" accounts for the bulk of the remaining half. It is exemplified by "Jam Today" (Peter DeVries),

"You're Too Hip, Baby" (Terry Southern), "Mending Wall" (Willard Marsh), "A Really Good Jazz Piano" (Richard Yates), and "The King of Jazz" (Donald Barthelme). All anti-story stories satirize romanticism and are most frequently organized around the dichotomy of a jazz musician's quest for acceptance (and a living wage) and a jazz fan's dream of authenticity (rigorously modern music uncompromised by concern for mass culture or the market).

> The Story goes like this: a musician of genius, frustrated by the discrepancy between what he can achieve and the crummy life musicians lead (because of racial discrimination, or the demand that the music be made commercial, or because he has a potential he can't reach), goes mad, or destroys himself with alcohol and drugs. (Bourjaily, 44)

The Story functions within *CTS* much as melody and harmony function within the polyphonic jazz of old New Orleans; it regulates the unfolding of the text. This concept can be verbally sketched by referring to the narrative codes Barthes develops in *S/Z*. Briefly, he observes that "unity," a textual effect, "is basically dependent on two sequential codes: the revelation of truth and the coordination of the actions represented." The hermeneutic (revelatory) code corresponds to melody. Because it is predicated on enigma—"suspended disclosure" or "delayed resolution"—this code urges readers to keep reading (decoding). The proairetic (action) code, on the other hand, corresponds to harmony. It sustains the narrative by bringing "everything together" in "the cadence of familiar gestures" (1974:29–30). In chapter 3, we shall return to and develop Barthes's analogy between classic narratives and classical music, but for now, it is enough to notice that *CTS* treats the melody and harmony provided by the Story—its tune and its changes—as "new music from the north." It perverts rather than replays.

Professional Dimension: Jazzing The Story

In other words, *CTS* does not abandon the Story, but it does jazz it up. More precisely, it looks writerly or modern, not readerly or tonal, because Ondaatje interrupts the orderly unfolding of the Story (the narrative as syntagm) by elaborating terms that he associates with Bolden's legend. For example, he invents a friendship between Bolden and photographer E. J. Bellocq. Without abandoning effects of forward motion—narratival movement toward resolution—Ondaatje forces a shift in interest center. Instead of retelling the Story (restating the melody), he uses the Story as a means to invention (creating solos). This strategy, a contribution of the author's disciplinary discourse and a valuable lesson for the mystorian, marks Ondaatje's status as an expert, a professional writer. Notice, however, that it was derived from (or was at least available within) Bolden's legend.

The jazzman always uses melody, harmony, or rhythm as a place to start improvising. This is a received truth of jazz. But in the particulars of Bolden's story Ondaatje also discovers a set of instructions that tells him exactly how to improvise on the Story. Legend has it that Bolden was the first jazz publisher. He wrote a gossip sheet. Marquis, Bolden's demythologizer, finds this information unsubstantiated; Ondaatje exploits it as a heuretic device. He writes:

> *The Cricket* existed between 1899 and 1905. It took in and published all the information Bolden could find. It respected stray facts, manic theories, and well-told lies. (24)

Since no scrap of *The Cricket* has ever been found, it provides Ondaatje with a *topos* for filling. "I'm really drawn to unfinished stories," the novelist told Mark Witten. "There's all those empty spaces you can put stuff in" (Witten, in Barbour, 99). *CTS* thus fulfills (or fills out) Bolden's story, and it does so by following the three-step recipe for concocting mythologies that it attributes to *The Cricket*. On the acknowledgments page of the novel, Ondaatje lists the sources of his *"stray facts."* They read like movie credits and include Ramsey and Smith's *Jazzmen*, Martin Williams's *Jazz Masters of New Orleans*, Al Rose's *Storyville, New Orleans*, tape recordings of jazz musicians from the Jazz Archives at Tulane, and files from the East Louisiana State Hospital. Other material, "expanded or polished to suit the truth of fiction," can be filed under the heading *"well-told lies"*: for example, the characters of Nora Bass (Bolden's wife), Nora's mother, Webb (Bolden's detective friend), or the pimp, Tom Pickett. Finally, under the category *"manic theories,"* we could single out again the "private and fictional magnets" that drew Storyville photographer E. J. Bellocq and Bolden together.

Ondaatje organizes *CTS* as he says Bolden organized *The Cricket*: by dropping its ingredients "into his pail of sub-history," shaking them up, and then spreading "them out like garbage"

(Ondaatje, 134). In a word, he *composts*; his method is to composition what dream logic is to rational thinking. Both include "not only condensation and displacement, but also secondary elaboration, a reworking of the bizarre material generated by the primary process into a coherent form" (Ulmer, 1991:6). Not surprisingly, Ondaatje's Bolden employs this exact same strategy as a means of making music on his cornet. In a monologue, he contrasts his aesthetic with that of rival musician. "Did you ever meet [John] Robichaux?" he asks himself.

> I never did. I loathed everything he stood for. He dominated his audiences. He put his emotions into patterns which a listening crowd had to follow. . . . When I played parades we would be going down Canal Street and at each intersection people would hear just the fragment I happened to be playing and it would fade as I went further down Canal. . . . I wanted them to be able to come in where they pleased and leave when they pleased and somehow hear the germs of the start and all the possible endings at whatever point in the music that I had reached *then*. (93–94)

Ondaatje to some extent realizes this dream of an alternative art form: first, by exploiting the technology of the book; second, by simulating and, thus, anticipating the emerging possibilities of electronic media. *CTS* is, on one level, a simple random-access machine; it reads like a codex, not a scroll. An assemblage of anecdotes, data, and short poems, it shivers the regular rhythms of the Story. It's directly analogous to John Zorn's recording "Spillane," a sequence of "disparate sound blocks" (originally stored on filing cards), each of which evoke "some aspect of [Mickey] Spillane's work, his world, his characters, his ideology" (Zorn, 9). But *CTS* and "Spillane" differ in one especially telling respect. Zorn admits that his music "is ideal for people who are impatient, because it is jam-packed with information that is changing very fast" (12). *CTS* relies on repetition with variation, permutations that unfold ever so slowly. I think of it as a simulated hologram and associate it with the "ambient music" of Brian Eno, perhaps because I often listen to Eno while writing, but more certainly because this anecdote of his arrests me.

> When I was in school—I went to a Catholic school—we were told that the host—the thing you get at Holy Communion—

could be broken into any number of minute parts and that each part was still the complete body of Jesus Christ, even if it was only a tiny fragment. This always puzzled me. I thought about that a lot as a fine theological point. And then when I was about 18, I went to a lecture by Dennis Gabor, who invented the hologram; he said that one of the things that's interesting about the hologram is that if you shatter it and you take a fragment from the whole, you will still see the complete image from that piece, only it will be a much less distinct and fuzzier version. It's not like a photograph, you see, where if you tear off one corner, all you see is that corner. The whole of the image is encoded over the whole of the surface, so the tiniest part will still be the whole of that image. And I thought this was such a fantastically grand idea, and for the first time it gave me some understanding of the Catholic idea of the host; there was some scientific parallel to it. (Eno, in Milkowski, 17)

The Bolden legend plays host to Ondaatje its author, but it also possesses him like a parasite or demon. In the diegesis or fictive story space of *CTS*, it's Bolden who's frequently pictured as the quintessential parasite, the unexpected guest. For example, when he leaves New Orleans to play a three-night gig at Shell Beach, he ends up annexing himself onto a couple, Jaelin and Robin Brewitt. They become a *ménage à trois*. In French, so perhaps in Louisana, *parasite* not only means to inhabit or take advantage of another, it means noise: "the static in a system or the interference in a channel" (Serres, x; see also *CTS*'s "dolphin epigraph").

Personal Dimension: Ground Zero

In a self-reflexive passage, immediately following the resolution of the narrative and a one-page résumé summarizing the "facts" of Bolden's life, Ondaatje accounts for the existence of *CTS*. He describes Gravier, Phillip, and Liberty—streets Bolden had traveled seventy years earlier—mentions that, today, people in that old neighborhood have not heard of the famous cornet player, and then reveals: "When he went mad he was the same age as I am now" (133). It's a startling passage, for not only does the novelist interpolate himself into his own fiction, he raises a fascinating question. Why are we as writers or readers drawn to (and, in a sense, drawn by) certain texts? Ondaatje images a possible answer as he invokes the metaphor of a mirror or speculum. He writes:

Why did my senses stop at you? There was the sentence, "Buddy Bolden who became a legend when he went berserk in a parade. . . ." What was there in that, before I knew your nation your colour your age, that made me push my arm forward and spill it through the front of your mirror and clutch myself? Did not want to pose in your accent but think in your brain and body, and you like a weatherbird arcing round in the middle of your life to exact opposites and burning your brains out so that from June 5, 1907 till 1931 you were dropped into amber in the East Louisiana State Hospital. Some saying you went mad trying to play the devil's music and hymns at the same time, and Armstrong telling historians that you went mad by playing too hard and too often drunk too wild too crazy. The excesses cloud up the page. There was the climax of the parade and then you removed yourself from the 20th-century game of fame, the rest of your life a desert of facts. Cut them open and spread them out like garbage. (134)

Were it not for this passage, *CTS* would be little more than an artful jumble of documentary materials, imagined dialogue and monologues, and poetic patches spread out in the manner of imagist poetry. It would read like the paper equivalent of an experimental film: mythic narrative rendered as especially lyrical *cinéma vérité* (multiple narrators; lots of cross cutting). And that would be admirable enough. But as the above passage indicates, *CTS* adds personal (idiomatic) information to the public and professional levels of discourse.

The autobiographical component of mystory is calculated to reframe the relation between subject and object. Put negatively and emphatically, it does not simply allow or encourage writers to share their personal experiences, to substitute subjective for objective discourse. It is not naïve. What is it then? What does Ondaatje teach us about autobiographical writing? Simply this: Mystory *shows* what theory *tells*. And that's the essential difference between heuretics and hermeneutics. For example, instead of explaining Althusser's concept of interpellation—the process by which we are constructed as subjects when we answer the call of ideology—Ondaatje visualizes his own identity formation. He pictures his solicitation by and response to Bolden as ego-ideal.

Ulmer labels such scenes "ground-zero anecdotes" (the Bomb, he says, represents "the principle of unsolved problems of every sort"). They are good to think with. They mark a place of memory, a site where imagination starts, because they are, paradoxically, sites where stories catastrophically end (Ulmer, 1989a:198). Ground-zero anecdotes demystify the desire that motivates research. They tell why we write what we write. But they are, at the same time, mysterious (representing the *mise-en-abyme* of narrative). On the one hand, Ondaatje satisfies our curiosity about the origins of *CTS*; he displays its "primal scene" and, thereby, makes his novel more than historical fiction. On the other hand, he suggests that *CTS* is a kind of mystery play, dramatizing a culturally significant icon for critical and inventive effects. Ondaatje seeks to understand himself by researching Bolden, a central figure or monument of his image-repertoire. But this is key. He responds to Bolden's legend not as a pilgrim (idolatrous), but as a tourist (fascinated), and it is this affective shift that makes *CTS* a memorial (a relay point in Ondaatje's memory) instead of a shrine (a place to stay and worship). Slaughter, it turns out, is an actual town in Louisiana. After Bolden's death, a train carried his body from the state asylum through Slaughter, Vachery, Sunshine, and, finally, to New Orleans's Holtz Cemetery (Ondaatje, 137). More importantly, Slaughter is a metaphorical topos; it's a place that Ondaatje passes through—alive.

Recipe

Let me summarize the ingredients and the basic steps for making a mystory:

1. Appropriate a popular icon, a "figure become mythical," as an object of study.
2. In the form of an anecdote or short skit (modeled after a scene from a medieval "saints" play), write out his/her/its story.
3. Research the icon in detail. Mystorian and jazz musician John Zorn says to "read books and articles, look at films, TV shows, and photo files, listen to related recordings, etc." (Zorn, 9).
4. Sift through the materials accumulated. Pick out an image, one that is especially striking. Set it aside; let ferment.
5. Compose a ground-zero anecdote. It should tell how the mystorian first learned about and became interested in the icon. More importantly, it should describe how, for all intents and purposes, this icon called or solicited the mystorian's attention and affections.
6. Allow the image selected in step 4 to ferment long enough, and it will become readable as a grammalogue (a trope or metaphor one can write with). Treat the grammalogue as a hieroglyph or

rebus that confuses the verbal and the visual, and it will suggest a specific method for arranging materials the mystorian has either gathered or invented.

7. Rewrite the story composed in step 2 by ordering materials (including the ground-zero anecdote) in a manner suggested by the grammalogue. This means that the mystorian should proceed by employing "pictogrammatical," not ratio-analytic, logic.

While *CTS* models mystory as an art practice directly applicable to a new kind of theoretical writing, *Silence*, by composer, author, and mycologist John Cage, is an *omnium gatherum* of theoretical texts informed by avant-garde practices. It is a cookbook for heuretics. (In the modern age, F. T. Marinetti disseminated futurist doctrine through a cookbook, and Ntozake Shange's novel *Sassafrass, Cypress & Indigo* uses cooking and playing jazz as mutually illuminating images. But as a literary form, the cookbook has been woefully neglected by theorists.) In the foreword to *Silence*, Cage discloses the aims of his scholarship:

> For over twenty years I have been writing articles and giving lectures. Many of them have been unusual in form—this is especially true of the lectures—because I have employed in them means of composing analogous to my composing means in the field of music. My intention has been, often, to say what I had to say in a way that would exemplify it; that would, conceivably, permit the listener to experience what I had to say rather than just hear about it. (Cage, 3)

Cage's practice of telling by showing is, of course, hardly revolutionary within the realm of art. It is T. S. Eliot's notion of the objective correlative; it was *de rigueur* for the Dadaists and surrealists. Cage's innovation, therefore, isn't the invention of a new methodology but the application of an established methodology to a new field. Cage appropriated what his friend Marcel Duchamp would have considered "normal science" for avant-garde artists, and he employed it to write and deliver lectures. Cage exploited art for pedagogical purposes. This, to make a point I shall not develop, marks his major break with modernism. In his desire to rid music of taste and memory and in his antipathy toward repetition, Cage is thoroughly modern (he finds no pleasure in jazz or rock and roll); in his attitude toward a mass audience (in his acceptance of didacticism), Cage announces postmodernism.

In *Silence* Cage explores the pedagogical potential of a wide variety of "art" styles and techniques. He composes a manifesto on the use of noise to make music, writes a mock field guide on contemporary music and mushrooms, weaves together multiple narrative lines to form a single text, pontificates on the concept of indeterminacy, repeats phrases for rhythmic effect, imagines a dialogue on experimental music between "an uncompromising teacher and an unenlightened student," converses with the deceased French composer Erik Satie, constructs a lecture out of questions and quotations, details a means of composing music using the *I-Ching* (*Book of Changes*), relates the history of experimental music in the United States, and arranges written text according to chance operations. Plus, he tells ninety anecdotes. One of my favorites goes as follows:

> Two wooden boxes containing Oriental spices and foodstuffs arrived from India. One was for David Tudor, the other for me. Each of us found, on opening his box, that the contents were all mixed up. The lids of containers of spices had somehow come off. Plastic bags of dried beans and palm sugar had ripped open. The tin lids of cans of chili powder had come off. All of these things were mixed with each other and with the excelsior which had been put in the box to keep the containers in position. I put my box in a corner and simply tried to forget about it. David Tudor, on the other hand, set to work. Assembling bowls of various sizes, sieves of about eleven various-sized screens, a pair of tweezers, and a small knife, he began a process which lasted three days, at the end of which time each spice was separated from each other, each kind of bean from each other, and the palm sugar lumps had been scraped free of spice and excavations in them had removed embedded beans. He then called me up to say, "Whenever you want to get at that box of spices you have, let me know. I'll help you." (193)

This anecdote, if read allegorically, illustrates two principles of textual arrangement. Tudor (the tutor) separates. Cage mixes; he makes *saturas*. But the anecdote also comments on interpretation. Given a *satura*, should readers set to work, try to sort it all out, or should they simply try to forget about it, get on with other matters?

For the moment, let's do a little more sorting. The spice anecdote represents a recurring theme in Cage's writings. They abound in references to food and dining. For example, in "What Are We

Eating? And What Are We Eating?" Cage writes an account of his travels with the Merce Cunningham Dancers by detailing what everyone ordered when they stopped to eat. And in *Silence*, he relates many anecdotes about studying, gathering, consuming, and, occasionally, vomiting mushrooms. He writes: "I have come to the conclusion that much can be learned about music by devoting oneself to the mushroom" (274). But, one might ask, why mushrooms? Cage remarks with a wink: The secondhand bookshops in which one purchases "'field companions' on fungi" are "in some rare cases next door to shops selling dog-eared sheets of music." This "logic" should alert us. The lessons mushrooms teach about music are the result of fortuitous allegory. (Heuretics is etymologically linked to eureka.) Hence, whether or not mushrooms really speak some truth about music is completely beside the point. To Cage, they are invaluable because they suggest methods for compos(t)ing.

Silence restates, extends, and applies the lesson of *CTS*. An ideology—a way of living or a mode of production—can be extrapolated from an idiom (or item). For example, mushrooms can yield aleatory music; the *satura* can yield jazz. Conversely, culturally sanctioned methods of arrangement channel or delimit particular interests; ideologies constrain idioms. Finally, it is impossible to demarcate fully what is personal, popular, or public; the three levels of discourse are too deeply imbricated. Mystory, then, may be understood as an experimental genre dedicated, not to sorting out the discourse systems that structure our lives and culture, but to writing out their overlap.

The next three chapters conclude with mystories. Each one is an experiment in traversing the overlap between one level of discourse and the other two; each one writes with (or writes out) a trope of jazz. They appear as follows:

Chapter 2. "A Jarrett in Your Text" focuses on personal discourse (the level of the individual); it plays off the trope of obbligato in order to question subjectivity.

Chapter 3. "*Rap*sody in Read: Ishmael Reed and Free Jazz" focuses on professional discourse (the level of institutions); it plays off the trope of rhapsody in order to question simulation.

Chapter 4. "The Tenor's Vehicle: *Way out West*" focuses on popular discourse (the level of ideology); it plays off the trope of *charivari* in order to question cultural politics.

This chapter includes no experiment because this section on how to write mystory functions as a menu, naming items selected and combined when writing heuretically. All mysteries are *saturas*, and just as there is no single right meal and no single right way to make jazz, there is no single right way to write heuretically. The experiments, then, actualize heuretic potential in the form of mystories, but they also suggest (and are blind to) unrealized possibilities. They are vital to the concerns of this text for two reasons. First, the experiments are designed to show that writing with the tropes of jazz (the heuretic composting discussed earlier) generates ideas; it produces knowledge effects just as surely as hermeneutics and critique (the conventional scholarship employed in the archeologies of each chapter). Second, the experiments are designed to emphasize matters of presentation. Or put contentiously, for all the energy critics and theorists devote to examining beautifully written, cinematic, dramatic, and musical texts, their own work rarely seems to profit from such study. For example, theory is hardly ever as stimulating as its objects of study. The texts of Derrida, Barthes, Cage, Deleuze and Guattari, and, more recently, Florida School theorists such as Ulmer and Robert Ray are notable exceptions to this rule. That's one of the main reasons they have caught the attention and imagination of so many readers. They proceed not only as if theory has things to say about art (for example, in "The Double Session," Derrida delivers a short, very complex course on Mallarmé's use of spacing), but as if art could revitalize theory by making it more attractive and engaging ("The Double Session" is itself something of a knotty poem, as allusive as Mallarmé's poetry). Jazz, too, is concerned with presentation. Or consider, if scholars want to learn how to popularize criticism and theory, they might take a lesson from rock and roll. If they want to study and profit from deep conflict—the desire to popularize and the equally strong desire to maintain respectability—jazz will do the trick.

༈

TWO

Obbligato:
Required Listening

Tropology: The Art of Improvisation

Strength lies in improvisation.
—Walter Benjamin (1978:65)

The variations were the real matter, not the theme.
—Dorothy Baker (39)

Nothing is so easy as improvisation, the running on and on of invention.
—Henry James (171–72)

Obbligato is—to borrow Barthes's neologism—an "amphibology": a "precisely ambiguous" term. Not merely polysemous (for all words have multiple meanings), it yokes together "two absolutely contrary meanings" (Barthes, 1977a:72–73). This is demonstrated by the following definition, written by Don Randel and taken from the *Harvard Concise Dictionary of Music*:

> Obbligato [It.]. Obligatory, usually with reference to an instrument (*violino obbligato*) or *part that must not be omitted*; the opposite is *ad libitum*. Unfortunately, through misunderstanding or carelessness, the term has come to mean a mere accompanying *part that may be omitted if necessary*. As a result, one must decide in each individual case whether obbligato means "obbligato" or "ad libitum." (343, emphasis added)

Unlike Barthes, who delighted in Janus words, for they occasion "a kind of *luck*, a kind of favor not of language but of discourse" (1977a:72), Randel appears perturbed. He can no longer differentiate the obligatory from the arbitrary with complete confidence. Obbligato has somehow deviated from its full, originary meaning. It has "come to mean" its opposite. Someone or something, either "through misunderstanding or carelessness," jazzed it up, behaved improperly toward it, so that the hymen between the compulsory (always associated with composition) and the voluntary (always associated with improvisation) has been breached.

Obbligato alludes to everything traditionally considered parergonal, supplemental, "*hors d'oeuvre*," or a matter of style. Within the verbal arts this includes prefaces, footnotes, marginalia, and illustrations; within the visual arts it includes frames, mats, and even the walls on which paintings are hung; within music—ornamentation: *agréments*, grace notes, and improvisation (Ulmer, 1985:92). In the next three paragraphs, I want to gloss these latter musical terms, not to explain obbligato, but as a short exercise in metaphorical substitution. My aim is to set in motion semantic reverberations; my method is analogous (in a naïve sort of way) to one favored by beboppers who, eschewing interpretation or "straight reading," often recompose (or compost) popular songs by substituting and breaking up chords.

The collective term "*agréments*" was introduced into French musical vocabulary around the time of Louis XIV's reign (1643–1715) and "finally adopted into all European music." It refers to a group of "signs or abbreviations" for signifying musical ornaments ("the practice . . . of embellishing musical works through additions to or variations of their essential rhythm, melody, or harmony"). *Agréments* are directly related to the *passaggi* of Italy, the *glosas* of Spain, and the *graces* of England. They were divided into the following categories: "(1) appoggiatura (also double appoggiatura); (2) trill; (3) turn; (4) mordent; (5) *Nachschlag*; (6) arpeggio; (7) vibrato." But this definition is potentially, maybe inevitably, misleading. *Agréments* seem to imply "the existence of unadorned compositions representing the pure intentions of their composers." This is hardly the case. *Agréments* not only graphically expressed musical figures that were, according to Randel, "indispensable features of many musical works of the 17th and 18th centuries," they reflected and reinforced a reconceptualization of music that we have inherited. One need not come from a musicological background to notice this: The assumption that variation is opposed to theme or that ornament supplements essence owes a debt of gratitude to the development of *agréments*. This codification system marks the institutionalization of improvisation and the further division of musical labor into the now received roles of performer and composer. Like ballet and courtly dance, which also developed at Versailles, *agréments* articulated—they helped naturalize—the monarch's efforts to consolidate and maintain power. They were, therefore, an expression of ideology—allied to a social regime or apparatus—just as surely as they were a technological achievement (an important chapter in the history of notation). More succinctly, *agréments* regulated musical production but were themselves effects of regulation. They depended on *civilization*, which is to say a complex network of power relations organized around the figure of Louis XIV. Without this network, the names given to various ornaments lost their meaning (signifiers became unhooked from their signifieds), so that today the "correct interpretation" of *agréments* "constitutes a considerable problem in performing music of the 17th and 18th century" (Randel, 10, 362–63).

Barthes helps explain the feelings I have when I say "grace." It is, for me, a "mana-word." "Ardent, complex, ineffable, and somehow sacred": It seems to "answer for everything" (1977a:129). I can, of course, cite its musicological definition—grace is a term early English musicians used to designate musical ornaments—and I understand the magical economy of grace notes. They are extra, they step outside of time, and they give without taking. I have also heard musicians—Count Basie, for example—play seemingly without effort. In other words, I have witnessed the operations of grace in jazz. I believe in swing. The "perpetual conflict" between it and clarity, John Cage writes, "is what makes hot jazz hot."

> The best performers continually anticipate or delay the phrase beginnings and endings. They also, in their performances, treat the beat or pulse, and indeed, the measure, with grace: putting more or fewer icti within the measure's limits than are expected (similar alterations of pitch and timbre are also customary), contracting or extending the duration of the unit. This, not syncopation, is what pleases the hep-cats. (92)

But what really makes the word "grace" resonate for me is a mnemonic aid designed to teach the Christian concepts of *charis* (grace) and *charisma* (gift). As a child attending Baptist Sunday School, I recited, "*GRACE*—God's *Riches At* Christ's *Expense*," and matched these five words with the fingers on my right hand. (Grace = God's potlatch.) Nowadays, this acrostic serves me. Which is to say, it serves theory. It raises what Derrida calls "the question of the gift, time—and the rest" (1992:1). To think, to conceptualize the possibility of grace—the necessary supplement or the superfluous necessity—is to solve the problem of the obbligato.

But what of improvisation? It is traditionally regarded as an activity *different from* playing obbligatos, because it is perceived as *more than* embellishment. Thus, improvisation revisits a couple of topics we have already encountered. First, it evokes a paradox. Improvisation makes the optional a matter of obligation. The improvisor can't play only what's required; he's bound to contribute a *certain excess*. For example, we can see Schuller playing off this theme when he defines improvisation within the context of jazz as

> [a] manner of playing extemporaneously, that is, without benefit of written music. Improvisation, if it is not absolutely essential to jazz, is considered to be the heart and soul of jazz by most jazz musicians and authorities. It is equatable with composing on the spur of the moment. (378)

Notice then that improvisation marks a line or a partition where excess becomes essence, the incidental becomes requisite, where ornamentation becomes composition. Not that we need to locate this line or struggle with the question, What is improvisation? Rather, the study of improvisation in jazz obliges us to ask: What counts as improvisation? By what means does interpretation become invention? What takes shape in the name of improvisation? These questions, because they signal a shift in focus from ontology to politics, prompt another observation. There is a *certain relation* between writing and the conditions of improvisation (its conventions, contexts, intentions, and so forth). Writing (recording technology) is not opposed to improvisation. It results from it. The term "obbligato," then, is useful because it makes explicit what's implied by other terms for ornamentation: namely, that any and all distinctions between composition and improvisation are socially constructed and ultimately incomplete.

Listening: Canonical Figures for C90

Ornament is confabulation in the interstices of structure. A poem by Dylan Thomas, a saxophone solo by Charles Parker, a painting by Jackson Pollock—these are pure confabulations as ends in themselves. Confabulation has come to determine structure.
—Kenneth Rexroth (in Parkinson, 182)

The following mix of recordings—here again programmed for a ninety-minute cassette—is an unabashed attempt to create a pocket-sized canon. Anyone interested in jazz should feel obligated to hear all of these performances. They are touchstones.

To assemble this list, I let jazzography—a science or body of knowledge—tell me what to include. Thus, plenty of enjoyable work, that regularly makes its way into my disc player, finds no place on this tape of essential tunes. I've also refused to play the role of iconoclast and sneak in titles that I dote on, but that leave all or most other experts cold. Critical consensus—agreement (or popularity) among the cognoscenti about aesthetic-historical significance—determined selection.

On the one hand, this tape is of course destined to fail. How could it be definitive? Jazz is simply too vast, rich, and slippery an art form to lend itself to a conceit as elementary as mine. But on the other hand, it cannot help but succeed. This tape—whether actually heard or not—will clue in readers interested in, but ill-informed about, jazz, and it will incite knowledgeable jazz fans to debate and, hopefully, to create alternative lists. Finally, this imaginary cassette is dedicated to two institutions. First is Theodor Adorno—not out of a jazz fan's sense of vengeance, but because Adorno was so obviously bereft of opportunities to hear music valued by jazzography. He probably would have loathed my selections. Second is the Chattanooga Public Library. From its stacks I borrowed Monk's *Two Hours with Thelonious*, Ellington's *The Golden Duke*, and Dizzy Gillespie's *In the Beginning*. That's how I was first able to hear "real" jazz.

Side I

01. Jelly Roll Morton (1926) "Black Bottom Stomp," *The Jelly Roll Morton Centennial: His Complete Victor Recordings*, Bluebird.   3:10

The first great jazz composer, Morton boasted a cock-sure grin, diamond implanted in his front tooth, and bohemian affectations assiduously cultivated.

02. Louis Armstrong (1928) "West End Blues," *Volume IV: Louis Armstrong and Earl Hines*, Columbia.   3:15

    Armstrong's opening gambit is easily the most admired cadenza in jazz history.

03. Bessie Smith (1929) "Nobody Knows When You're Down and Out," *The Collection*, Columbia.   2:57

    Born around 1894, Smith left Chattanooga, her home-town, as a teenager to travel with Ma Rainey. By 1925, she was the highest paid black musician in history— the Empress of the Blues.

04. Thomas "Fats" Waller (1929) "Ain't Misbehavin'," *The Joint Is Jumpin'*, Bluebird.   2:56

    Eudora Welty dubbed this stride pianist "Power-house"—not without good reason.

05. Benny Goodman (1936) "Moonglow," *The Original Benny Goodman Trio and Quartet Sessions, Vol.1: After You've Gone*, Bluebird.   3:22

    Syncopated elegance, streamlined swing: Goodman's chamber group defined musical felicity as the fine bal-ance between exuberance and control.

06. Count Basie (1938) "Jumpin' at the Woodside," *The Complete Decca Recordings*, Decca.   3:08

    If God had said, "Let there be swing," this would have been the result.

07. Coleman Hawkins (1939) "Body and Soul," *Body and Soul*, Bluebird.   3:00

    Less a deconstruction of one song's harmonic struc-ture, than the retooling of the tenor saxophone for jazz possibilities.

08. Billie Holiday (1939) "Them There Eyes," *The Quin-tessential Billie Holiday*, Volume 6 (1938), Columbia.   2:48

    To repeat an observation made by Simon Frith (in Music for Pleasure*), Holiday was the greatest* metteur-en-scène *American popular music has ever produced.*

Which is to say, she responded to song lyrics as great actors respond to dramatic parts. Here she's having a ball.

09. Duke Ellington (1940) "Ko-Ko," *The Blanton-Webster Band*, Bluebird.   2:39

    Perhaps more than any American composer, Duke Ellington explored the potential of the phonograph record.

10. Charlie Parker (1945) "Ko Ko," *Bird: The Savoy Original Master Takes*, Savoy.   2:53

    Modern jazz, bebop, starts here, on a composition that bears no relationship to Ellington's neoprimitivist masterpiece.

11. Woody Herman (1947) "Four Brothers," *The Thundering Herds 1945–1947*, Columbia.   3:15

    Bebop popularized and made danceable by a taut arrangement and an impeccable front line of saxophones.

12. Bud Powell (1949) "Tempus Fugue-it," *The Best of Bud Powell on Verve*, Verve.   2:25

    Powell's fleet right hand thought like Charlie Parker's alto sax.

13. Ella Fitzgerald (1950) "Someone to Watch Over Me," *Pure Ella*, GRP Decca.   3:13

    Duets with pianist Ellis Larkins; the precursor to the song-book series.

14. Thelonious Monk (1951) "Straight No Chaser," *The Best of Thelonious Monk: The Blue Note Years*, Blue Note.   3:08

    More than any other bopper, Monk defined his calling not in technique—chops 'n' changes—but in sound, structure, and rhythm.

15. Sarah Vaughan (1954) "Polka Dots and Moonbeams," *Swingin' Easy*, Verve.   2:33

    The Divine One inhabited tunes, refashioning them in her own image.

Total playing time 44:42

Side II

01. Art Blakey (1954) "Doodlin'," *The History of Art Blakey and the Jazz Messengers*, Blue Note.   6:44

    Catchy tunes, inspired improvisations, and drums that pack more wallop than a final exam at Los Alamos.

02. Miles Davis (1959) "So What," *Kind of Blue*, Columbia.   9:02

    Cut number one from the most famous album in the history of jazz. It blazed new paths for improvisers.

03. Charles Mingus (1959) "Boogie Stop Shuffle," *Mingus Ah-Um*, Columbia.   3:41

    Makes audible what happens when a lapsed pentecostal uses jazz as a form of psychoanalysis.

04. John Coltrane (1964) "Part One: Acknowledgement," *A Love Supreme*, Impulse!   7:48

    Coltrane's sax is transcendent, while the rhythm section—especially Elvin Jones's polyrhythms—is palpably immanent.

05. Anthony Braxton (1976) Cut Three, *Creative Orchestra Music 1976*, Bluebird.   6:43

    Parade music, avant-garde certainly, but with a slightly inebriated Crescent-City totter to it.

06. Ornette Coleman (1979) "Sleep Talk," *Of Human Feelings*, Antilles.   3:31

    Harmolodics—Coleman's idiomatic approach to improvisation—marries street rhythms—the funk associated with James Brown, Sly and the Family Stone, and George Clinton.

07. Henry Threadgill (1986) "Good Times," *You Know the Number*, RCA Novus.   6:33

    Three coordinates triangulate Threadgill's trajectory: second-line fervor, rampant experimentalism, and fastidious attention to detail.

Total playing time 44:02

Archeology: Is Improvisation Possible?

We believe that a thing is valuable to the extent that it is improvised (hours, minutes, seconds), not extensively prepared (months, years, centuries).
                    —*F. T. Marinetti (in Apollonio, 194–95)*

NICHOLS: *Where's the arrangement?*
ARMSTRONG: *Arrangement? Man, nobody writes down Dixieland. You just let it happen.*
NICHOLS: *Suppose it happens great one time and you'd like it to happen exactly the same way. What do you do then?*
ARMSTRONG: *Just like tappin' a nightingale on the shoulder, sayin' "How's that again, dickie bird?"*
                    —*Louis Armstrong and Red Nichols*
                    (The Five Pennies, *1959*)

Jazzing Jazz

Because the majority of books written about jazz fail to deal "with the music itself in anything more than general descriptive or impressionistic terms," they are, in Schuller's view, glosses: adornments, ornaments, and embellishments. They are tangential to the "sound objects" they purportedly describe. Instead of analyzing "techniques and actual musical content," the authors of these books "concentrated on the legendry of jazz" (Schuller, vii).

This section on the archeology of the obbligato trope is neither a critique of nor an apology for amateur criticism, the sort of writing replaced by "genuine musicological research." But it does take the professional's perception of amateurs as a starting place for examining how "jazzing up"—a precisely ambiguous figure—controls all representations of jazz; how it enables us to think jazz into discourse. Here again, we shall see that the vocabulary Schuller uses to describe inadequacies in jazzography echo vocabulary used to characterize jazz. Schuller loves jazz, but not discourse that jazzes up jazz.

All musicological discourse about jazz is enabled by a fundamental contradiction, and Schuller's prefatory remarks to *Early Jazz* are exemplary. They suggest that analytical discourse on jazz—what I call *jazzology*—proceeds only by effacing the implications of its central claim for jazz. In other words, Schuller's rhetoric rings true as it affirms the exalted status that jazz grants to improvisation, while his analytical discourse functions as science only as it rejects or represses knowledge of the unsettling textual effects of improvisation. Jazzology arises as jazz writing purges itself of the very qualities it assigns to jazz. Jazzology is stubbornly disingenuous. It admits the obbligato trope—acknowledges that improvisation undoes any distinction between what is essential and what is incidental—even as it depends on the assumption that essential/incidental distinctions are, if not self-evident, then at least readily available to the professionally trained ear.

But what if this professional ear—whose emblem might be Nipper, RCA's ever-faithful mascot—stopped operating and started hearing differently? What if it considered that the claims regularly made for jazz could teach jazzography (all writing about jazz) a lesson? Just what could it mean to improvise, to make jazz, on a page? In this chapter, I engage these questions. The archeology that follows explains how the obbligato trope enables us to *write about* jazz; later sections, which use the grammatological theory of Jacques Derrida and the example of Ralph Ellison's *Invisible Man*, suggest and then model a way to *write with* jazz.

Touched by Grace

Marjorie Perloff, in her study of the textual strategies of the futurists (a movement coterminous and sharing deep affinities with the Jazz Age), calls improvisation "an art that depends not on revision in the interests of making the parts cohere in a unified formal structure, but on a prior readiness, a performative stance that leaves room for accident and surprise." Her definition develops Gerald L. Bruns's statement: "Improvisation is the performance of a composition at the moment of its composition. . . . [I]t is discourse that proceeds independently of reflection. . . . It is deliberate but undeliberated" (Bruns, in Perloff, 102). Bruns, in turn, recalls Bill Evans. As part of his liner notes to Miles Davis's *Kind of Blue* (1959), Evans introduced what is perhaps the most famous analogy of improvisation in jazz:

> There is a Japanese visual art in which the artist is forced to be spontaneous. He must paint on a thin stretched parchment with a special brush and black water paint in such a way that an unnatural or interrupted stroke will destroy the line or break through the parchment. Erasures or changes are impossible. These artists must practice a particular discipline, that

of allowing the idea to express itself in communication with their hands in such a direct way that deliberation cannot interfere.

The resulting pictures lack the complex composition and textures of ordinary painting, but it is said that those who see well find something captured that escapes explanation.

This conviction that direct deed is the most meaningful reflection, I believe, has prompted the evolution of the extremely severe and unique disciplines of the jazz or improvising musician.

Why "extremely severe and unique"? Because the jazz musician's task isn't how to replicate (interpret) the styles of precursors. Given time enough and space, anybody—make that any classicist—with enormous technical powers can manage that. No, his task is how to misinterpret, recall while playing unlike, the innovators of the past—and still land gigs. The jazz musician perceived as innovative, like Nietzsche's "strong poet," is one who aberrantly reads a conventionalized version of a previously recognized innovation. Walking the line between redundancy and incomprehensibility, he devises nonidentical repetitions of already received styles of playing and already established texts (traditionally, the chord sequences of Tin Pan Alley "standards"). The jazz innovator offers what will be received as perverse readings or spontaneous compositions (for within the realm of jazz, interpretation and invention remain scarcely differentiated activities). Ultimately, he attempts to dislodge an established manner of playing—a sanctioned hermeneutic—by parlaying what is, in fact, a radical hermeneutic into an authorized reading.

This struggle between interpretation and invention motivates all representations of jazz, from historical accounts of the music's development to stories of key players. But improvisation as an artistic practice is rarely, even tacitly, examined. Derek Bailey, guitarist and author of a wide-ranging book on the subject, writes: "Improvisation enjoys the curious distinction of being both the most widely practised of all musical activities and the least acknowledged and understood" (ix). Perhaps this is because few jazzographies regard it as a problem.

William Zinsser's biography of Willie Ruff and Dwike Mitchell provides an exception that proves this rule. In one memorable scene, it stages a soft critique of improvisation. "You have a story," Zinsser told a journalist, "that is essentially, extraordinarily dramatic—two black men in China [1981], one of whom is explaining jazz, which is a totally oral tradition based on improvising, to the oldest literate and literal society in the world" (qtd. in Beuttler, 21). Ruff, who plays French horn, describes improvisation—"the lifeblood of jazz . . . something created during the process of delivery"—to a group of faculty and students at the Shanghai Conservatory of Music. He then joins Mitchell, a pianist, and they improvise on a simple blues theme. The audience is nonplussed, having never heard anything like this in their lives. Their language doesn't even have a word for "improvisation." After the performance, Ruff is questioned, and Zinsser records the exchange:

> An old professor stood up. "When you created 'Shanghai Blues' just now," he said, "did you have a form for it, or a logical plan?"
>
> "I just started tapping my foot," Ruff replied, tapping his foot to reconstruct the moment. "And then I started to play the first thought that came into my mind with the horn. And Mitchell heard it. And he answered."
>
> "But how can you ever play it again?" the old professor said.
>
> "We never can," Ruff replied.
>
> "That is beyond our imagination," the professor said. "Our students here play a piece a hundred times, or two hundred times, to get it exactly right. You play something once—something very beautiful—and then you just throw it away." (17–21)

Clearly, this dialogue represents a near limit case of improvisation as the disruption of readerly expectations. Two paradigms clash—in a most congenial sort of way. But what or whose expectations are disrupted? From one perspective, improvisation contests presuppositions on which the Chinese base the creation and performance of music. The old professor seems positively baffled by jazz. From another perspective, the old professor (a personification of Writing-as-Inscription) challenges the value of Mitchell and Ruff's improvisation.

Unfortunately, Zinsser does not present Ruff's response to the old professor's politically correct suggestion that jazz is homologous not to oral African culture, but to disposable American culture. Nevertheless, his narrative prompts a couple of observations. First, the meaning of improvisation—what it denotes and connotes—is socially determined and, therefore, can always be read as an articulation of ideology. Second, improvisation is a sign operative within certain semiotic systems. If it has meaning, that meaning derives from and depends upon a particular cultural context. So we might ask: Within textuality or, more specifically, within our electronic culture, what is said of improvisation? As one might expect, individual answers vary. They do, however, fall into three general categories:

1. Improvisation is ultimately impossible within the realm of writing (i.e., in cultures possessing any sort of "recording technology").
2. Improvisation, which refers to a number of methods used to generate spontaneous compositions, may be translated into the register of writing; in fact, it is an effect of writing (inscription of all sorts).
3. Improvisation is the name of a problem, a problem useful for writing. Explaining these positions is a needful task. Additionally, it provides an occasion for surveying the basic topography of jazz fiction: that variety of "amateur" writing that regularly feels obligated to aspire to the condition of improvisation.

Impossible Music

How should jazz fans respond to Pierre Boulez's declaration? He writes: "It is necessary to deny all invention that takes place in the framework of writing. . . . Finally, improvisation is not possible" (Boulez, in Attali, 145). First, there's the temporary refuge of jingoism. We might smirk and recall Eddie Condon's response to an earlier French pundit: "I don't see why we need a Frenchman to come over here and tell us how to play American music. I wouldn't think of going to France and telling him how to jump on a grape" (Condon, in Balliet, 1986:5). More rational jazz fans might notice that Boulez's comment includes but isn't limited to jazz and that, moreover, it isn't original. His statement rings changes on an ancient theme. It succinctly repeats an argument central to Plato's *Phaedrus*, recalling the polemic Socrates advances against writing.

Still another rationale for Boulez's assertion might emphasize the paradigm shift that accompanies technologies of writing (which include, but are not limited to, phonetic and nonphonetic systems of notation, electronic recording media, and even the trace movements of people: dancers, athletes, wanderers, and warriors). Writ-

ing and the culture of repetition that it engenders precludes improvisation. For example, this book only and always quotes. It's nothing but permutations of characters in the alphabet, words from the
dictionary, ideas of my culture. And the jazz musician is no different. He never actually improvises. He reworks what's given. Improvisation is an idea, one that's actually inconceivable.

At first glance, it might appear that this line of reasoning
would find few adherents among the ranks of jazz writers. But this
is hardly the case. Writing about the impossibility of improvisation
is a seldom-acknowledged but time-honored practice within jazzography. For example, consider Lawrence Ferlinghetti's poetry "conceived specifically for jazz accompaniment." Here we encounter
antipathy toward "the framework of writing" analogous to the
antipathy jazz musicians have historically shown toward recording
technology. Ferlinghetti regards the labor of composition with profound distrust. It merely supplements the spontaneity of live performance. And his writing aspires at least to the condition of jazz.

To anyone familiar with and sympathetic to Derrida's critique
of Rousseau's *Essay on the Origin of Languages*, Ferlinghetti's
stated goal of composing poems receivable as "spontaneously spoken 'oral messages' rather than as poems written for the printed
page" sounds suspiciously like a romantic attempt to efface archi-
writing (*différance*) in order to conjure a totally oral culture where
improvisation is imaginable (Ferlinghetti, 48). The inevitable fail-
ure of this project—*and it is predicated in order to fail*—accounts
not only for much work by Ferlinghetti and other Beat poets, but
for the dominant tone of jazzography. Most stories and poems about
jazz seem motivated by a sense of loss. Its effects are overt in the
numerous elegies written for departed jazz musicians, but feelings
of loss also take other forms. Responding to a poem Frank O'Hara
composed the day after Billie Holiday died, Andrew Ross makes a
point applicable to a variety of jazzography: Mourning for unrecu-
perable "presence" has ideological as well as aesthetic consequences. Jazz discourse, in which "nostalgia-stuck desire" is acted
out, ends up paying tribute to the modernist text "with its own
epiphanic moment to record the loss, in the past, even the very
recent past, of a culture of authenticity" (66).

Adore? No. Adorn? No.

This is why Theodor Adorno's landmark essay, "On Popular
Music" is, fundamentally, a lament. Its author assumed the mantle

of Jeremiah, the weeping prophet of Israel's exile, when he heard the harsh music of Babylon (or as New York Dolls singer David Johansen would later call it, "Babble On"). Let me summarize Adorno's position on jazz and discuss his reliance on the obbligato trope.

As a matter of course, jazz musicians and jazz fans place boundless trust in the powers and pleasures of improvisation, but they routinely register feelings of loss by decrying the sufficiency of notational systems and recording technologies to "capture" what is most essential and ephemeral in the music they love. For example, Derek Bailey declares: "any attempt to describe improvisation must be, in some respects, a misrepresentation, for there is something central to the spirit of voluntary improvisation which is opposed to the aims and contradicts the idea of documentation" (ix). Schuller questions the correspondence between the primary material object of jazz, the record, and the historian's ultimate object of study, improvisation.

> Whereas we are interested primarily in the *Eroica* and only secondarily in someone's performance of it, in jazz the relationship is reversed. We are only minimally interested in *West End Blues* as a tune or a composition, but primarily interested in Armstrong's rendition of it. Moreover, we are obliged to evaluate it on the basis of a single performance that happened to be recorded in 1928 and are left to speculate on the hundreds of other performances he played of the same tune, none exactly alike, some inferior to the recording, others perhaps even more inspired. Jazz improvisation constitutes "work in progress"; and it ought to give the jazz historian pause for thought that certain artists never played their best performance of a given piece in the recording studio. (x)

Thus, those who love jazz dream of plenitude and presence. They read written descriptions of the music, peruse musical scores, and hear radio broadcasts and recordings as a promise of imminent fulfillment. Improvisation will come. For Adorno, though, jazz was a cruel joke—a false promise offering that which was not and could never be.

Adorno understood jazz as embellishment—"a veneer of individual 'effects'" pasted on the standardized form of popular song—and he challenged the emphasis jazz fans place on "the music's improvisational features" (Adorno, 1941:18, 17). He maintained that such features—"mere frills"—masked "the fundamental characteristic of popular music: standardization" (17). To his ears, the ears of the displaced person, what normally passes for improvisation is "the more or less feeble rehashing of basic formulas." Real improvisation, should it occur, for instance "in oppositional groups which perhaps even today still indulge in such things out of sheer pleasure," is already impoverished by its dependence on popular song form. Jazz and popular music (the two are interdependent commodities of the culture industry) are the aural equivalent of automobiles mass produced by the Ford Motor Company. Adorno substituted the concept of the *embellished standardized product* for what Schuller calls *"the music itself."*

Even though Adorno lived until 1969, his knowledge of jazz stalled sometime around Benny Goodman's 1938 Carnegie Hall concert. He was unaware of or, more probably, not interested in attempts made by modern and avant-garde jazz musicians to push the boundaries of their idiom and develop nonidiomatic forms of improvisation. Hence, we could disallow his classic leftist formulation as, at best, hasty, and, at worst, wrongheaded. We could declare it facile, a *reductio ad absurdum* argument equally applicable to the "serious" music Adorno lauded, or we could typify it as nothing more than an embellishment of the one-note, anti–mass culture theme Adorno harped on till the end of his life. Better, we can observe that Adorno's characterization of jazz depends on a favored trope of jazzography. He hones in on and attacks, not *music itself* (although that is included as part of his target), but an *image*, enlisted by supporters and detractors alike, that brings jazz into language.

For example, notice how the following passage from a jazz appreciation textbook works off exactly the same image Adorno employs:

> Early jazz musicians often began improvising simply by embellishing the melodies of pop tunes. Eventually, the embellishments became as good as and more important to a performance than the tunes themselves. In some performances, all that remained was the original tune's spirit and chord progressions. What is today called improvising was referred to by early jazz musicians as "messin' around," embellishing, "jassing," "jazzing up." (Gridley, 57)

Convention dictates that discourse becomes jazzography by summoning images of embellishment, variation, grace notes, improvisation, ad-libbing, or ornamentation. Collapsing distinctions between metonym and metaphor, these images come to count as *jazz itself*. The issue, then, is not whether to use the obbligato trope in representing jazz, but what valence to assign this trope. Those critical of jazz declare that the music equals ornamentation (that is, –[jazz = adornment]), the ultimate elevation of style over substance. Those sympathetic to jazz utilize two strategies. They reverse the polarity of the obbligato trope and valorize it as the vindication of style over substance, improvisation (spontaneous creation) over composition (labored deliberation), and the primitive over the civilized (that is, +[jazz = adornment]). Or they have a second option. Boosters can also maintain that jazz might originate as ornamentation, but that *good* or *real* jazz can never be reduced to a series of embellishments (that is, jazz > embellishment).

We, therefore, receive Adorno's opinion as truth—as a blow against jazz and, by extension, as a blow against mass culture—precisely to the extent that we feel it scores a blow against a trope organizing our conception of jazz. In other words, Adorno's argument succeeds to the extent that it valorizes "improvisation," identifies a public that perceives jazz as improvised music, and, then, convinces this public that they are sadly mistaken. Jazz is the culture industry's substitute for "real improvisation." It is nothing more than embellishment. Improvisation within the realm of mass culture is impossible. Hegemony—hierarchies of power—simply won't allow the flexibility that jazz claims it has. Adorno thus sang the blues because jazz seduces us into believing that capitalism grants more options than it actually does. An ever-ready iconoclast, he attacked mass culture by turning the public's image of jazz against itself.

Gotta Write to Sing the Blues

We now shift our focus to another position regarding the possibility of improvisation within "the framework of writing." Some jazzographers, perhaps taking a cue from Samuel Johnson's historic refutation of Bishop George Berkeley, point to the scores of jazz discs stocked in record stores. Surely they provide ineluctable proof that improvisation exists.

A more subtle argument employs the logic of structuralism. It goes like this: Improvisation is a construct. It operates within our culture, and it is an effect of relational difference. That is, we know what improvisation is because we know what it isn't. It isn't composition. Conversely, we understand composition as "not-improvisation." The two terms are bundled together like atoms forming a compound; their meanings result from the pairing, not from inherent qualities of the separate elements. Improvisation, then, according to this structuralist line of reasoning, is ultimately a consequence of writing; it is thinkable only within textuality.

Keep this in mind, however. It's preposterous to assume that all who believe in improvisation know the language of structuralism. Rather, it is reasonable to accept that structuralism is a language sufficient to describe the social context that makes such believing possible. Let me substantiate this point in a somewhat circuitous manner, by appealing to an essay written by two scholars. In "Miles Davis Meets Noam Chomsky," Alan Perlman and Daniel Greenblatt explain the jazz solo through an analogy that likens improvisation to "linguistic performance." Their stated goal is to oppose the "commonly-held assumption among people whose acquaintance with jazz is casual or informal that the music is made up out of nothing, invented out of thin air":

> Just as the speaker of a language makes instinctive use of the lexicon and structure of his/her language when s/he speaks or writes, the musician accomplishes his/her aims through mastery of and spontaneous resort to a basic vocabulary of musical figures, interspersed with quotes and connected by scales and arpeggios. It is the musical figures, or "licks" (played, of course, on the correct scale- and chord-tones) that give a jazz solo its distinctive jazz sound, in the same way that speaking English implies the use of the available word stock of the language, including bona fide loan words and recognizable neologisms. The basic lexicon of jazz licks is not large—there are perhaps two or three dozen that most players rely on—but, since any lick can be played over any chord, beginning with any scale/chord-tone and repeated indefinitely up and down the entire range of the instrument, the number of improvisational possibilities becomes enormous. (169, 175–76)

While Adorno would have probably agreed with the basic description offered here, he would not have agreed with its tone. What Perlman and Greenblatt label "improvisational possibilities," Adorno simply called "tricks." Jazz musicians were, to him, sophists who used grammar to produce glamour. The issue, then, isn't only a matter of spin. It's a question of paradigms. The work of Perlman and Greenblatt—like comparable work produced by Gary Tomlinson—situates the question of jazz improvisation within the debates over oral, literate, and electronic culture, debates that have animated theory for the last thirty years.

Apologists for improvisation most often understand the lexicon of jazz as directly analogous to the mnemonics of epic poetry: Louis Armstrong is to jazz what Homer is to poetry. But this comparison needs qualification. Think back a few pages to Zinsser's assertion that jazz arose within "a totally oral tradition." He's simply wrong. As surely as Elizabethan drama was made possible by the printing press, jazz was made possible by electronic culture, by what Walter Ong calls "secondary orality." Its development parallels that of cinema. The radio, phonograph, and even the telephone (whose lines carried the signals of live-remote broadcasts) established the material conditions within which African Americans— not mythic Africans—created jazz.

Improvisation, then, is not just one of the names that writing assigns to *orality*, but one of the names writing assigns to its *other*. Within literacy, improvisation is opposed to composition; it's the repressed term in a hierarchy, designating that which is auxiliary and ephemeral, that which is artfully (artificially) tacked on to some real item, to an original. (After all, no one is publishing books and articles arguing for the value of composition or the complexity of classical music.) Everyone who accepts the possibility of improvisation, therefore, begins by receiving the terms of this structuralist logic; which is to say, these terms are already in place when jazz arises, diachronically, in history, or synchronically, in performance. Most jazzographers seek either to invert the "classical" composition/improvisation hierarchy or to elicit respect for improvisers. This latter aim informs the subject matter of William Matthews's "Bmp Bmp"; the following lines, taken from the middle of the poem, describe a jazz solo built on the tune "Yes We Have No Bananas."

> Bechet's in mid-surge as usual
> by his first note, which he holds, wobbles
> and then pinches off to a staccato spat
> with the melody. For a moment this stupid,
> lumpy and cynically composed little money-
> magnet of a song is played poor and bare
> as it is, then he begins to urge it out
> from itself. First a shimmering gulp
> from the tubular waters of the soprano sax,

> in Bechet's mouth the most metallic
> woodwind and the most fluid, and then
> with that dank air and airborne tone
> he punches three quarter-notes
> that don't appear in the song but should.
> (Matthews, 146–47)

Of all the poets associated with jazz, Matthews was one of the best. But however unique, "Bmp Bmp" exhibits a couple of features common to jazzography, and especially to jazz poetry. Obviously, it is writing *about* jazz: discourse that represents the culturally assigned, politically privileged signifiers governing the representation of this music. As such, it resonates for the "hip," those cognizant of its codes, or as Lee Meitzen Grue puts it: "Particular artists known for a certain sound—singers for certain songs—evoke the metaphor of their lives; their names, the titles of the songs, invest the poems with myth not available without these references" (Grue, in Feinstein and Komunyakaa, 259). Jazz poetry—actually most writing about jazz—constitutes something of a test for readers, granting pleasure by admitting us into (or prompting us to imagine others barred from) a body of knowledge, a "science."

Additionally, "Bmp Bmp" exhibits another characteristic of jazzography. It aspires to the condition of its subject matter, which is another way of saying Matthews seems desirous of making jazz on paper the way other poets want to paint with words. He takes jazz as a paradigm for writing. Another poet, John Taggart, writing of his first truly successful poem, explains:

> The first jazz that made itself available to me was "The Drum Thing" on John Coltrane's *Crescent* album. . . . It's tempting to say the music gave me the poem. The contribution of the music, however, was more an instigation, a prompting to begin, than a complete template. (Taggart, in Feinstein and Komunyakaa, 273)

James Nolan extends this notion of jazz as a prosthesis for writing poetry. In the following passage he raises the question of what constitutes jazz poetry (Is it intersemiotic mapping?), then responds by invoking the conception of his own poems: the result of words and jazz coming together. His comments, like Taggart's, appear in the "Biographical Notes and Statements of Poetics" that forms an appendix to *The Jazz Poetry Anthology*:

Is a jazz poem one that uses some of the structural elements of jazz, that is, call-response, repetition & variation of theme, improvisation within form, etc., or is it one that sounds good when read right with jazz accompaniment, like Barry Wallenstein's stuff? I decided to send you what I have, in the past, felt inspired to perform *with* jazz because the poem answers *to* jazz the way a child answers to its mother. So these are the poems that jazz begat. Words got to fooling around with jazz . . . and these poems were born. (Nolan, in Feinstein and Komunyakaa, 268)

Dismissing the problem of formal definition, Nolan suggests that the jazz poem is determined by the conjunctive activity that generates it. It esteems *invention*—what we might call "creative (mis)reading" or what theologians once called "heuretics"—over *imitation* (mimesis) or *interpretation* (rereading or hermeneutics). Disrupting readerly expectations becomes its raison d'être, "the anxiety of influence" its covert subject. The improviser, whether poet or musician, is a "strong poet," horrified at the possibility of "finding himself to be only a copy or a replica" (Bloom, 80).

Conjunctive activity—the *fooling around* of words and jazz—is, of course, a synonym for improvisation (jazzing up). It's also a well-known euphemism (fooling around = jazzing up = copulation), one calculated to evoke an etymology. The word "jazz," as several scholars note, is connected in sound and original meaning to "jizz" and "gism," American vernacular for semen. "Gism"—in various parts of the South a "gravy" or "cream sauce"—connotes "spunk": "strength, talent, genius, ability" (Merriam and Garner, 385–86). "Jizz," writes Robert Farris Thompson, "appears to derive from the Ki-Kongo verb *dinza*, 'to discharge one's semen, to come.' *Dinza* was creolized in New Orleans and elsewhere in black United States into 'jizz' and 'jism'" (1983:104). E. J. Hobsbawm corroborates. He writes: "the jazz fan, however knowledgeable, is fundamentally a lover" (12).

The Bad Seed

The third and final position on the possibility of improvisation within "the framework of writing" unsettles notions of intentionality and human subjectivity by insisting that improvisers are played or written (by ideology) just as surely as they play or write (texts). Improvisation, therefore, becomes "improvisation": the emblem of a problem, an enigma useful for writing; not the emblem of a solution, the name of a method used in writing. Perhaps I can make this point clearer. Let's recall Randel's definition, cited at the beginning of this chapter. Randel, in effect, recognizes "obbligato" as the musical confusion of compulsory and voluntary. It is both a "part that must not be omitted" and "a mere accompanying part that may be omitted if necessary." "Improvisation"—which is to obbligato what narrative is to anecdote—functions similarly. It, too, is indeterminate. "Jazzing up" breaches the hymen—the partition—that separates what is central from what is eccentric. Coleman Hawkins's "Body and Soul," Charlie Parker's "Ko Ko," John Coltrane's "My Favorite Things," and a host of other improvisations: Though based on other people's songs, they're hardly versions of those songs. Rather, they serve notice that authorship and composition are both concepts—and tenuous concepts at that.

So then, "improvisation" or the trope of the obbligato forces a choice. We must either embrace or deny undecidability. We can seek to affirm the impossibility of making ultimate distinctions, in which case, as Marx put it, "all that is solid melts into air." Or we can strive to ignore the arbitrariness of culturally drawn boundary lines that, for example, separate author and performer or composition and improvisation. Most jazzography makes this latter choice. By validating improvisation over composition, it represses knowledge of the obbligato trope, and ends up paying homage to the "classical" opposition that keeps improvisation and composition distinct. (The emergence of classical music depended on, and coincided with, notions of authorship that resulted from the emergence of print culture.) But one might ask, what could it mean to employ the obbligato trope as the model for a kind of writing that does not oppose composition (an authored original) to improvisation (a more-or-less perverse representation)? How might one perform the myth of undecidability? In "STRINGFOUR" and "STRINGFIVE" Richard Kostelanetz presents one quick answer to these questions. Here's a line from the latter of these two poems:

Stringfiveteranciderideafencerebrumblendivestablishment-
entertaininteger- (121)

Instead of attempting to create a stable "work" (the labor of signifieds), Kostelanetz generates "text" (the play of signs). He does this by two means. First, he breaks the contract—a kind of hermeneutic pact—between artist and audience. In doing so, he positions readers, not as consumers giving the poem a final "expression," but as producers coauthoring or completing the poem (Perloff, 117). He obliges readers to assume the role of *player*. Second, Kostelanetz breaks another contract: the mimetic pact between representor and represented—subject and object. His poems certainly do not answer "*to* jazz the way a child answers to its mother." In fact, it's questionable whether they have a mother, much less whether that mother is jazz. Perhaps we should conceive of them as jizzography: as seeds disseminated, ready to come into meaning. They look, I suspect, exactly like a recurring nightmare Socrates must have endured, the one that fulfilled his every fear about writing and the one that made his hair fall out.

Paradigm: A Lesson from Ellison's *Invisible Man*

> For me, Francis Ponge is someone first of all who has known that, in order to know what goes on in the name and the thing, one has to get busy with one's own, let oneself be occupied by it.
>
> —*Jacques Derrida (1984:26)*

> After adornment the next most striking manifestation of the Negro is Angularity.
>
> —*Zora Neale Hurston (54)*

The Rinehart episode of Ralph Ellison's *Invisible Man* (ch. 23) allegorizes the trope of obbligato. It dramatizes a dilemma reached in any search for identity. The scene begins when the protagonist— reeling from the death of his comrade, Brother Clifton, and fleeing the wrath of the Black Nationalist, Ras the Destroyer—spots "three men in natty cream-colored summer suits . . . wearing dark glasses." Visions of ordinariness, they prompt the Invisible Man to nothing less than an epiphany. "I had seen it thousands of times," he writes, "but suddenly what I had considered an empty imitation of a Hollywood fad was flooded with personal significance" (1947:364).

Like a shot, Ellison's protagonist hurries into a drugstore and grabs the darkest lenses he can find. Plunged into blackness, he moves outside and is immediately stopped by "a large young woman" wearing a "tight-fitting summer dress." She reeks of "Christmas Night perfume."

"Rinehart, baby, is that you?" she said.

Rinehart, I thought. So it works. She had her hand on my arm and faster than I thought I heard myself answer, "Is that you, baby?" and waited with tense breath.

"Well, for once you're on time," she said. "But what you doing bareheaded, where's your new hat I bought you?"

I wanted to laugh. The scent of Christmas Night was enfolding me now and I saw her face draw closer, her eyes widening.

"Say, you ain't Rinehart, man. What you trying to do? You don't even talk like Rine. What's your story?"

I laughed, backing away. "I guess we were both mistaken," I said.

She stepped backward clutching her bag, watching me, confused.

"I really meant no harm," I said. "I'm sorry. Who was it you mistook me for?"

"Rinehart, and you'd better not let him catch you pretending to be him."

"No," I said. "But you seemed so pleased to see him that I couldn't resist it. He's really a lucky man." (365)

Stopping at the first hat shop he sees, the Invisible Man purchases "the widest hat in stock" and returns to the street as Rinehart, a character whose name Ellison took from a blues by Jimmy Rushing (O'Meally, 90). Rinehart, however, as Gary Lindberg rightly observes, is not actually a character at all (he never "appears"), but "merely a mask and a set of roles" (248–49). Subsequently, the Invisible Man is taken as "Rine the runner and Rine the gambler and Rine the briber and Rine the lover and Rinehart the Reverend" (Ellison, 1947:376). As he "begins trying to place Rinehart in the scheme of things," he reflects:

He's been around all the while, but I have been looking in another direction. He was around and others like him, but I had looked past him until Clifton's death (or was it Ras?) had made me aware. What on earth was hiding behind the face of things? If dark glasses and a white hat could blot out my identity so quickly, who actually was who? (372–73)

Identity always forces a choice. One must either embrace or deny undecidability: reject ultimate distinctions between *rind* and *heart* (for they are always purchased at the cost of violence) or reject the "vast seething, hot world of fluidity" (for it is gained only at the expense of stabile identity) (376).

What's the Invisible Man's choice in this matter? Well, I'm not going to say. Readers who can't answer this question for themselves simply haven't done their homework. They should read *Invisible Man*, or, failing that, they could read virtually any criticism on the novel. Everybody seems willing to discuss the problem of identity as emblematized by the Rinehart figure. That is, everyone except me. I've become less interested in Ellison's substantial philosophical contributions (the "heart" of the novel?), than in his more obvious means of setting philosophical issues in motion (the novel's "rind"?). Like the Invisible Man (and Poe's Dupin), I wonder more about what's hidden in plain view—one's signature for example.

Proper names, like musical sounds, lack any apparent semantic content. In theory, they denote but do not connote. They belong, as Umberto Eco puts it, to "a linguistically poor universe" (1976:86–87). Thus, lacking the gravity of other words, they perpetually drift and slip, threaten continually to become *improper* nouns (for example, Rine becomes rind). "At stake in this oscillation," writes Robert Ray, "is the power of any given language to control its signification, to delimit where meaning begins and where it leaves off" (1994:287). It's no wonder, then, that Ellison declared: "a concern with names and naming was very much part of that special area of American culture from which I come" (1964:149). As an African American writer, Ralph Waldo Ellison regarded proper names (the sometimes dubious "gifts" of others) as political sites, raising issues of property and propriety. Playing with names was, therefore, an activity fraught with consequence. Of what sort, Pierre Boulez describes:

> Play is sometimes amusing, but it can also be deadly serious, since it questions the necessity of creation. Play may help us to shirk fundamental issues; it may also go to the very heart of the truth, and of our own uneasiness, by revealing the huge accumulation of culture with which we are more or less bound to live, and indeed to "compose": playing with this culture means trying to abolish its influence by making it quite clear that one has mastered all its mechanisms—from outside—even the most perverse. (356–57)

To play with the proper name is to write with the obbligato trope on the level of personal discourse, the proper name representing, as we have seen, issues of identity and authorship, the difficulty of keeping "rind" and "heart" separate. The proper name designates that which is personal (one's own style: an affirmation of individuality) and that which is political (what one is "bound to live with": an indication of ideological imposition).

Proper names, it turns out, are puzzles; they're good for compos(t)ing in much the same way that the tunes of Tin Pan Alley are good for jazz improvisation. Ellison learned this lesson in childhood (even before he discovered the vocation barely latent in his own name) and applied it to writing *Invisible Man*. The entire novel is, in effect, structured by Rinehart, a personification of the obbligato trope if there ever was one. The proper name transformed into a common noun becomes prescriptive of a newly invented genre: mystory. To the reader "trying to keep the beat, to follow the melody, or analogously to pursue the aspirational story line," Ellison's name games present "absurdist intrusions." Rineheart repeatedly disrupts linearity with "threatening moments of chaos." But to the reader willing to slip into the breaks and look around (i.e., to the reader willing to behave like the Invisible Man), "rinehart" offers an alternative order. As a literary form, mystory (the traversing of rind and heart) is analogous to jazz. It is concerned with melody as well as breaks, what Lindberg calls "the orderly, historically relevant plots as well as the purer perception available during performance disruptions" (249–50).

Another author who has learned how to write with the proper name is Jacques Derrida, but here again, his signature experiments—notably *Signsponge* and *Glas*—have been examined, almost exclusively, for their philosophical concepts, not for the way they confuse hermeneutics (philosophical work) and heuretics (textual play). Of Derrida's most experimental texts, Robert Ray writes:

> When these books and essays are mentioned at all . . . they are typically discussed for their "content," as if their unusual forms were at best only irritating impediments to arguments capable of being glossed in plainer language. In fact, they seem to share the ambition that John Cage announced for his lectures: "My intention has been, often, to say what I had to say in a way that would exemplify it; they would, conceivably, permit the listener to experience what I had to say rather than just hear about it." (1994:281)

Indeed, as Ray insists, we might understand Derrida's work as a "continuation of French surrealism." The avant-garde has regularly appropriated ideas from philosophy (Marx) and psychology (Freud) for its projects. Derrida has returned the favor by raiding the avant-garde for textual strategies and forms: "The tolerance of chance, the investment in verbal games, the Mallarméan yielding of the initiative to words—these tactics seem less sui generis when placed in the tradition of the exquisite corpse, Dali's 'paranoiac-critical activity,' *frottage*, the irrational enlargement of the object, and automatic writing" (282–83).

If we seek a connection between jazz and Derrida, surrealism is one place to look. Robert Goffin, a Belgian lawyer who authored the first article on jazz (1919), was, as I mentioned in the last chapter, a friend of Apollinaire and an expert on his poetry. But the association between jazz and surrealism is stronger than acquaintance. Krin Gabbard writes:

> The first concert treatment of jazz in French music was the opening performance of Erik Satie's 1917 ballet *Parade*, for which Jean Cocteau had written the scenario and Picasso had designed Cubist sets and costumes. In *Parade* Satie, who had been drawn to jazz as a music that "shouts its sorrows," mixed Afro-American sounds with music originally scored for sirens, typewriters, airplane propellers, and a lottery wheel. In the program notes for *Parade*, Guillaume Apollinaire used the word "surrealism" for the first time. Audiences were properly scandalized. (1991a:95)

Goffin no doubt approved. He understood jazz as surrealism by other means; vanguard art comprehended jazz. In fact, the same thinking (often accompanied by radically different aesthetics) continues today. For example, Gabbard links "quotation"—blowing a few bars of some "classic melody" in the midst of an improvisation—to collage, and he argues that it turns the modern jazz solo into an avant-garde strategy. Quotation enables artists to adopt a stance of "ironic detachment" ("affect a 'hip' or 'cool' attitude") toward institutionalized music even as they "strive to gain legitimacy for themselves and their music" (102). Which is to say, Charlie Parker's music was opposed to the music of bourgeois drawing rooms in much the same way that Dadaist "word salads" and Wyndham Lewis's writings were opposed to the literary productions of mass culture: *Saturas*, both musical and literary, function satirically. Gabbard's point, anticipated as an intuition by Goffin, makes perfect sense. His essay on quotation is a model of well-reasoned cultural criticism, extremely useful as an explanation. But it isn't jealous of the jazz/avant-garde strategies that it so clearly delineates. Which should prompt us to wonder. Derrida has modeled philosophy informed by artistic experimentation. How might cultural criticism effect a similar transformation?

Assignment: Jazzing the Personal Dimension

Here we have an answer to the puzzle that has prevented many a willing experimenter from taking up the project of theory. If one was not to undertake close formal analyses as in the mode of calculation nor to decipher signs as in the conjectural paradigm, then what else was there to do? The mystorical answer is, to make a text. The mystorian reads any and all works as a set of instructions for making something (not necessarily something of the same kind).
—*Gregory Ulmer (1989b:315)*

In a text that exemplifies what it declares—thus permitting readers to experience what you have to say rather than just read about it—respond to the following questions: What does your signature teach? What can you make it say, about writing? How does your name suggest a solution to the problem of improvisation: writing with the obbligato trope, composing jazz on paper?

In order to complete this assignment, draw on what you've learned from the heuretic strategies of Ralph Ellison and Jacques Derrida. You may also want to refer to several other sources:

1. "The Signature"—in the "Experiments with Texts" chapter of Robert Scholes, Nancy Comley, and Gregory Ulmer's *Text Book*;
2. Ulmer's "'Derrida at the Little Bighorn'—A Fragment," the final chapter in *Teletheory*;
3. Robert Ray's "The Signature Experiment Finds Andy Hardy," an essay in *Deconstruction and the Visual Arts*;
4. Sun Ra's methods for pushing interpretation (hermeneutics) to invention (heuretics), described in John F. Szwed's *Space Is The Place* (61–87). An avid reader, Sun Ra was aware of earlier discussions of renaming in African American literature, in works by

Frederick Douglass, Booker T. Washington, Jean Toomer, Elijah Muhammad, Ralph Ellison, James Baldwin, and Malcolm X (80).

After reading commentary and studying recommended models, explore the words and information that may be generated out of your own name ("proper" as well as nicknames). Then, write a "mystory" that suggests how the materials discoverable in your name fulfill John Coltrane's dream of a kind of writing (composting as composing) that allows for "more plasticity, more viability, more room for improvisation in the statement of the melody itself" (Mackey, 1986:79). Obviously, this mystory will focus on the personal level of discourse. For it is on this level that we unclench our teeth and start improvising. But you should not avoid referring to appearances of your signature in both public and private discourse.

To begin the experiment, force your name to yield a "key list" of terms and topics. Translate your proper name into ordinary discourse. That means you ought to use every available means to find the common words bound up in your name. Check dictionary definitions in the original language of your heritage, as well as encyclopedic dictionaries relevant to your names. You may also use poetic techniques to generate words out of your names—puns and anagrams, for example. Perhaps you might want to include graphics that illustrate or emblematize what you discover.

Several of the readings suggest analogies that might guide your experiment. *Text Book* (from which this assignment is extrapolated) recommends thinking of the signature project as a written version of one's coat of arms (a kind of improvised blazoning). Additionally, this project might prompt an association with the nicknaming process (an activity that, you might recall, enjoys privileged status among jazz musicians); this, in turn, might lead you to reflect on signs of fate or codes of destiny embedded in your signature. Are you "well-named"? Finally, remember that the goal of this project is to seize all of your names—and whatever materials they provide—in order to turn (trick or trope) them into a theory (a general description) of heuretics. Instead of interpreting your name, employing already received methods of interpretation, show how it suggests a solution to a problem: how to improvise; how to push interpretation so far that it becomes invention.

In other words, after you've read what your name says, use this information to suggest a new way to write: your own—and thus idiomatic—method for improvising. For example, remember the form of the well-made essay, the one you learned in freshman composition class? Its shape was an inverted triangle and its length about five hundred words? It required a clear statement of thesis, supported by cohesive paragraphs that logically combined to create a coherent argument or presentation. For now, ignore that model. Craft an essay that displays a new sort of form, one that follows instructions once latent but now manifest in your name.

A message to skeptics. Of course, this signature experiment could be considered self-indulgent and pretentious. That's because, in following the lead of the jazz musician and in forsaking a self-effacing stance of disinterest (a stance characteristic of both "classical" science and music), we appear to have foregrounded subjectivity. It looks like we've gone on a mad quest to "know ourselves." This, however, is not the case. Jazzography teaches us that the most brilliant improvisations are always signature experiments. Jazz is created when received traditions (constraints imposed by an institution) creatively conflict with materials from an improviser's past (autobiography). The jazz musician always arrives at the gig cognizant that he is, as it were, already "written" by ideology. Jazz—years before postmodernism advertised the "death of the author"—problematized subjectivity and, thus, cozy distinctions between what is self-effacing and what is self-indulgent. The signature experiment, therefore, prompts students to experience their status as "prewritten texts." Names, it turns out, do not designate identities so much as they mark a terrain where the idiomatic and the ideological blur. Creating texts out of signatures requires students to make something out of what their culture has dealt them. The results could "sound" like practice or, maybe, like art. But that's a risk you'll have to take.

Take some refuge, then, in the knowledge that perceptions of your work rest with your readers (a teacher, peers, an invisible audience). They will determine its value. Poet and jazz critic Philip Larkin held that John Coltrane's music sounded like practice. And it's practically a time-honored tradition for enemies of jazz to label improvisations as a sort of musical masturbation. Chalk up their disparagement to racism if you want. But it's more likely that they understand good musicianship as interpretation: absolute self-sacrificing devotion to a score. Improvisation, especially when it is sensed as extreme, clashes with everything they hold true and dear.

Experiment: A Jarrett in Your Text

CONTACT MIKE . . . CONTACT MIKE
—Laurie Anderson (54)

In December 1965, with my personal life and fortunes at
low ebb. I went to Rome. One day I visited many
churches. I was overawed to observe that in each one
there were urns containing the remains of saints and sol-
diers. How incredible that persons of such opposite
beliefs—each in his own way attempting to influence our
world—could end up in exactly the same place—a jar.
—Ornette Coleman (1987:n.p.)

When I was a painter, my most successful paintings I left
outside and let them get rained on. The ones that weren't
so successful I just gave away, but my most successful
ones rotted, returned to leaves and twigs. I'm just inter-
ested in decomposition. I want to be buried in New
Orleans, because it's the only place in America that lets
you rot.
—Jim Dickinson (in R. J. Smith, 1992:22)

Text—this text almost mad in its need to obey the law of
my (im)possible signature—always begins at a stopping (stopper-
ing or corking) place. It represents the end of false starts for the
one who inscribes it. Like the mason jars that lined my Grand-
mother Jarrett's pantry—full of pole beans, okra, corn, tomatoes,
bread 'n' butter pickles, and all kinds of preserves (peach, pear,
watermelon rind, blackberry, and muscadine, to name only
five)—it silently marks the work (it is the trace) of canning. (In
the South, "puttin' up stuff in cans" means putting stuff in jars.)
And like mason jars—signed and dated, covered and sealed with
paraffin (like tomes or tombs "sealed unto the day of redemp-
tion"), which wait standing with their strong, well-formed legs
locked at attention—the text-as-jar, a cornucopia, exists to
become part of a feast.

But you will notice (for you have opened my jar, are feasting
now), the text-jar is not used up. It fills itself as fast as it is emptied.
To emphasize this point, consider the following biblical passage
that describes Elijah the prophet's visit to the drought-stricken
town of Zarephath and to a widow whom God promised would provide sustenance:

[Elijah] arose and went to Zarephath. And when he came to the gate of the city, indeed a widow was there gathering sticks. And he called to her and said, "Please bring me a little water in a cup, that I may drink." And as she was going to get it, he called to her and said, "Please bring me a morsel of bread in your hand." Then she said, "As the LORD your God lives, I do not have bread, only a handful of flour in a bin, and a little oil in a jar; and see, I am gathering a couple of sticks that I may go in and prepare it for myself and my son, that we may eat it, and die." And Elijah said to her, "Do not fear; go and do as you have said, but make me a small cake from it first, and bring it to me; and afterward make some for yourself and your son. For thus says the LORD God of Israel: 'The bin of flour shall not be used up, nor shall the jar of oil run dry, until the day the LORD sends rain on the earth.'" So she went away and did according to the word of Elijah; and she and he and her household ate for many days. The bin of flour was not used up, nor did the jar of oil run dry, according to the word of the LORD which He spoke by Elijah. (I Kings 17:10–16)

Clearly the jar of Zarephath forms this passage's cynosure. It is a hedge against the wasteland. Because of its fecundity (always enjoyed "out of season" and removed from the place of generation), death becomes pregnant. The oil that flows out of its mouth or orifice (associated with the anointing or sanctifying work of God and his prophet) produces new life.

"Can it!"

I am way ahead of myself, so I stop.

I stop to start. I "close (a finger hole of a wind instrument) or press down (a violin string, etc.) to produce a desired tone" ("stop," *Webster's New World Dictionary*). But my stopping will not be noted, or rather notated, in this particular manner again. Instead, it is sufficient to see that every punctuation mark, every white space, the breaking off of every letter to make another heralds (like a band of angels) a stopping. They all mark my signature.

ᨰᨒᨰ

My model for this experiment in composition is Derrida's *Signsponge*. Hence, I use my "own signation to investigate [to invaginate] a field of study." To make my intentions transparent (so they will be perfectly clear) and straightforward, merely observe that I ret ("to impute, ascribe, or attribute"—OED) to composition an

FIGURE 2.1

essentially jar-like function. This essay, therefore, tests sound principles of canning. It is itself a recipe for making the most heavenly (literally God-like) jams and jars, and it follows this recipe:

JAMES MICHAEL JARRETT JAM
(straightforward version)

1 signature	1 literary object (*saturas* or Menippean satire)
1 problem (how to trope a proper name into an improvisational style)	1 pinch of content

Write an introduction using the generative principle of signature and add a pinch of content. Cook until moderately thick. Write the recipe. Remark the proper name's generative principle by exposing the grid of common nouns produced through etymological and associative exploration (homonyms, anagrams, and such) of the signature. Copiously elaborate the terms of the grid into a text by straining the Menippea (the literary object) through the grid. Season and serve as a specific example of an inexhaustible, general compositional principle.

The above recipe (which both goes before and follows this essay) follows the following recipe for "Muscadine Jam." It was recorded by Mrs. S. R. Dull (who signs her foreword as Henrietta Stanley Dull) for her book *Southern Cooking*—a text "gleaned from over forty years of . . . experience" and written in response to "the need for an authoritative source of information on the preparation of foodstuffs the 'Southern Way.'" Mrs. Dull's cookbook was a wedding gift.

Muscadine Jam

5 lbs. fruit	3 lbs. sugar

Pulp grapes and put pulp to cook in small quantity of water; cook until broken. Put through coarse strainer to remove seed. To the hulls put sufficient water to boil until tender. Mix the two together, add sugar and cook slowly, stirring often to prevent scorching. Season with any spices liked. (333)

Inexplicably, Mrs. Dull omits any reference to the jars that traditionally hold jam. Many reasons could be suggested, but several possibilities seem especially promising:

1. The jars are present, but because they constitute the received container of jam making, they are invisible.
2. The jars are absent. Dull—"the first lady of cooking in Georgia"—can only conceive of jars in Tennessee (or they are absent just to spite Wallace Stevens).
3. The jars are both absent and present, and the absent/present opposition is jammed by the jars. Mrs. Dull's omission typifies logocentrism's habit of establishing dualisms, that is, of privileging content over form, inside over outside, and presence over absence.

My signature, though, explicitly demonstrates the interpenetration or at least the interdependence of jams and jars. As Cage wrote: "If any thinking is going to take place, it has to come out from inside the Mason jar" (108).

My Papa Jarrett was named James—James Lloyd. But when I think of James, my first name, the memory usually recalled is not an image of Papa, but of the hand-tinted photograph that hung over the bed I slept in when visiting my grandparents. This pho-

FIGURE 2.2
Dad, Papa, Adam (child), and me

tograph, which both comforted and frightened me as a child, portrayed my Uncle James—who died of leukemia when he was three years old. My father—Richard Eugene, the only surviving son and oldest of three children—never saw his brother, so, of course, neither did I.

On December 10, 1953, my parents named me James Michael Jarrett. They decided that I would be called Michacl (a law routinely broken by telephone solicitors who call me Jim). When I sign my signature, however, I sign it as James M. Jarrett, because my father said that was best. Thus, in signing my name, Michael all but erases itself, and James—the mark of the ghostlike, absent child—appears. I mark his absence, his never appearing, as his mark in turn marks mine. My Papa Jarrett is dead, too.

James, the Hellenistic version of Jacob (Iakobos), means supplanter (supplement) or literally "heel-catcher." A man always in a tight spot—a jam—Jacob usually improvised a way to get out of sticky situations. For instance, at his birth, foreshadowing the Olympic games (now held in gyms), Jacob hamstrung his older twin Esau. Nevertheless, God loved Jacob and hated Esau (Romans 9:13). God thought Jacob had the potential to become a real gem.

When I was in junior high school, people called me names. One was Carrot Jarrett. Another was Micajarrett, one word, said real fast. And I loved it, for its rhythm and for its association with mica.

No mineral matched mica. Its thin, somewhat flexible, crystalline layers (called isinglass), which could be separated into transparent planes with one's fingernail, fascinated me. I looked at the freckles it made in granite. I searched for it in the red Georgia clay around my house. And I marveled at the tops of electric fuses—little windows of mica resistant to heat and electricity. If Jacob was God's gem, mica was mine.

Mica, actually Michael, asks the question, "Who is like God?" I know the answer well. Its emphatic "nobody"—an answer that certainly demonstrates its asker's unwillingness to elicit the banter of light conversation—booms like Pavarotti singing through an expensive microphone (or like "Em-eye-kay-ee [that's Mike D of the Beastie Boys] on the em-eye-see"). But herein lies a problem. Who asks the question of Michael, and to whom is the question addressed? What questions are raised in my signature? What can I make of its apocalyptic scene, this code that decodes? The first atom bomb was nicknamed Mike. And Michael was the most popular boy's name in the United States the year I was born, which, by

the way, was the same year Julius and Ethel Rosenberg were executed for passing secrets about Mikes to the Russians. (Mike and
Ike; isinglass and Eisenhower.)

⌁

Gently but firmly tap on Jarrett, and it will easily open up, making
its contents available. Cut it in half with a jarrit ("a wooden javelin,
about five feet long, used in games by Persian, Turkish, and Arabian
horsemen"—OED), and it will reveal two parts as distinct as the
seed of a *jaret* (a *"variété de prune"*—*Littré*). It will neatly divide
into a common noun—"jar"—and an uncommon verb—"ret." But
before I investigate jar/ret (reveal its contents to you), notice my
mother's maiden name—"Jordan." Its origin is uncertain, but

> the suggestion has been made that *Jordan* is short for *Jordan-
> bottle*, and meant originally a bottle of water brought from the
> Jordan by crusaders or pilgrims; that it was thence transferred
> to "a pot or vessel used by physicians and alchemists," and
> thence to the chamber utensil. But the earlier steps of this
> conjecture apparently rest upon nothing but the later form of
> the word (which may actually be a corruption of something
> else), and the external probabilities of such an origin. (OED)

Thus, "jordan" involves a complex series of displacements, until
finally patriarchal law (the law of Dick Jarrett and the OED) puts a
lid on the whole subject, screws meaning down, and declares that,
henceforth jordan shall be:

1. a kind of pot or vessel formerly used by physicians and
   alchemists,
2. a chamber-pot,
3. applied derisively to a person (OED),
4. or, in a word, a jarrett.

Jarrett supplements jordan. The alchemist's vessel of healing/poi-
son becomes a piss-pot. The little jar relegates the jordan to "The
Lady's Dressing Room," declares it unclean—a *pharmakos*—or at
very best a "frail *China* Jar [ready to] receive a Flaw" (*Rape of the
Lock*, canto II). But undeniably a trace or whiff of jordan remains,
for after all a jarrett is a jordan as we have seen, and as I shall point
out again.

    I married Pamela Gail Dill. She now signs her name Pamela

Gail Jarrett. Did I take her name? Was it freely given? Did I erase
her name? Does it palimpsestically remain? What is the nature of
the idiomatic law by which dill (a plant of the carrot family) disap-
pears into the abyss of a pickle jar only to emblazon itself upon the
label or signature of the jar? In what way do the three boys she bore
resemble (remark) a pickle jar, which at once carries the genetic signature of both mother and father? These are questions I shall only
pose, preserve (for later) by placing them into this text-jar, this
jahr's text.

⌒

As I noted earlier, Jarrett—to measure out, sound out, or partly
open its principle of generation—yields a "jar" and a "ret." *Jar*, in
its noun form, rates three separate entries in the OED (a kind of jar
in its own rite). (1) It signifies a harsh, inharmonious, grating sound
or combination of sounds, which by extension signifies dissension,
discord, dispute, and want of harmony. "To jar," writes Jean Jacques
Rousseau,

> is to lose the intonation; that is, to change improperly the just-
> ness of the intervals, and, consequently, to sing false. There
> are some musicians, whose ear is so just, that they form no jar,
> but such as are rather uncommon. Many others do not jar for
> another reason, since, to lose the tone it must first have been
> found. To sing without a key, to bawl, force the voice too high
> or too low, and to have more regard to the extent than to the
> justness, are methods almost sure to spoil the ear, and at the
> same time to jar. (210)

(2) Jar also designates a vessel without spout or handle (or having
two handles) usually more or less cylindrical in form, and hence, a
measure of volume, and (3) something (like a door) "on the turn,
partly open." *Ret*, a verb, signifies several actions: (1) accusing,
charging, reckoning, imputing, and ascribing, (2) soaking (especially
flax or hemp) in water and exposing to moisture, in order to soften
or season, and (3) rotting (for example, hay spoiled by water). Ret is
also an obsolete form ("3 sing. pres. indic.") of "read." Jarrett, I ret,
equals (among other things) a rotten, slightly opened jar. A jarrett is
a jordan—a truly jarring fact.

In French, the definition of *jarret* is expressed as: (1) "bend of
the knee, popliteal space, ham (in man); hough, hock (of horse,
etc.)," (2) "knuckle (of veal); shin (of beef)," and (3) "unevenness,

bulge, break of outline (in curve of arch, etc.)" or "an elbow, knee-joint (of pipe)" (*Heath's Standard French and English Dictionary*). Phrases employing my signature are as follows:

Plier le jarret, to bend the knee.

Avoir du jarret, to be strong in the leg.

Couper les jarrets à quelqu'un, to take the wind out of someone's sails.

S'avancer le jarret tendu, (i) (of courtier, etc.) to advance making a leg, (ii) (of fencer, etc.) to advance on his toes.

Couper les jarrets à un cheval, to hamstring a horse.

Also, note that *jarrettes* are socks or half-hose. The verb *jarreter* refers to the act of putting on one's garters or stockings or to stripping a tree of its side branches.

∽∾∽

Obviously, then, I find myself attracted to Menippean satire, to *saturas* of all sorts, because my signature makes the genre possible. I say this, rather write this, because as I study the Menippea, it seems purely fanciful (that is, pataphysical) to think that my signature—myself as subject—can remain outside, *hors d'oeuvre*, any text. Therefore, I insert my signature into the genre (or jar) called Menippea, but in so doing, I lose my identify, my title of ownership over the text. I let james michael jarrett—a chain of common nouns—"become a moment or a part of the [Menippean] text" (Derrida, 1984:56).

On the simplest level this means that I like satire for its jars. For example, Petronius, in the *Satyricon*, has his character, Seleucus, ask:

> What are men anyway but balloons on legs, a lot of blown-up bladders? Flies, that's what we are. No, not even flies. Flies have something inside. But a man's a bubble, all air, nothing else. (Petronius, 50)

People, to Seleucus, are empty jars, and whatever Petronius's position on this issue, one thing is clear. The *Satyricon* concerns itself with what was later called the Cartesian jar/jelly split. Swift worked the same image, in *A Tale of a Tub*, when he wrote:

> in most corporeal beings, which have fallen under my cognizance, the outside hath been infinitely preferable to the in;

whereof I have been farther convinced from some late experiments. Last week I saw a woman flayed, and you will hardly believe how much it altered her person for the worse.

Yesterday I ordered the carcass of a beau to be stripped in my presence, when we were all amazed to find so many unsuspected faults under one suit of clothes. Then I laid open his brain, his heart, and his spleen; but I plainly perceived at every operation, that the farther we proceeded, we found the defects increase upon us in number and bulk. (333)

This often cited passage presents a jarrish or jordanean episteme. It forcefully argues that people are jelly jars—tubs. It implies that *A Tale of a Tub* should be renamed *A Tale of a Jarrett*.

The Menippea features tuns of other famous jars. Here are a few examples. Rabelais organized the whole of *Gargantua and Pantagruel* around "the Holy Bottle of Bacbuc." Sir Thomas Browne wrote a piece entitled *Urne Buriall*. Voltaire wrote *CANdide*. Sterne has Mr. Shandy call the mind of Susannah, his servant girl, "a leaky vessel" (vol. IV, ch. 14). And Carlyle, following Swift's lead, wrote *Sartor Resartus* or the *Canner Recanned* or the *Jarrer Rejarred*.

But identifying jars in Menippean texts is like making jelly using commercial pectin. It works, but it's nothing to be proud of. Anyone equipped with a box of sure-jel can move into cannery row. James Michael Jarrett, though, offers much more than this. As a sock or half-hose, *jarretts* resemble the cornucopia, a horn of plenty, whose sheer abundance—*copia*—jars my mind, creating cognitive dissonance, overloading or jamming all channels.

The Menippea, too, in its encyclopedic storing up of information, jams signals. It most often features itself as Godlike—as right, in the sense of always correct—a beautiful, well-heeled angel (messenger) sent to warn mankind of coming apocalypse. It hooks into meaty issues, exposes rottenness, calls a jordan a jordan (really puts them in a pickle if done right), and hamstrings (delimbs) evil doers. Inherently conservative, it keeps the door to a traditional past ajar. In other words, if the Menippea had its way, everything would be unscrewed: virginity would be endlessly recovered.

Make no mistake, though, the Menippea rettes people of villainy, but it soils itself as it cans and contains putrification. At one and the same time, it desires to poison and to heal by jarring texts (people, language, and reality), by making them bend the knee. Some say it would jam everyone into one mold; others say it has no mold, that it only jars what it does not want or what it fears. Like all jars

it has no spout.
It is without spout.
Its spout is off.
It spouts off.

As a literary genre, Menippean satire has seen the "excremental vision" (Norman O. Brown's term for the jarrettean moment). Again, *it contains rottenness*. It knows its way around jakes (outhouses were supplanted by modern, giant underground jordans called septic tanks). And it prefers "to fall at jar"—that is, to dissent or vary—on and about the outlying districts or margins that society and language inscribe. Aristotle rammed this point home when he wrote in chapter four of the *Poetics* that comedy arose in the outlying districts from those who led the phallic songs. Comedy (here synonymous with jarrettean literature) is suburban. Like canning and Wycherley's country wife, it grew up on the farm; it is a pharmacotic bumpkin, tracing out margins.

Or look at it another way. The Menippea is a kind of jazz, and jazz is a kind of Menippea, forming a body of work that aurally satirizes mainstream, Caucasian music, art, and culture. Of the time jazz appeared, F. Scott Fitzgerald wrote:

> It was characteristic of the Jazz Age that it had no interest in politics at all. It was an age of miracles, it was an age of art, it was an age of excess, and it was an age of satire. (14)

When jazzmen really cook—let out all the stops and ham it up—the result is a high-quality jam. This jam, what Duke Ellington called "such sweet thunder," jars ("cuts") established (generic) ways of playing tunes, because it foregrounds the solo or group improvisation. Stated succinctly, jazz and the Menippea follow the law of the signature (a hymen marking the fold of ensembles and solos); classical music and literature (for example, romance and tragedy) follow the law of the preestablished score.

What about this essay? Does it follow the law of the subject (the idiom) or the law of the object (the recipe)? Hopefully, by miming the motions of signation, it folds the two laws together. If this is the case, perhaps a new recipe for essaying is called for, one that can be written only after all cooking, canning, and jamming is done.

THREE

Rapsody:
The Counterfeiters

Tropology: The Art of Passing

Bring me a penny, that I may see it. And they brought it.
And he saith unto them, Whose is this image and super-
scription? And they said unto him, Caesar's. And Jesus
answering said unto them, Render to Caesar the things
that are Caesar's, and to God the things that are God's.
                                    —Mark 12:15b-17a

*Rap*sody: the variant spelling of this trope is calculated to evoke several semantic layers. The term, notes Walter Ong, combines *rhaptein* ("to weave or stitch together") with *oide* ("song") and, thus, signifies "the stringing together of poems" (13). Originally, it referred to an epic poem or to part of one "suitable for recitation at one time" (OED). Later, according to Pat Rogers, it signified a miscellany or literary medley "pieced together without close or integral connection" and, hence, by extension and perhaps through a false etymology with "rapture," an "effusive outpouring of sentiment" or "uncontrolled fervour" (1972:246–47). Hugh Holman, synthesizing various meanings of "rhapsody," states that it is marked by emotional intensity and "free, irregular form, suggesting improvisation" (379–80).

Hamlet uses the word. Back home in Denmark after abandoning his university studies in that hotbed of Reformation thought, Wittenberg, Germany, he speaks to his mother of those who turn "sweet religion" into "a rhapsody of words" (III, iv, 46–49). He, thus, recalls Martin Luther's criticism: Catholicism had deteriorated into empty ritual, vain repetition. A precocious and conservative semiotician, Hamlet chides Gertrude for advancing a linguistic practice that turns ultimate, metaphysical reality into empty letters—chains of signifiers without transcendental signifieds—strung together like rosary beads to make mere syntax. He realizes that rhapsody is ultimately a pagan practice, the antithesis of "sweet religion," because it reverses the direction of sublation. Instead of lifting metaphors (signifiers) into concepts (signifieds), it turns philosophemes into allosemes. "Sweet religion" *renders* (signifier to signified); rhapsody *rends* (signifier from signified).

Rogers notes that shifting attitudes toward rhapsody provide an index to aesthetic norms throughout literary history, and he credits Shaftesbury with remotivating the term, even with precipitating "the admiring tone which the word picked up in the wake of Romanticism." But it is in his study of Jonathan Swift's "On Poetry: A Rhapsody" (1733) that Rogers makes a more important observation. He mentions it only in passing—perhaps because it threatens to upset rhapsody as a stable concept (constructed, as we shall see, on the supposition that semblance and reality are always ultimately distinguishable). Early printed versions of Swift's poem went by the title "On Poetry: A Rapsody." Dropping the "h" from "rhapsody" made evident a "slangy double pun" (Rogers, 1983:869–78). First, *rap*sody suggested a "rap" or knock on the head (from *rhepo*, to slap or smite with the palm of the hand). Second, it evoked the "rapp": a "counterfeit coin, worth about half a farthing, which passed current for a halfpenny in Ireland in the 18th century, owing to the scarcity of genuine money" (OED). "The fact is thus," writes Swift in *The Drapier's First Letter*, "many counterfeits passed about under the name of rapps" (424).

But how can we label the rapp a counterfeit when everyone, knowing that it was "false," allowed it to circulate as genuine money? What is the nature of its "falseness"? The rapp is a ready-made. It imitates not real money but an authorization, the moment when real money was issued by the British Treasury; "not a visible thing," writes Hugh Kenner, "but an invisible event: perfectly invisible: it never happened" (83). The rapp anticipates Marcel Duchamp's *Fountain* (an image of blocked circulation—conflating art, sewage, and lucre—that pictures the museum as a clogged colon) and Andy Warhol's *Campbell Soup Can* (perhaps *the* icon of pop appropriation). More obviously, though, it provides a striking antecedent for the "money" of J. S. G. Boggs, a conceptual artist (like Warhol, from Pittsburgh) who, in the early 1990s, made news when he began exchanging hand-drawn bills—which he called "notes"—for currency authorized by various treasury departments. Not surprisingly, Boggs met with official opposition. He was arrested for counterfeiting in England and Australia, and while in Cheyenne, Wyoming, Secret Service agents seized fifteen of his maverick bills. Swift would have approved. His life and work indicate an obsession with counterfeiting. As Kenner recalls: Swift "earned the undying gratitude of his countrymen for exposing, under an assumed name and in an assumed character [Drapier], a scheme for flooding Ireland with counterfeit halfpence, and in his will he endowed a mental hospital" (97).

The rapp is, therefore, remarkable for a couple of reasons. On the one hand, by linking words with money, it renews and recasts an ancient metaphor. Since Zeno, linguistic and economic symbolization and production have been regarded as homologous, if not dual effects of an internalized "numismatic 'epigrammatology.'" Coinage, tyranny, and philosophy developed at the same time and in the same place, arguably, by means of a shared logic of symbolic exchange (Shell, 38, 152–54). On the other hand, associating the economy of literature—literature as an economy—with the specific case of the rapp proclaims a new order of simulacrum, even as it anticipates the emergence of yet another order. The gold coin, according to a presumed "natural law of value," referred unequivocally to a status (allowing one to distinguish between "genuine" and "counterfeit"). The rapp abolished difference. Like the first paper money Marco Polo saw when he visited Cambaluc, China, it was based on "the commercial law of value," referring only to equivalences (and, hence, creating the conditions of production). But unlike backed currency, the rapp was indeterminate, based on "the structural law of value"; it was less a sign (of "serial production") and more a code capable of generation (Baudrillard, 1983:83–106). If the rapp could become legal tender, what couldn't?

The history of music parallels "these mutations of the law of value" (83). For example, classical music, like phonetic writing, follows from the assumption that signs can refer unerringly to sounds. It corresponds to the first order of simulacrum; art—which synthesizes or counterfeits nature—lives entirely off of the gap between semblance and reality (95). Jazz—born of the industrial revolution, mechanical reproduction, and the obliteration of the concept of "original"—belongs to the second order. Pop to the third order. It is, Adorno argues, completely code-generated (1941:18).

I have come to associate rap—for example, the Beastie Boys's *Paul's Boutique* (Capitol, 1989), L. L. Cool J's *Mamma Said Knock You Out* (Def Jam, 1990), or Public Enemy's *Apocalypse 91 . . . The Enemy Strikes Black* (Def Jam, 1991)—with *rap*sody: first, because it feels genuine and, second, because it involves the tactical deployment of digital codes (sampling) to make music. Rap, despite claims to the contrary, doesn't so much represent the ultimate in pop honesty, as it marks a late instance of pop substituting codes of passion for codes of realism. Predicated on an ideology of transparency, it generates the effect of authenticity by combining production techniques that signify cunning with performances that signify conviction. Rap is, in a word, rhapsodic: syncretism animated by zeal. Formally, it recommends making records out of other people's records to create what Charles Aaron describes as "a *rhythmic* construct of patched-together drum beats and bass fragments, animated by snatches of melodic figures" (23). Thematically, it recommends speaking the "truth."

Listening: Wailing Saxes for C90

> *Rapturously, rhapsodically, the number rose to madness.*
> —*Rudolph Fisher, "Common Meter" (27)*

This anthology focuses on the saxophone, the most rhapsodic of jazz instruments. To mangle a phrase coined by Erik Satie, it shouts both sorrow and ebullience. Designed for a ninety–minute audio cassette, it presents work by some of the most significant players in the history of jazz, and it illustrates a wide range of approaches to soprano, alto, tenor, and baritone saxes. Unfortunately, since the saxophone is practically ubiquitous in jazz, it also omits a multitude of phenomenal players and performances. For example, I'm grieved that there was no room for Don Byas, Zoot Sims, Hank Mobley, Steve Lacy, Dexter Gordon, or Serge Chaloff. The listener's task, then, is to focus on what is here, while letting included selections prompt further inquiry.

Side I

01. Carlos Ward (1985) "The Wedding," from Abdullah Ibrahim, *Water from an Ancient Well*, Enja/Tiptoe.   2:38

    A simple melody, harmonies of Protestant hymns, bound together by an arrangement reminiscent of Ellington-Strayhorn.

02. Benny Carter (1961) "The Midnight Sun Will Never Set," *Further Definitions*, Impulse!   3:55

    Unabashedly gorgeous composition by Quincy Jones, featuring solos by Coleman Hawkins, Dick Katz, and Carter.

03. Charlie Parker (1947) "Drifting on a Reed," *The Legendary Dial Masters, Vol. 2*, Stash.   3:00

    Yes, it's the title track of this book.

04. Joe Henderson (1963) "Blue Bossa," *Joe Henderson: The Blue Note Years*, Blue Note.   7:58

    Instead of delineating "meaning," this tenor saxophonist employs improvisation as a means of displaying possibilities.

05. Archie Shepp (1980) "Backwater Blues," *Trouble in Mind*, SteepleChase.   2:39

    A duet with pianist Horace Parlan that lovingly affirms African rhythmic sources and blues feeling.

06. Sidney Bechet (1939) "Summertime," *The Port of Harlem Jazzmen*, Blue Note.   4:10

    Before John Coltrane and Steve Lacy, Bechet was the sound of the soprano saxophone.

07. Art Pepper (1980) "That's Love," *Winter Moon*, Galaxy.   4:50

    A real anomaly: an artistically satisfying jazz-plus-strings recording.

08. David Murray (1991) "Song from the Old Country," *Shakill's Warrior*, DIW/Columbia.   7:01

    Listening to this organ combo raises most people's cholesterol level.

09. Stan Getz (1964) "Corcovado (Quiet Nights)," *The Girl from Ipanema—The Bossa Nova Years*, Verve.   2:28

Not the first, but the most popular meeting of American jazz and Brazilian samba.

10. Gerry Mulligan (1971) "Grand Tour," *The Age of Steam*, A&M.   4:19

    Although it is probably composed of brass, Gerry Mulligan's baritone sax sounds like it's made of chocolate. Or at least that's an adequate metaphor for its patented creamy buzz.

11. John Lurie (1980) "Harlem Nocturne," *The Lounge Lizards*, Editions EG.   2:04

    Self-consciously revisits the diegesis of film noir.

Total playing time 45:02

Side II

01. Lester Young (1939) "Lester Leaps In," *The Essential Count Basie, Vol. 2*, Columbia.   3:10

    Prez didn't craft instantly memorable melodies so much as he rode unforgettable riffs.

02. Sonny Rollins (1956) "St. Thomas," *Saxophone Colossus*, Prestige.   6:45

    A infectious calypso that foils any attempt to keep still.

03. Ben Webster (1964) "Stardust," *See You at the Fair*, Impulse!   2:24

    Bill Clinton's desire to become President of the United States was blatant compensation for not being able to play tenor sax like this.

04. World Saxophone Quartet (1980) "I Heard That," *Revue*, Black Saint.   3:23

    In effect, a gospel quartet that uses horns in place of vocal chords.

05. Eric Dolphy (1961) "'Round Midnight," from George Russell, *Ezz-thetics*, Riverside.   6:33

    Monk's most famous composition rendered as a cri de coeur.

06. Johnny Hodges (1966) "Isfahan," on Duke Ellington,
    The Far East Suite, Bluebird.   4:04

    The model for all achingly lyrical ballads.

07. John Coltrane (1963) "My One and Only Love," *John
    Coltrane and Johnny Hartman*, Impulse!   4:54

    *Proof positive that Coltrane wasn't afraid to play
    pretty.*

08. Jimmie Lunceford and His Orchestra (1937) "For
    Dancers Only," *For Dancers Only*, Decca/GRP.   2:37

    *Sy Oliver's charts jump, trumpets scream, and the sax-
    ophone section perks like a well-tuned machine.*

09. Wayne Shorter (1964) "Infant Eyes," *Speak No Evil*,
    Blue Note.   6:43

    *Incorporates blues and gospel elements into the basic
    vocabulary of bop.*

10. James Carter (1993) "Lunatic," *JC on the Set*,
    DIW/Columbia.   4:18

    *A contemporary phenomenon, Carter also manifests
    affection for the bar-walking honkers of the 1940s.*

Total playing time 44:51

Archeology: How Was Jazz Made Audible?

*"That business about progress in art is ancient non-
sense," Etienne said, "but in jazz as in any art there's
always a flock of fakers. Music that can be translated
into emotion is one thing, but emotion which pretends to
pass as music is another."*
                                                      —*Julio Cortázar (69)*

All glamor is bound up with some sort of trickery.
                                          —*Theodor Adorno (1941:29)*

Assay Office

The history of jazzography is, for all intents and purposes, one
massive attempt to repress the implications of *rap*sody. Instead of
considering that authenticity in music might be a question of poli-

tics—an effect of hegemony—jazzography has repeatedly concerned itself with erecting and policing real/fake distinctions. To substantiate this claim, one need look no further than Henry Osgood's *So This Is Jazz* (1926). It was, as I mentioned in chapter 1, the first book by an American to make jazz its object of study. An attempt to validate jazz as "serious" music, it elevated the "superior" compositions of Paul Whiteman and George Gershwin—for example, "Rhapsody in Blue"—over the "quaint" improvisations of "nameless" folk musicians. But while the wisdom of hindsight (and the added motivation of political correctness) might prompt us to dismiss its polemic as, at best, misguided and, at worst, racist and elitist, we should also notice how Osgood gained an audience and established the terms of jazz discourse. By doing so, we stand to learn something not only about jazz and jazzography, but about the cultural politics of modernism.

Osgood, like his immediate successors—Robert Goffin, Wilder Hobson, John Hammond, George Frazier, Car Van Vechten, Frederic Ramsey, Charles Edward Smith, Hugues Panassié, Winthrop Sargeant, and André Hodeir—cast the critic in the role of assayer. And he rendered jazz in culturally receivable—that is, in essentialist and oppositional—terms. Instead of presenting jazzography as yet another case of "experts" *determining* what will and will not pass as genuine (a matter of politics), he represented it as a site where experts accept responsibility for *distinguishing* the genuine from the counterfeit (a matter of ontology). Osgood's discourse—subjective judgments of taste disguised as objective assessments about style and form—was structured by American myths about "passing."

Of Numismatics and Jazzography

Schuller agrees. After picturing most early jazzography as a kind of embellishment of "music itself" and the "body of writing" that accumulated around jazz as an "amalgam," he notes a curious phenomenon. The "amalgam" circulated like a bizarre type of currency. It "was allowed to pass for scholarship and serious analysis" because of "the humble, socially 'unacceptable' origin of jazz" and "the widely held notion that a music improvised by self-taught, often musically illiterate musicians did not warrant genuine musicological research" (vii). By some twist or trick—some trope—jazzography comes to signify an impoverished or bankrupt economy where an imitation (a rapp, simulacrum, or double) can pass as genuine.

Watch my words closely, though. I am not suggesting that Schuller regards all jazzography as counterfeit. Clearly, this is not the case. He generally trusts the adequacy of musicological discourse to represent acoustical phenomena (his book is proof enough of this fact). I am declaring that his preface to *Early Jazz* tells a personal version of an institutional myth, one that explains how jazzography invented itself. Put allegorically, I am saying that Schuller imagines the field of jazz writing as something like Ireland in the eighteenth century: the site of an elaborate confidence game; a space where counterfeits pose real threats by consistently passing for—contesting and confusing—that which is genuine.

Schuller aims to distinguish the authentic from the spurious by presenting readers with an example of "genuine musicological research": "a systematic, comprehensive history dealing with the specifics of the music" (vii, viii). That task completed, we should be able to measure jazz writing against an established (immutable) standard. Schuller's text, *Early Jazz*, will serve as the discourse equivalent of an assay office; fraudulent imitations of "scholarship and serious analysis" will be seen for what they are.

But what are they? Schuller avoids words I have used, adjectives such as "fraudulent," "counterfeit," and "spurious." He prefers "fascinated," "well-meaning," and "amateur." For him, jazzography fails when it exhibits "critical gaps or misjudgments," falls "prey to basic misconceptions," attends to the "general descriptive or impressionistic," and misses "elusive essentials." Schuller never once lists counterfeiting—imitating serious scholarship with an intention to defraud—as one of the jazz author's nefarious practices. His point is stated more subtly. "Well-meaning amateur criticism and fascinated opinion" may have passed "for scholarship and serious analysis," but they did so, not through artfulness (for they had none), but by permission! Bias prompted tolerance. Since jazz lacked "academic credentials"—had a "humble, socially 'unacceptable' origin" and was produced by "self-taught, often musically illiterate musicians"—it "did not warrant genuine musicological research." Therefore, the writing that jazz happened to elicit, although it counted for very little and was "hardly sufficient to produce a serious interest," "was allowed to pass for [that is, to stand 'in place of' absent] scholarship" (vii).

In the following pages of this archeology, I want to sketch, first, how jazzography attempted to establish authenticity in jazz by conceptualizing it through a genuine/counterfeit opposition; additionally, I want to explore how this same opposition informed and enabled jazzography. In Schuller's representation of *jazz writing*, he again employs an image conventionally used to conceptualize *jazz music* (a counterfeit of "legitimate" music), *records* (counterfeits of "live" performances), and *writing* or *notation* (a counterfeit of an "objective truth"). One may, therefore, read my comments on jazzography as an oblique discussion of logocentrism: the philosophical position that thinks itself into existence by differentiating original from copy, real from image, and object from symbol (and by privileging the first term in each of these pairs). I provide readers with another "popularized" account of what has already been theorized extensively in such works as Marc Shell's *The Economy of Literature*, Jacques Derrida's *The Truth in Painting*, and Jean Baudrillard's *Simulations*. Throughout this section, I employ the trope of *rap*sody as an exegetical tool for writing about jazzography. In subsequent sections of this chapter I concentrate on the possibility of writing with *rap*sody.

Two Sides of Jazzography

The aesthetic economy that determined musical legitimacy and musical common sense during modernism prompted two initial responses to jazz. One response signified its provisional acceptance (*"Jazz is great fun; it's culturally relevant, too!"*). The other side signified a refusal or reluctance to grant jazz full admittance into mainstream American culture (*"Jazz is hardly worthy of serious consideration!"*). Both sides are readily apparent in this passage from Winthrop Sargeant's *Jazz: Hot and Hybrid*, a swing-era study that Theodor Adorno called "the best, most reliable and most sensible book on the subject" (1984:121):

> The attendant weakness of jazz is that it is an art without positive moral values, an art that evades those attitudes of restraint and intellectual poise upon which complex civilizations are built. At best it offers civilized man a temporary escape into drunken self-hypnotism. . . . It is a far cry from the jazz state of mind to that psychology of human perfectibility, of aspiration, that lies, for example, behind the symphonies of a Beethoven or the music dramas of a Wagner. (in Ramsey and Smith, 339; this passage was deleted in later editions of *Jazz: Hot and Hybrid*)

Little perspicacity is required to locate the economy of fear underwriting this passage. Its political progressivism seems awfully close to a symbolic attempt to "accommodate and expunge the black presence from the host community" (Hebdige, 44–45). But if this double-coded, racist subtext is only barely latent in Sargeant's statement, it is woefully manifest in the writings of others who were, in the early days of jazz, regarded as liberals. For example, Gilbert Seldes, managing editor of *Dial* and a booster of the Harlem Renaissance, wrote:

> I say the negro is not our salvation because with all my feeling for what he instinctively offers, for his desirable indifference to our set of conventions of emotional decency, I am on the side of civilization. . . .
>
> Nowhere is the failure of the negro to exploit his gifts more obvious than in the use he has made of the jazz orchestra; for although nearly every negro jazz band is better than nearly every white band, no negro band has yet come up to the level of the best white ones, and the leader of the best of all, by a little joke, is called Whiteman. (Seldes, in Dodge, 312)

Interestingly and most tragically, after Roger Pryor Dodge cites the latter of these two passages in "Consider the Critics" (1939), his survey of jazzography, he chides Seldes, not for racist presuppositions founded on a romantic image of African American as primitive, but for an inexcusable critical lapse—an admiration for the Paul Whiteman Orchestra. Dodge declares that Seldes's concluding remark, "admittedly slight in witty intent, will ever strike back at its author as a more humorous error in art judgment!" (312–13). In Dodge's eyes, Seldes erred aesthetically, not ethically. Dodge agrees with Seldes—at least to a point. He, too, accepts the amorality of the African American, stating that "the Negro may have been indifferent to our emotional decency," but he adds: "the vital part of our centuries of musical experience" has gone into "Negro jazz" (312).

Although Dodge and Seldes's use of the possessive pronoun "our" scarcely needs glossing, we should observe that power hinges on this word. In *The Grandissimes* (1879), a novel set in New Orleans at the time of the Louisiana Purchase, George Washington Cable has a Creole patriarch, Agricola Fusilier, observe:

> [W]hen we say, "we people," we *always* mean we white people. The non-mention of color always implies pure white; and whatever is not pure white is to all intents and purposes pure

black. When I say the "whole community," I mean the whole white portion; when I speak of the "undivided public sentiment," I mean the sentiment of the white population. (59)

Dodge and Seldes inherit the narrative position that Cable exposes (and that functions to create and sustain the binary opposition "black/white"). Moreover, they bank on the dividends it pays.

But unlike Seldes, Dodge refuses to accept the formula: amoral people yield uncivilized music. Instead, he opts for another solution. Jazz is valuable to the extent that it exhibits "our [Western] harmony and musical form" (312). It is interesting to the extent that it is "indifferent to our set of conventions of emotional decency." Or stated differently, Dodge is reassured by the dependence of jazz on convention (song form and harmony); he is titillated by its deviations from decorum (its emphasis on syncopation). This is why he finds it more interesting than the standard productions of Tin Pan Alley. It simultaneously meets what Adorno identified as the two demands of popular music: that is, it's material that falls "within the category of what the musically untrained listener would call 'natural' music," and it's stimulating enough to provoke "the listener's attention" (1941:24). Jazz, for Dodge, holds forth the possibility of an art form that is, potentially, at once popular and avant-garde—which is to say, thoroughly modern. Taking this argument one more step, we reach an astounding conclusion, one that reverses and supplements the conventional perception of jazz as the white co-optation of black music. According to Dodge and Seldes, Negro jazz is worthy of attention—it will be allowed to pass for Music—precisely to the extent that it recuperates white musical experience. It is a quaint but also threatening counterfeit of "real music," part of a feedback loop. White people create Music, black people—like children—imitate it (play around with it), and, then, white people consume this refracted representation of themselves. For example, mark how this process is employed to represent the development of the cakewalk, a nineteenth-century dance:

There is a theory that the plantation cakewalk originated when colored servants *imitated others* doing the minuet. Whether or not that's true, the cakewalk *gravitated right back* to white folks by way of minstrel shows. Even high society behind their cloistered doors "kicked up high" for fun without the incentive of a simple cake for a prize. (Harris, 30, emphasis added)

"The negro," wrote George Jean Nathan in 1919, "with his unusual sense of rhythm, is no more accurately to be called musical than a metronome is to be called a Swiss music-box" (in Dodge, 306). Thus, the Negro becomes the archetypical mimic, a Yahoo capable of aping the motions of civilization (one will recall that the Houyhnhnms, the talking horses of *Gulliver's Travels*, contend that Gulliver probably does not speak so much as imitate their speech). And jazz becomes a counterfeit of Music. Why? For one thing, it is regarded as performed, not composed. In an oral culture, distinctions between performance and composition collapse or, rather, they have not yet emerged. In a literate or an electronic culture, where copyright laws uphold an industry predicated on music publication and an ideology founded on the private ownership of property, performances repeat compositions (originals). However unique it may be, an improvisation is always viewed as a performance (valued or vilified as a sort of ingenuous counterfeit). It may qualify as a musical object worthy in its own right—but "in a legal sense," writes Simon Frith, it is "composerless." The improviser sells, not songs, but "his or her unique *approach* to songs" (1981:17).

Jazzography gained currency as it referred to, even reinforced, an epistemology predicated on making real/fake distinctions. In circulating two radically different aesthetics, though, it undercut its own philosophical presuppositions and suggested that what passed for genuine (both within writing and music) was a reminder of politics, not a reflection of essence. One aesthetic, as we have seen, pointed to the dependence of jazz on European harmony and form. While it readily admitted and frequently emphasized indispensable African contributions to the music, it measured the worth of jazz against musical standards established by what Seldes identifies as "several thousand centuries of civilization." This "sweet" aesthetic, which imputed value to jazz as it replicated "the conventions and material formulas" of classical music, dominated jazzography in its early years (Adorno, 1941:24). Another aesthetic, associated with "hot" music and the swing era, characterized jazz as the repudiation of such "civilized" standards. It emphasized the dependence of jazz on African and Caribbean rhythms, and while it readily acknowledged that jazz and classical music shared European conceptions of melody and harmony, it frequently called attention to the harmonic-melodic tendencies (for example, the blues scale or microtones) that distinguished jazz from classical music. It assumed that "Negroes assimilated only those harmonic-melodic tendencies that permitted the integration of their African tradi-tions," or it assumed that the European musical elements employed in jazz either did not adversely affect the music (civilize or domesticate it), or that they were successfully perverted by the music (Schuller, 39). In short, this aesthetic represented jazz as a distinctly American parody or aberrant reading of "civilization"; it imputed value to jazz to the extent that it replicated or reinforced privileged cultural representations (stereotypes) of the Negro as primitive.

In his study of jazz aesthetics, *The Imperfect Art* (1988), Ted Gioia criticizes those who imagine the jazz musician as "one who creates beauty out of pure ignorance" (or forges music in "the smithy of his soul"), and he pays special attention to how this romanticist assumption informed the opinions of Hugues Panassié, Charles Delaunay, and Robert Goffin ("the founding fathers of jazz studies") as well as later-born critics, such as James Lincoln Collier, who wrote about Ornette Coleman and the jazz *avant-garde* (Gioia, 44, 28). But while Gioia's examination of jazz as a "primitivist" art is thorough, making reference to a mythology that finds early expression in the writings of both Montaigne and Rousseau, his motivations are different than mine. Gioia wants to express a truth about jazz music. "In point of fact," he writes, "jazz is not primi-tive art. Nor . . . is it imitative of primitive art" (45). I, on the other hand, want to illustrate a contention about jazzography: trace its rhetorical strategies. In order to accomplish this task, I turn to a specific example.

The White Negro

"[T]he undisputed impresario of the Harlem Renaissance," Carl Van Vechten was an aesthete who practiced a kind of cultural one-upmanship by making "*approving* critical judgments about the very new and the very off-beat" (Moore, 95; Huggins, 94). A dandy, he did everything in his power to invert Victorian values and pro-tect what he perceived as exotica from the encroachments of the vulgar. This Des Esseintes from Cedar Rapids delighted in chal-lenging what James Weldon Johnson called "the Nordic superiority complex" (qtd. in Moore, 99); he fashioned a distinctly American version of the French passion for "*les choses Africaines.*" Although his aesthetic judgments often seemed capricious, subject to the fluctuations of an overdeveloped palate—for example, he champi-oned the Aeolian Hall premier of Gershwin's *Rhapsody in Blue* and at roughly the same time asserted that whites had no business singing spirituals—his lapses from conventional standards of decorum could not have been more calculated or more consistent (96–98).

Van Vechten discovered the title for his novel about Harlem in an old term referring to the topmost gallery of a theater. He called it *Nigger Heaven* (1926). In it he draws a picture of the sociopolitical position of modern African Americans by developing—by extending and, ultimately, remotivating—his title as a metaphor. He has the protagonist and "New Negro," Byron Kasson, exclaim:

> We sit in our places in the gallery of this New York theatre and watch the white world sitting down below in the good seats in the orchestra. Occasionally they turn their faces up towards us, their hard, cruel faces, to laugh, or sneer, but they never beckon. It never seems to occur to them that Nigger Heaven is crowded . . . that we sit above them, that we can drop things down on them and crush them, that we can swoop down from this Nigger Heaven and take their seats. (89–90)

Memorable and disturbing—and redolent of Herman Melville's *Confidence Man*—this image of avenging angels could not be any more striking. It is as if, with one hand, Van Vechten points to the "seal-brown" face of his character Byron Kasson, and with the other points at his own white face. Then, in his best, most sincere imitation of Louis Armstrong, this Janus-faced fop sings a version of "What Did I Do (to Be So Black and Blue)?" Like the novel as a whole, this image of a simulated black man talking about the prejudices of white men underscores its own duplicity. It simultaneously critiques and exemplifies the exploitation of blacks by whites with an ambiguity that will remain unmatched until the Rolling Stones, bohemians cut from the same bolt as Van Vechten, record "Brown Sugar" (1971) and Randy Newman, one of pop music's greatest minstrels, records "Sail Away" (1972).

More importantly, by showing how easy it is to pass for black (the narrator's game) or white (a game played by several of the novel's characters), Van Vechten comes close to demonstrating that race is an effect of politics: in Baudrillard's words, a matter of acting or *simulation*—threatening "the difference between 'true' and 'false,' between 'real' and 'imaginary'" (1983:5). If blackness can be manufactured, then it ceases to be imaginable as a fact of nature, a biological reality. Race becomes a matter of politics, a case of the state apparatus invoking biology to do its bidding.

Then again, Van Vechten only comes close to my argument. Because he is content to exaggerate the radical separation of what is claimed ("*I* am *black*") and what is seen ("*That man* looks *white*")—intent and effect—he ultimately rests upon a belief that "difference is always clear, it is only masked" (Baudrillard, 1983:5). "Each sign . . . refers unequivocally to a status" (84). Passing, for Van Vechten, is a type of counterfeiting (dissimulation—acting like one isn't what one is), not simulation (showing that identity is a matter of acting). He opposes the ideology that backs statements such as those made by Seldes (his junior by thirteen years) and Dodge. Van Vechten represents jazz as a symbolic inversion of "civilized" music; he sanctions the Negro-as-primitive. But he seems unwilling or unable to consider the possibility that racial difference is artificially generated by laws (judicial, scientific, social) that determine who will, or will not, pass for black or white.

For example, Van Vechten describes Mary Love—a light-skinned Negro who could have easily "passed for white"—as one who "admired all Negro characteristics and desired earnestly to possess them," but who, "through no fault of her own,"

> had lost or forfeited her birthright, this primitive birthright which was so valuable and important an asset, a birthright that all the civilized races were struggling to get back to—this fact explained the art of a Picasso or a Stravinsky. To be sure, she, too felt this African beat—it completely aroused her emotionally—but she was conscious of feeling it. This love of drums, of exciting rhythms, this naive delight in glowing colour—the colour that exists only in cloudless, tropical climes—this warm, sexual emotion, all these were hers only through a mental understanding. (89–90)

Mary "lost or forfeited her birthright," not when she lost "natural rhythm," when she no longer found joy in loud colors, or when her steamy sexuality froze in the more temperate climate of Harlem. For she had lost none of these stereotypically Negroid characteristics. She lost her birthright—primitiveness—when she found or developed self-consciousness.

To Van Vechten, self-consciousness is a nonbeneficial adaptation to civilization, and Mary, at least at this point in the novel, is a counterfeit. She is a fake Caucasian (a Negro who can pass for white); she is a fake Negro (a primitive who has lost her birthright).

Thus, it becomes one of her author's major tasks to define genuineness and, then, restore it to her. But who could be more self-conscious, more of a fake, than Van Vechten? In his fiction, he's a narrator signifying and yet deprecating self-consciousness; in life, a dandy plotting every social move, obsessed with aesthetic sensation—tiny details of refinement—and yet affecting nonchalance? And this is a key point. By underscoring difference even as he simultaneously calls attention to ethnocentrism and the politics of passing, Van Vechten models an enabling contradiction of modernism: the desire to achieve transcendence by making ultimate distinctions, and the desire to affirm that such distinctions are contingent, effects of a culturally inherited vocabulary.

Unlike Dodge, Seldes, and their intellectual father, Lemuel Gulliver, Van Vechten does not aspire to the perfect rationality of the Houyhnhnms (who fear that Yahoos are hideous copies of themselves). Rather, convinced that he is already and irreversibly a Houyhnhnm (a disfigured, postlapsarian Yahoo), he casts the African American as primitive (a model Yahoo) and himself as one called to stay the advances of civilization. He writes a fictive critique of ethnocentrism that repeats a gesture Derrida identifies with the eighteenth century: the "humility of one who knows he is unacceptable." *Nigger Heaven*, like Rousseau's *Confessions* (and, later, Lévi-Strauss's *Tristes Tropiques*), imagines non-European peoples "as the index to a hidden good Nature, as a native soil recovered, of a 'zero degree' with reference to which one could outline the structure, the growth, and above all the degradation of our society and our culture." Or, in other words, Van Vechten's novel pictures "Nigger Heaven" as the ideal from which civilization has fallen; it penitentially shoulders the burden "of constituting the other as a model of original and natural goodness, of accusing and humiliating" itself. It is enabled by remorse—the "remorse that produces anthropology" (Derrida, 1976:114–15).

White Knights

Guilt associated with an assumed loss of essence or presence accounts for much ethnomusicological endeavor. But, typically, guilt finds more overt expression in the form of rebellion. For example, after sketching the life story and contributions of Charles Seeger, whom he calls "the guiding spirit of modern American ethnomusicology," Kerman singles out "middle-class antagonism towards conventional middle-class culture" as "the typical factor in the ideological makeup of ethnomusicology" (11, 159). Alan P. Merriam, who defined ethnomusicology as "the study of music in culture," asserts that postwar ethnomusicology was informed by the "White Knight" and the "Dutiful Preserver" concepts (in Kerman, 13, 159). Indeed, if Seeger and others—for instance, Alan Lomax (author of *The Folksongs of America* and the definitive biography of Jelly Roll Morton)—were progenitors of the "Dutiful Preserver Concept," often identifying with the conditions of "poor whites," then Van Vechten and others—for instance, John Hammond—were classic "White Knights" who admired the Negro's mythic ability to transcend poverty and oppression through music. "I have often been accused of chauvinism because of my preference for Negro musicians," wrote Hammond in his autobiography. "I suppose I must have seemed so to English readers [of *Melody Maker* magazine], but I was being honest. . . . As any musician will tell you, great improvisation depends on . . . the drive of proper rhythmic support. I said so again and again in print, prompting some people to call me 'nigger lover,' or to think I must be black" (58). Of Hammond, Count Basie said, "He's been a hell of a man. And he has never asked for a nickel from me or any of those people he's done so much for. . . . All he wanted to see was the results of what was supposed to be happening" (Basie, 296).

The 1930s, Andrew Ross observes, was a decade with an "ethnological feel" (48). "[W]riters and artists had set out on exhaustive fact-finding travels all over the country, imbued with the documentary spirit of studying a hitherto 'unseen' native culture that could be cast as either 'folk' or 'proletarian' in character." Charles Seeger exemplified this group. Although he had little direct bearing on jazzography, he provides counterpoint to its development. Put anachronistically, Van Vechten was *hip*; Seeger was *beat*. He identified with the disenfranchised (for example, agricultural workers in Sacramento Valley), advocated pacifism in 1917, and opposed the institutionalized elitism of university music departments. At one point in his life, after teaching at the University of California, he stopped composing music and "took his family in a homemade automobile house-trailer to rural North Carolina, so that he could play free sonata recitals in churches and Grange halls" (Kerman, 155–56). To folk culture Seeger offered "civilization"; to the masses he offered an "authentic" folk culture. Like other intellectuals of his time, he was motivated by opposing urges. He professed a desire, as he put it, to "look at things from below up," but he remained a "reluctant natural aristocrat" (159). He espoused predictable leftist political affiliations (a flirtation with communism in the '30s) and, then, secured administrative posts in "two of Roosevelt's programmes to combat the Depression, the Resettlement Administration and the Works Progress Administration" (156). While in Washington, he used his government positions to encourage the recording of folksongs; later, through his son, Pete, he succeeded in bringing folk music to the masses (159).

Van Vechten and Hammond also seemed motivated by mutually exclusive desires: egalitarian urges and highbrow reflexes. As boosters, they hoped to popularize jazz (share it with the middle class); as hipsters, they wanted to keep it untainted by the masses (shelter it from the effects of conventionalization). Their attempts to live out workable responses to conflicting motives served to produce enormous amounts of creative energy. For example, Hammond was, in his own words, "an inheritor of the guilt and therefore the obligations of wealth." His mother was a Vanderbilt: a "reformer fired with . . . energy, certain in the right, oblivious to physical infirmities which all right-minded flesh could overcome" (23). She communicated this missionary zeal to her only son. He signed and recorded an amazing roster of musicians for Columbia Records: Billie Holiday, Count Basie, Lester Young, Teddy Wilson, Charlie Christian, Benny Goodman (who married Hammond's sister), Bob Dylan, Bruce Springsteen, Aretha Franklin, and George Benson. From one perspective, these artists virtually define American popular music. From another perspective, their fame refers to Hammond's power (Stowe, 54–64). For example, I love Billie Holiday when she moans and Bob Dylan when he bellows. Possibly, they thrill me exactly as they did Hammond; he just "discovered" them first. But I wonder. Isn't it equally likely that my "natural" affections are an ultimate dissemination of Hammond's tastes? "[T]he arbiter of African-American musical authenticity," he shaped what would pass or count as a good jazz or pop voice—very often against the grain of formerly accepted standards of propriety (Stowe, 52).

On December 23, 1938, Hammond produced a concert—billed and recorded as *From Spirituals To Swing*—and brought jazz to Carnegie Hall. In recounting the events of that historic evening, he recalled a one-word imperative issued by Van Vechten. Let it serve as a metaphoric epithet for all those who heard their vocation in music "raw" and "uncivilized."

It is doubtful where [sic] the concert could have started less auspiciously. The plan had been to have me make some opening remarks, and then play an excerpt from the recordings of the Turner expedition in Africa, showing a kind of ethnic relationship between African tribal music and American jazz and folk music (something I would never venture today). I was so nervous that my voice couldn't be heard, and I remember Carl Van Vechten yelling "louder" from his front row perch, whereupon I gave a signal to the sound man to increase the amplification. He misread the cue and instead put on the record of wild African chanting, while I was still talking to the audience. Everybody broke up, of course, but from then on it was a continuous ball, beginning with the three boogie-woogie pianists and ending some three and a half hours later with the first concert presentation of Count Basie's big band. (Hammond, 1987:1)

To summarize, we have identified two distinct patterns for responding to and representing jazz. Not so coincidentally, these patterns also correspond to dominant listening patterns that David Riesman found operating among pop consumers in the 1950s (8–9). First, there was a tendency to assimilation, to connect jazz with "civilization." We might label the amateur critics committed to this aesthetic nascent jazz musicologists. Second, there was a tendency to enlist jazz as a means of differentiation or resistance, to connect it with primitivism. The amateur critics committed to this aesthetic are best labeled nascent "comparative musicologists" or, to employ a term Jaap Kunst introduced in 1950, "ethnomusicologists." From this latter, more sociological and left-leaning orientation came the jazzography of Hammond and Van Vechten and, later, Amiri Baraka, Eric Hobsbawm, and Frank Tirro. Schuller's musicological study, because it explains jazz by mapping it onto "civilized music," finds its paradigm in the former tradition.

Passing Muster

Several points should now be evident.

1. The images that bring jazz into language signify the appropriation of music by ideologically motivated systems of discourse. The most elemental sort of co-optation takes place at the level of words, metaphors.
2. At least two groups "discovered" a homological relationship—a "symbolic fit"—between jazz and their own values; by filling

jazz with significance—linking it with preferred signifiers then reading back this meaning onto their own systems of representation—they sought the power to determine who could authoritatively speak of and for jazz. They manufactured identity by representing and, subsequently, by possessing the sign *jazz* (cf. DeVeaux, 525–60; Hebdige, 113ff.).

3. For all its "actuality" anterior to linguistic sense, jazz enters discourse as a projection or objectification of warring systems of representation. It signifies an arena of negotiation where power manifests itself as a privileged reading: the right to treat *jazz* as signified not as signifier; the right to treat unauthorized readings as counterfeit.

4. By creating, then policing a boundary between the real and the fake, "jazzology"—the musicological and ethnomusicological discourse of jazz—installed itself as a kind of science. Stated differently, jazzology is a historical consequence of the assumption that one can distinguish between genuine and counterfeit; it is an effect of suppressing traces of origin ("the counterfeiter's central strategy"—Kenner, 160) in order to situate a discourse as genuine. Looking again at Schuller's comments, we can now see that what "was allowed to pass for scholarship and serious analysis" actually determined what would later count as *genuine*. Genuineness was not some foreknown quality possessed by texts. It was a by-product, or better, a spoil of war in the battle that determined the meaning of the term *jazz*.

Fake Book

We find ourselves in a quandary. Should we accept Schuller's writing—a musicological study of early jazz—as *genuine*? Obviously, he believes we should, and we could find others to agree with him. For example, jazz and social critic Nat Hentoff regards Schuller as part of a "nucleus of technically trained critics . . . developing a durable body of analytical jazz criticism" (Hentoff, 250). But given our observations about the process by which a system of representation comes to count as genuine, should we accept the testimony of Hentoff? Why not dismiss him as Schuller's accomplice? Dare we suspect that Schuller's text might be a counterfeit—an imitation of "genuine musicological research," merely passing for "scholarship and serious analysis"? How do we know that Schuller is not deceiving us, perhaps even deceiving himself? Maybe without believing in musicology, he is merely playing with it, simulating it, in order to seduce readers. Could he be an *amateur* passing for a *professional*? Is he so overwhelmed with love for jazz that his desire compels him to pose as, to affect all the signs of, a serious scholar?

Strictly speaking, there is no generally accepted name for the study of jazz. "Ethnomusicology," Kerman notes, "is popularly understood to mean the study of non-Western music" (13). Musicology—which "was originally understood (as *Musikwissenschaft* still is) to cover thinking about, research into, and knowledge of all possible aspects of music"—

> in academic practice, and in broad general usage . . . has come to have a much more constricted meaning. It has come to mean the study of the history of Western music in the high-art tradition. . . . Furthermore, in the popular mind—and in the minds of many academics—musicology is restricted not only in the subject matter it covers but also in its approach to that subject matter. (I say "restricted" rather than "constricted" here, for this approach is not the result of any paring down of an earlier concept.) Musicology is perceived as dealing essentially with the factual, the documentary, the verifiable, the analyzable, the positivistic. (11–12)

Schuller's text, then, can only imitate the motions of "genuine musicological research." It can cast out or conceal its metaphorical basis, disguise discourse that is generally descriptive or impressionistic, and, thereby, force the merely rhetorical to submit to the authority of science. And it can employ the discourse of science—the dialectic of positivism—to describe jazz. But it cannot be musicology, precisely because jazz has not been institutionalized as *Music*; it is not part of the high-art tradition of Western music.

When Schuller states that his "book is directed particularly to the 'classically' trained musician or composer, who may never have concerned himself with jazz and who cannot respond to the in-group jargon and glossy enthusiasm of most writing on jazz," he in effect labels his own text a counterfeit: a rapp (ix). If *Early Jazz*, or any other utterance about jazz, is "allowed to pass for scholarship and serious analysis," it must play the part of discourse that is playing the part of musicology. It must mark itself as a counterfeit of a counterfeit in order to be allowed to pass as genuine. Hence, Schuller faces a mandate that cannot be carried out (except through a trick: by *faking*). His text must ultimately exclude classical music, for it must demonstrate how jazz differs from classical music. But at the same time, for his text to be taken seriously, it must employ a discourse system that would exclude his object of study, one that was devised for the express purpose of representing classical music.

Schuller has cut a deal with jazz. If it will permit musicology to adopt it, colonize it, make love to it, dress it up, jazz it up, and so on (choose or invent a metaphor), then the nagging question of its legitimacy and literacy can be amended. Jazz will gain the ratio-analytical language of science and, thereby, order its credentials and increase its desirability. Leonard Feather summarizes the benefits of such a bargain:

> Many have tried to explain jazz in words; all have failed. But the more persuasive writers and lecturers, impressing their audiences with the subject's validity as material for serious discussion, have drawn into the orbit of jazz appreciation a number of potential converts, willing to listen with a broader mind, a more receptive ear. (19)

By feigning musicological discourse—the representation of music warranted as truth in this episteme—jazzology aims to seduce. It hopes to lure receptive ears. Like all writing about jazz, *like all writing*, it works off—assumes and produces—desire. As Stephen Longstreet remarks, in a passage Kennington and Read use as the epigraph to *The Literature of Jazz,*

> There were a raft of books published about jazz history, a lot of them bad, some of them very good as to facts and dates and names; a few were readable, the rest mostly for the fanatics and so packed with names, dates and written either in professors' English or reporters' prose that you had to love the stuff a lot to wade through it. But it all helped, it all made the subject serious because people are impressed by the printed word about anything. (in Kennington and Read, iii)

Summary by Allegory

We have seen that, within the workings of a complex economy, the body of jazz literature is conceived as counterfeit. More accurately, it is imaged as hermaphroditic discourse: an amalgam of amateur criticism passing as (that is, carrying the marks of) both "general descriptive or impressionistic" writing and "scholarship and serious analysis."

Hermaphroditus, readers may recall, was the son of Hermes and Aphrodite. One day, while bathing in a fountain, he was spotted by the local nymph Salmacis. Smitten, she immediately fell in love. But Hermaphroditus rejected her. At her prayer, however, when Salmacis embraced Hermaphroditus, the gods united them in a single body. Although we may question the subsumption of the name Salmacis by the name Hermaphroditus, we could consider the nymph as but a catalyst in the metamorphosis of Hermaphroditus. The offspring of Hermes and Aphrodite was always an indeterminable figure. In his/her name, Hermaphroditus bears an image of duality; difference is played out (created and exhausted) in its space.

By an interesting twist, Hermaphroditus's father—Hermes or Mercury—is associated with the amalgam (an alloy of mercury with another metal), and as the inventor of the lyre (which he fashioned from a tortoise shell and exchanged with Apollo for the caduceus, a symbol of the medical profession), Hermes is also associated with music. He is the messenger of the gods, the trickster—a *conductor* "obligated in the way of a relay that may not keep its charge but must pass it on" (Lyotard and Thébaud, 35). He is the patron of prose and rhetoric, thieves and lying, philosophy and "hermetic" knowledge; he is identified with Theuth, the god of writing, and Thoth, the Egyptian god of wisdom (cf. Derrida, 1981:84ff.). His union with Aphrodite (by definition, the goddess of amateurs, and by means of a pun, the goddess of things Afro-) produced an archetypical counterfeit (a word that derives from the French *contrefaire*, to imitate). Hermaphroditus could pass for either male or female, both male and female, and neither male nor female. S/He should be the god of jazz. Or, if we want a god with Yoruba origins, we could use Obatala, another deity of dual sexuality, and the (Afro-Cuban) Santeria god/ess of creation.

I suspect that I have done violence to Schuller's intentions. I have certainly taken Schuller's metaphor places it would not have otherwise gone. By means of a trick, I have twisted it, prompted it to behave improperly, jazzed it up. This section has been something of a *rap*sody.

Paradigm: A Lesson from Cocteau's *Flâneur*

MCA: I was in a cab in Singapore. Some rap came on the radio, a good friend of mine. The driver didn't know that I rhymed. He said, "I hate rap music. I

> hate that." I'm like, "Why?" And he said, "Any-
> body could do it. Anybody could do that. That's
> not music." I said, "That's the whole point. Any-
> body can do it. It's not elitist.
> ADROCK: It's not illegal.
> MIKE D: The highest praise that [you can give] any kind
> of music—coming from both the punk rock and the
> hip-hop sides—is that you're actually creating
> music that inspires other people to make music, as
> opposed to sit back and say, "O.k, I'm in the audi-
> ence." That's like the best shit you could ever pos-
> sibly achieve. That's what it's about, right there.
> —Beastie Boys

> [T]he goal of literary work (or literature as work) is to
> make the reader no longer a consumer, but a producer of
> the text.
> —Roland Barthes (1974:4)

To address the question, *What might it mean to employ jazz as a paradigm for writing?* we might survey the avant-garde's stance toward jazz during modernism. As Marjorie Perloff has noted, "the *ethos of avant guerre*" finds a counterpart in the desire to blur boundaries—"between art and science, between literature and theory, between the separate genres and media"—that informs much of the intellectual activity during our own time. The avant-garde (a catchall term for futurism, vorticism, dada, surrealism, and constructivism), interrupted by the Holocaust and World War II, reemerges in postmodern theory, "disillusioned or cool." Roland Barthes, for example, turns out to be a late-born futurist (Perloff, 195). But what happens if we recast Perloff's insight—which is itself a refinement of Marx's opening insight in *The Eighteenth Brumaire of Louis Bonaparte*—and view postmodernism's revival of avant-garde experimentation from a more specifically jazz-informed perspective? We might begin with this observation: Jazz funerals in New Orleans have what is called a first line and a second line. The first line, composed of mourners and a band, marches slowly with the deceased to the cemetery. On the way back, though, a second line forms; the music picks up and the dancing starts. Postmodernism is the return of modernism as second line (or as *party line*, to evoke Avital Ronell's telephone metaphor). Recovering the historical uses of jazz by the avant-garde might suggest unexplored uses for jazz within postmodernism. Potentially, though, there's an even bigger lesson to be learned from such study. The avant-garde's stances toward jazz—indicative of attitudes about mass culture—suggest possible stances that critical theory might adopt toward popular culture.

So how did the avant-garde respond to jazz? Taking Paris in the 1920s and '30s as exemplary, Bernard Gendron identifies three figures and three positions that typify the options available to vanguard artists interested in jazz. First, there is Darius Milhaud, composer of *La création du monde* (1923). Second is Igor Stravinsky; third, Jean Cocteau. Milhaud, who first heard jazz in a Harlem club, which he claimed "had not yet been discovered by the snobs and the aesthetes," assumed the posture of *"authenticist."* He presented himself, at least for a time, as a faithful interpreter of jazz, though his asserted relationship and commitment to "authentic music" (to music with "roots in the darkest corner of negro soul") was disputed (Gendron, 14). Stravinsky took an altogether different posture, that of the *bricoleur*. Nevertheless, as Gendron notes: "the similarities between the modernist authenticist and *bricoleur* are more significant than the differences. However much their postures diverge, both Milhaud and Stravinsky ultimately approach jazz in the manner of the Baudelairean *flâneur*" (14). As such, they represent "the consumption side of the modernist aesthetic practice," compulsively making raids on "the new, the not-yet-fashionable, the outré, the evanescent on the margins of culture" (16). Cocteau was also a *flâneur*, but his posture toward jazz and other "sounds and sights of modern life" was wholly different from either Milhaud's or Stravinsky's. Pleased that jazz had jarred modernism away from "obsolete aesthetic practices," he nonetheless urged avant-gardists to reflect on the problems of appropriation. He suggested that they resist the temptations of slavish imitation and brainless co-optation. "It is useless to badly pastiche the fox trot," Cocteau wrote. Jazz has lessons to teach—"attention to rhythm, economy of means, simplicity, and unpretentiousness"—but mapping its formal principles into or onto French art is counterproductive (20–21).

Whereas Milhaud recommended mimeticism (artistic renewal through imitation) and Stravinsky recommended hermeneutics (artistic renewal through interpellation and interpretation), Cocteau recommended heuretics—although he, of course, did not employ the term. Gendron again:

> It is clear that, except as a temporary tactic, Cocteau rejects the posture of the *bricoleur* as well as that of the authenticist.

> For the Cocteau *flâneur*, the consumption of jazz functions as brute stimulant of, rather than as an aesthetic exemplar for, the modernist production that follows upon it. (21)

Cocteau consumed jazz for reasons different than the Baudelairean *flâneurs* of modernism. Instead of using jazz as a fashion plate, a means of keeping aloof from mass culture, he incorporated it as part of his program "to form a new avant-garde" that took a middle path between high-culture aesthetes and left-leaning modernists. Consequently, he did more to promote jazz than any other Parisian avant-gardist (19). Milhaud and Stravinsky, on the other hand, abandoned jazz when it migrated inward, from the margins of bohemia.

Cocteau is, therefore, tremendously important for two reasons. First, while not abandoning mimesis and hermeneutics as effects, he models an alternative way to write *with* jazz. Second, by using jazz as an impetus to invention, he, in effect, reverses the direction of co-optation (thus making it a nonissue). While most modernists involved with jazz employed it as shock tactic—miming it or incorporating it into their art in order to scandalize the bourgeoisie and jump-start their own careers—Cocteau worked the concept of inspiration with vigor (17). In a very real way, he didn't use jazz so much as he offered himself up as host, to be used or possessed by it. But while this posture may seem more mystical than material—a case of the avant-garde getting old-time HooDoo religion—it doesn't have to be (although there's something to be said for flying in the face of materialist logic).

The Baudelairean *flâneur* assumed that in "shopping" he was the one doing the consuming (modernism maintained a clear demarcation between production and consumption); Cocteau—anticipating postmodernism and perhaps thinking about the *flâneuse* (the "streetwalker")—realized that the shopper was both consumer and consumed (production and consumption are purely structural designations). Her or his biggest problem was choosing (assuming choice is possible) what to shop for, what to be co-opted by. Cocteau chose jazz because it was, to him, "modern"—a word, he said, that "brings to mind the image of 'a negro prostrate before the telephone'" (20). My question: Is this man or woman talking on a party line?

Jazzographers tend to take one of three possible stances toward their object of study, and while it's oversimple to assume a one-to-one correspondence between a writer's stance and his or her form, such a generalization does have explanatory value. Thus, we might notice that writers, who follow Milhaud's lead, fashion texts that are passable as genuine representations of jazz. Musicology and realistic fiction are just the most obvious examples of this authenticist or rhapsodic approach; there are also alternative metalanguages (feminist, thematic, Marxist, etc.) that typically maintain the real/fake dichotomy. The authenticist represents real knowledge as a matter of being (*"I know because I'm black"*), feeling *("I know because I'm hip"*), or doing (*"I know because I blow"*). Members of the Harlem Renaissance (Langston Hughes), white rebels (Carl Van Vechten), Beats (Robert Creeley), and Black Power advocates (Julian Bond): one could argue that all of these jazz-associated groups created identities for themselves by redefining authenticity in their own terms. Through inverting classical norms, they embraced the emotional and formal liberties of rhapsody, but maintained, even reinforced, an epistemology predicated on making real/fake distinctions.

Parody is another stance jazzographers take toward their object of study. It ironizes authenticist discourse and is one of two manifestations of *"rap*sodic form." Parody follows from the methodology of the Baudelairean *flâneur*. It is a type of passing (just as the one who passes is a type of parody), functioning as an immanent critique of epistemological certainty. For example, among anthologized jazz texts, Marshall Brickman's "What, Another Legend?" lampoons the nascent ethnomusicology championed by Ramsey and Smith's *Jazzmen*. Leonard Feather's "I Invented Jazz Concerts!" reads surprisingly like the very sort of first-person critical histories its much-read author popularized. Steve Allen's "Crazy Red Riding Hood," one of a series of *Bebop Fables*, satirizes the argot of hipsters. And Donald Barthelme's short story "The King of Jazz" targets attempts to bring jazz into language. In it a jazz fan—responding to the query, "What's that sound coming in from the side there?"—describes the inimitable sound of Hokie Mokie, by improvising a series of clarifying questions:

> "You mean that sound that sounds like the cutting edge of life? That sounds like polar bears crossing Arctic ice pans? That sounds like a herd of musk ox in full flight? That sounds like male walruses diving to the bottom of the sea? That sounds like fumaroles smoking on the slopes of Mt. Katmai? That sounds like the wild turkey walking through the deep,

soft forest? That sounds like beavers chewing trees in an Appalachian marsh? That sounds like an oyster fungus growing on an aspen trunk? That sounds like a mule deer wandering a montane of the Sierra Nevada? That sounds like prairie dogs kissing? That sounds like witchgrass tumbling or a river meandering? That sounds like manatees munching seaweed at Cape Sable? That sounds like coatimundis moving in packs across the face of Arkansas? (357)

This metaphorical *tour de force* calls attention to what Barthes labels "the normal practice of music criticism," translating "a work (or its performance) . . . into the poorest of linguistic categories: the adjective" (1977b:179).

The second manifestation of *rap*sodic form, following from the stance taken by the Cocteau *flâneur*, seeks to do with writing what jazz does with sound. It adopts jazz or, better, a jazz trope as a metaphorical vehicle for structuring writing. For example, if we take *rap*sody as a trope, as a highly compressed lesson telling us what and how to write, then we get text that is, in Barthes's phrase, "subject to certain correspondences, arrangements, reappearances" (1986:281). Barthes observes this form in Proust's *À la Recherche du temps perdu*. I want to point it out in Sterling Brown's "Cabaret." This poem may represent jazz as emotionally intense, as music marked by unleashed "frenzy," "moans and deep cries." But a rhapsodic theme does not distinguish it. Authenticist jazzography conventionally presents jazz in this manner, as "music played with real feeling" (Frith, 1988:45). The determining feature of "Cabaret" is its form and the effects this form produces. Brown writes with *rap*sody, meaning he works a trope representing jazz as a stimulus to textual production. He strings contrasting images together with a song. He pictures a 1927 Chicago cabaret, where "Rich, flashy, puffy-faced . . . overlords sprawl" and gawk at the "shapely bodies" of "Creole Beauties from New Orleans." And he imagines a parallel setting on the Mississippi Delta, where "Poor half-naked fools, tagged with identification numbers . . . huddle, mute, uncomprehending, / Wondering 'how come the good Lord / Could treat them this a way.'" Between these scenes, which Brown subjects to a kind of written equivalent of crosscutting, are woven the lyrics of a blues tune that, if read "straight," idealizes life on the river. The result is a caduceus-like pattern or, to mix my metaphor, a text (from *textus*, fabric, the plural of *texere*, to weave).

Assignment: Jazzing the Professional Dimension

Walter wished he could play like that lady stitched.
—Fatima Shaik (/)

There are ten thousand of us in New York alone. Why don't you come across the line? You're light enough.
—Carl Van Vechten (183)

Assume but update the role of the Cocteau-style *flâneur*, and out of this role write a *rap*sodic essay that takes as its object of study an "art text" (a film, novel, painting, recording, play, building, etc.) whose "author" has, either explicitly or implicitly, claimed that his or her work follows from an "art text" of another field.

But why write a *rap*sody? Because, at its most general, this assignment calls for an investigation of the phenomenon of "passing" (a term fraught with significance) as it operates within the realm of aesthetics. Writing a *rap*sody is a means of learning by doing; scholars have to figure out for themselves (show in form and tell in discourse) how one might do an essay version of the very phenomenon they are investigating. Thus, on a more specifically professional level, this assignment calls for an investigation of "passing" as a way to stimulate invention (heuretics). It solicits alternatives to imitation (mimesis) and interpretation (hermeneutics), alternatives to playing the roles of authenticist and Baudelairean *flâneur*, although both of these time-tested methods of "passing" may be employed on the way to something else.

Perhaps, we could think of essays that succeed in fulfilling this assignment as *rapps*. While brazenly counterfeit (in that they look nothing like authorized discourse), they are passable for being so audacious. "An inventive culture," writes Ulmer, "requires the broadest possible criterion of what is relevant" (1994:6). Finally, a question to ponder: Do you understand the economic effect of *rapps*, why their circulation in Ireland had to be stopped? They stimulate rampant inflation; they can destroy an economy.

Experiment: Rapsody in Read— Ishmael Reed and Free Jazz

It's like making one part of your mind say, "Ooh-bla-dee." And make the other part of your mind say, "What

> *does he mean?" In other words, it's two different*
> *melodies.*
> > —Rahsaan Roland Kirk, "Medley,"
> > Does Your House Have Lions?

> *Writing does not simply weave several threads into a sin-*
> *gle term in such a way that one might end up unraveling*
> *all the "contents" just by pulling a few strings.*
> > —Jacques Derrida (1981:350)

When Bukka Doopeyduk, protagonist of Ishmael Reed's first novel, *The Free-Lance Pallbearers* (*FLP*), becomes a star in the world of HARRY SAM, a jazz critic from the *Deformed Demokrat* writes the following headline:

AFTER BEING STUMPED BY CECIL TAYLOR AND ARCHIE SHEPP
IT DID THIS CRIPPLED MIND SOME GOOD TO SEE OL BONES
(Reed, 1967a:82)

Later, several months after playing "to standing-room-only crowds in the Hamptons, Provincetown, Woodstock, and Fremont, Ohio," Bukka receives HARRY SAM'S ultimate accolade—an invitation that makes him turn "somersaults over its contents."

YOU ARE INVITED TO A BAD TRIP
AT THE HARRY SAM MOTEL. MUSIC BY CHET BAKER
FUN, STROBOSCOPIC LIGHTS, HOOPLA HOOPS AND
FRANK PRANKS (SMILE)
a driver will call for you at 12:00 A.M.
August 6th, 1945 (83)

The critic's headline and Sam's invitation name three actual historical jazz musicians: a pair of black, East Coast musicians and a white, West Coast trumpet player. [*1. Con abbandono. But what if the proper names in the headline and the invitation pre-sent readers with nothing more than a case of* homophony *(that is, "music in which one voice leads melodically, being supported by an accompaniment in chordal or a slightly more elaborate style," but also "music in which all the voices move in the same rhythm"—Randel, 227)? After all, in the semantic universe of proper names, homonyms abound. Plenty of names in* FLP *match up with names one can actually find in the phone book of any large city. Readers may even have friends or acquaintances who share some of these names.*] Taken together, they constitute a coded reference to the opposition free jazz versus cool jazz, and if read as ironic—as metacomments on the novel and the political milieu the novel portrays—they reveal Reed's aesthetic. Reed satirizes Chet Baker. Any entertainer who performs at the Harry Sam Motel—that is, at the author's version of the White House—is part of the novel's satiric target. And Reed identifies his artistic aims with two of the leading exponents of what was variously called "avant-garde jazz," "the new thing," or "free jazz," and that in 1967, the year *FLP* was published, included such other luminaries as Ornette Coleman, Sun Ra, Albert Ayler, and Bill Dixon.

[*2. Con affetto. Consider this parenthesis, the one above, and the parentheses below—numbered, titled, and set off in brackets for your convenience—as rhapsodic raving, a recurring emotive moment sending shutters of rapture—or rupture—through this essay.*]

Admittedly, two rather oblique references to specific musicians in a novel do not establish an aesthetic norm, and an ironic reading of those references does not necessarily warrant broad theoretical speculation. More evidence is needed if we are to connect *FLP* with free jazz. That evidence is readily available.

[*3. Con agitazione. Rhapsody, I remind readers, literally means to "stitch together songs." Homer's* Odyssey, *as Milman Parry and Albert Lord have shown, is recorded speech fragments, sewn together.*]

Throughout his career, Reed has alluded to jazz and jazz musicians, as a casual glance through his poetry, fiction, or collection of essays, *Shrovetide in Old New Orleans*, will reveal. He has also written articles specifically about jazz: for example, "Bird Lives" (1973), a review of Ross Russell's biography of Charlie Parker; "*Music: Black, White and Blue*" (1972), a review of Ortiz Walton's sociological study of "Classical American Music" (that is, jazz); and "The Old Music" (1975), a treatment of New Orleans music that draws parallels between early jazz and Voodoo rites. But in addition to manifesting a general knowledge of jazz, Reed has insisted upon his acquaintance with the major innovators of free jazz. Of his time in New York, he has written:

> Walking down St. Mark's Place in New York's East Village I was often able to observe key members of several generations of the American "avant-garde," before breakfast, or chat with

Archie Shepp, Ornette Coleman, Sun Ra, Bill Dixon, Albert Ayler, Cecil Taylor, and members of a splendid generation of young painters. (1977:111)

Indeed, it is important to emphasize that Reed has associated with a large number of artists—musicians, painters, actors, dancers, filmmakers, and writers—but it is equally important to note the particular group of musicians he singles out for specific mention and support.

[*4. Con alcuna licenza. On the copyright page of* FLP *there is an anonymous statement that declares: "All of the characters in this book are fictitious and any resemblance to . . ." etc. Maybe the indisputable fact that three names within the space of two pages coincide with three actual names listed in any good encyclopedia of jazz is too good to be true: a remarkable fluke, a fortuitous accident, a magical isometric moment where one set of textual voices and rhythms perfectly synchronize with the voices and rhythms of another set.*]

Little more than five months before the publication of *FLP*, Reed wrote an article for *Arts Magazine*, entitled "The Black Artist: Calling a Spade a Spade." In it he comments on the Black Arts movement in New York. He discusses the work of LeRoi Jones (later Imamu Amiri Baraka), Joe Overstreet, and Chester Wilson, but fully one third of the piece is devoted to observations on the work of Archie Shepp, Sun Ra, and Albert Ayler. Reed compliments Shepp's staging of a "Jazz allegory *Junebug Graduates Tonight*" for its hilarious "debunking of Marxist clichés," recommends "Arkestra" leader, Sun Ra, for his "interstellar bopping" and "not-to-be-believed theater," and singles out Ayler—a saxophonist whose brief career ended in a mysterious death by drowning in 1970—for praise redolent of *FLP*'s style. "[T]hem cats is hard," says Reed, referring to Ayler's band. "Got blood in their eyes as they 'spit up craziness,' honk eschatologically and do the hymnal violin sawing of American broadside music" (1967b:49).

[*5. Con alma. Strung throughout a text, proper names form a sort of ongoing test for the reader. They can reinforce cultural ties or effectively designate a barred entrance to a discursive ideology. If the reader recognizes the name* ("Wasn't Chet Baker the trumpet player who played sort of like Miles but looked like James Dean?"), *then it has functioned, in Althusser's phrase, as an ideological agent of* interpellation; *if the proper name is unknown* ("Chet Baker? Who's he? Some guy you slept with?"), *then the "call" offered by the name was, in effect, declined. The reader "de-inter-pellated" himself from one ideology, suggesting that he was already constituted by and within another ideology. In either case, as Jim Collins insists, identity is the direct result of "conflictive interpellation" (41).]*

One should no longer doubt that Reed intimately knows and admires jazz and specifically the type of jazz associated with Taylor and Shepp. Couple this with his observation that one of the "glaring problems" facing African American writing "is that there isn't as much variety among critical approaches as there is in the writ-

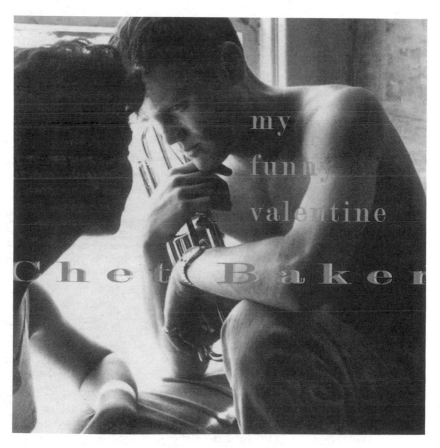

FIGURE 3.1
Album cover of Chet Baker's *My Funny Valentine*
(courtesy of Capitol Records/Pacific Jazz)

ing the critics are examining," and we practically have a mandate to approach his work through a more "experimental" approach (1977:140). What follows, then, is an investigation of a shared aesthetic: the possibility that the discourse of Reed and free jazz form a conspiracy, a breathing or blowing together (Mackey, 1986:76).

[6. *Con amabilità. To entertain the notion that three names—Cecil Taylor, Archie Shepp, and Chet Baker—could not signify three jazz musicians might seem frivolous, a pedantic, hermeneutical game. But it is far from that, for it touches upon a much larger question, one that affects our reading, not only of* FLP, *but of absolutely any text. Namely, if words refer, by what means do readers determine—stop and start—reference? It is a serious and practical question: the rapsody of reading. Marc Shell, in* The Economy of Literature, *notices that its answer—indeed, much critical thinking—rests on assumptions about the relationship between economic and verbal symbolization. He detects a "'constitutional' relationship between the origin of money and the origin of philosophy itself," and he argues that "[w]e should not underestimate the significance of the development of money for the study of other media of symbolization and transfer, such as verbal metaphor" (11, 36). "Coins," Shell reminds us, "were the first widely circulating publications or impressions in history" (64). "Symbolon, in fact, meant not only pactual token but also word; and, as Plato knew, the development of money corresponds to the development of a new way of speaking," one predicated on symbolic exchange and absence.*]

Several cautions, however, are in order. First one from Reed—he asks:

> How could somebody look at the black poetry of the last twenty years . . . and say that black poetry is . . . based upon "black speech and music" when an examination would show that the majority of language material is American or English and that the poets and novelists have been influenced by not only music but graphics, painting, film, sculpture—all disciplines and all art forms—and write about all subjects?
>
> They [the critics] say music because they are socialist realists and music is the most popular art form of the masses. You can be influenced by music while you're asleep but reading is hard work. Of course listening to Cecil Taylor, Bill Dixon, and others is hard work, too, but when these critics talk about "music" they don't mean those musicians. (1977:140–41)

[7. *Con amore. E. J. Hobsbawm writes: "relatively few [jazz] fans write poetry to or about the beloved," but "when they do, it tends to rely excessively on the magic of names which vibrate only for other lovers" (12).*] This statement serves as both a warning to, and a validation of, this type of investigation. On the one hand, it further substantiates what we have already witnessed. Cecil Taylor, Bill Dixon, and others are, to Reed, musicians wholly set apart from the mass of musicians championed by "socialist realists." On the other hand, Reed reminds us that any work of art results from multiple determinations. Because no hierarchical relationship between the making of music and the writing of literature can be demonstrated, we cannot speak of *FLP* as the literary equivalent of free jazz, or of free jazz as the musical equivalent of Reed's fiction or poetry.

[8. *Con anima. Many Greeks, including Herodotus, believed that coinage was invented in Lydia during the reign of Gyges the first tyrant. "Like Midas, his neighbor who turned all things into gold with a touch, Gyges turned all things into gold by his ability to purchase them with gold minted into coins" (Shell, 12). Money made it possible for him to rule with an invisible hand.*]

We can, however, imagine the possibility of a poetic shared by *FLP* and free jazz as a way to organize our thinking about Reed's fiction and the jazz avant-garde. Therefore, in the first half of this double-threaded experimental essay I shall look at the form of free jazz and employ a list of its commonly accepted characteristics to structure my observations about Reed. In the second half, I shall examine the sociopolitical implications of the Reed/free jazz aesthetic.

[9. *Con ardore. Heraclitus interprets economic exchange as the very image of metaphorization—the exchange of meanings. Unlike Plato, who sought "metaphysical stillness . . . above the supposedly escapable movements of commodities," Heraclitus focuses on "those changes that never 'harden'" (50–51). Marx follows him, when, in the* Grundrisse, *he declares: "Language does not transform ideas. . . . Ideas do not exist separately from language" (1973:162–63).*

"*Logic,*" *Marx writes in the "Critique of the Hegelian Dialectic and Philosophy as a Whole," "is the money of mind." It is "alienated thinking, and therefore thinking which abstracts from nature and from real man: abstract thinking" (in Shell, 1978: 37). Marx, as Shell points out, is "uneasy that a special logic, the money of the mind, informs and cannot be expelled from" his thinking (157). His problem: how does one proceed after overcom-*

ing, what Eco calls, "a metaphysics of the referent"? (1976:70).]

It is usually held that free jazz had its gestation in the early work (mid-1950s) of Cecil Taylor and Sun Ra, but that it was the white plastic saxophone of Ornette Coleman that gave it birth. Thomas Pynchon fictionalizes this event in *V.* when he describes McClintic Sphere's debut at "the V-Note":

> He blew a hand-carved ivory alto saxophone with a 4½ reed and the sound was like nothing any of them had heard before. The usual divisions prevailed: collegians did not dig, and left after an average of 1½ sets. Personnel from other groups, either with a night off or taking a long break from somewhere crosstown or uptown, listened hard, trying to dig. "I am still thinking," they would say if you asked. People at the bar all looked as if they did dig in the sense of understand, approve of, empathize with: but this was probably only because people who prefer to stand at the bar have, universally, an inscrutable look. . . .
>
> The solos of McClintic Sphere were something else. There were people around, mostly those who wrote for *Down Beat* magazine or the liners of LP records, who seemed to feel he played disregarding chord changes completely. They talked a great deal about soul and the anti-intellectual and the rising rhythms of African nationalism. It was a new conception, they said, and some of them said: Bird Lives. (1961:48–49)

The term "free jazz" took its name from *Free Jazz*, Ornette Coleman's landmark recording of 1960. A thirty-six minute continuous and simultaneous improvisation by two quartets, it has been called "perhaps the boldest album in the history of jazz" (Lyons, 391). Of it, Martin Williams wrote:

> [N]ot only is the improvisation almost total, it is frequently collective, involving all eight men inventing at once. And there were no preconceptions as to themes, chord patterns or chorus lengths. The guide for each soloist was a brief ensemble part which introduces him and which gave him an area of musical pitch. Otherwise he had only feelings and imagination—his own and those of his accompanists—to guide him. (liner notes to *Free Jazz*)

[*10. Con brio. Returning to the three proper names in question, let us assume that "Cecil Taylor," "Archie Shepp," and "Chet*

Baker" actually do refer. What then? FLP, as a satire—a referential text supposedly self-conscious and critical of its own referential status—collapses. We find ourselves in the midst of a classic double bind, similar to the one where the Cretan says, "All Cretans are liars." If we assume a fundamental fictiveness for the text, take the disclaimer printed on the copyright page seriously, then there is no satire (at least not in the ordinary sense of the word). FLP becomes an exercise in textuality. But if we assume that FLP actually designates "real people," then it begins with the out-and-out truth that it lies. Someone told us that all its characters are fictitious, but this is clearly not the case. The book, as promised, cannot be trusted. Its satire is unreliable, undercut by its own (dis)honesty.]

Paradoxically, the only fixed requirement of free jazz was free playing. Coleman, in the liner notes to *Change of the Century*, said "There is no single *right* way to play jazz." Reed, for all intents and purposes, could be seconding him when he has the protagonist of *Yellow Back Radio Broke-Down* declare:

> No one says a novel has to be one thing. It can be anything it wants to be, a vaudeville show, the six o'clock news, the mumblings of wild men saddled by demons. (1969:36)

It is hardly shocking that both Reed and Coleman have been accused of being, in Reed's phrase, "crazy dada niggers" (35), who create "anti-art"—"anti-novels" and "anti-jazz." For example, when *FLP* was first published, it was variously called, "another piece of self-indulgence," "impossibly bizarre and wholly directionless," "unsettling and decidedly exhausting," and "diarrhea of the typewriter" (Settle and Settle, 1982:39, 41, 37). In a prescient bit of criticism, someone even wrote, "Ishmael Reed makes poor music—perhaps just practicing—putting down screeches and grunts," the result being "a very self-indulgent piece of prose that reads as if the author didn't care whether anybody could like or understand it" (39, 37).

[11. Con calore. Suppose that we bracket off the statement on the copyright page, assume that someone, say an overscrupulous attorney, positioned it there to protect the ever-contentious Reed. Then, certainly, the names in the book could designate referents outside FLP. If these names were not homophones (but how could they not be?), "Cecil Taylor" would be a coded reference to a specific pianist (who never changes) named Cecil Taylor, and "Bukka

*Doopeyduk" would, of course, refer to Bukka Doopeyduk, some-
one with whom I have no acquaintance. In this version of* FLP—
*actually an inconceivable textual universe—words would have
one and only one referent. There would be a word for every thing
(at every moment, in every conceivable mode of presentation), a
thing for every word; no slippage of signification would be allowed,
no exchange, no generalization would be possible. There would be
no writing.*]

Compare this response to Reed's work with an excerpt from a
Down Beat review of an album Coleman recorded prior to *Free
Jazz*:

> I have listened long and hard to Coleman's music . . . have
> tried desperately to find something valuable in it, something
> that could be construed valuable. I have been unsuccessful. . . .
> Coleman's music, to me, has only two shades: a maudlin,
> pleasing lyricism and a wild ferocity bordering on bedlam. . . .
> "Beauty" from the Atlantic recording *This Is Our Music*
> descends into an orgy of squawks from Coleman, squeals from
> (trumpeter) Cherry, and above-the-bridge plinks from (bassist)
> Haden. The resulting chaos is an insult to the listening intel-
> ligence. It sounds like some horrible joke, and the question
> here is not whether it is jazz, but whether it is music. (qtd. in
> Lyons, 374)

The similarity of these dismissals indicates a host of biases, but it
emphatically demonstrates a critical inability (or refusal) to grapple
with the central issue of privileged and nonprivileged forms. Free
jazz and *FLP* tease out critical assumptions that normally remain
unexpressed, if not repressed.

[*12. Con carita. On the other hand, the possibility of multiple
signification (one signifier serving a number of signifieds) would
also keep* FLP *from functioning as a satirical text. For instance if
"Chet Baker" can refer to any number of Chet Bakers now living,
dead, or soon to be born, then the text cannot possibly have any
semblance of a stable satirical target.*]

As Taylor argues, free jazz is not just a negative freedom from
traditional ideas of harmony and time, but also the positive freedom to structure music in new ways. He states, "This [music] is
not a question of freedom as opposed to non-freedom, but rather a
question of recognizing different ideas and expressions of order"
(qtd. in Lyons, 379–80). The real question, then, is not whether

Coleman's "molten, unchained improvisations" are "music," or whether Reed's HooDoo *conjurings* are "literature." The question is, what kind of music, what kind of literature have these men created, and how can we describe their accomplishments? [*13. Con celerita. Is Reed referring to the Chet Baker born Chesney H. Baker on December 23, 1929, in Yale, Oklahoma, or is he referring to a former next-door neighbor of mine, the kid I used to play with in the 1960s? Is he referring to the Chet Baker that Charlie Parker admired and chose as his trumpet player, the Chet Baker who played in Gerry Mulligan's pianoless quartet in 1952, the Chet Baker who entered Rikers Island prison to serve time for possession of narcotics in the late 1950s, the Chet Baker who died while I was writing an early draft of this essay, or the Chet Baker I saw at the Film Forum in* Let's Get Lost? *Or could it be that he is not referring to a person at all, but to a "an abstract entity which moreover is only a cultural convention": a particular received representation? (Eco, 1976:66). (In that case, wouldn't the assertion that "all of the characters in this book are fictitious" be correct?) Given this possibility, which texts should the reader ignore and which should he privilege? How many Chet Bakers can there be and* FLP *remain legible?*] Answers to this question yield the following outline, which details structural characteristics of free jazz and Reed's fiction. It reworks observations made by LeRoi Jones (Amiri Baraka) and Len Lyons.

First, free jazz reworks and extends the language of bebop. In his sociopolitical analysis of African American music, *Blues People*, Leroi Jones (Amiri Baraka) reminds his readers that free jazz uses "the music of the forties [bebop] . . . as an initial reference" (Jones, 1963:225). And Ornette Coleman, discussing his composition "Bird Food," writes the following of Charlie Parker, the patron saint of bebop:

> Bird would have understood us. He would have approved our aspiring to something beyond what we inherited. Oddly enough, the idolization of Bird, people wanting to play just like him, and not make their own soul-search, has finally come to be an impediment to progress in jazz. (liner notes to *Change of the Century*)

Reed acknowledges certain reference points as well. We have already witnessed some of these, but we would not be far off the mark to perceive *Mumbo Jumbo*, ostensibly a madcap detective story about a conspiracy to knock, dock, co-opt, swing, bop, and rock the creative spirit of African Americans, as one long homage to intellectual and spiritual forbearers. One should also note that Reed, in the introduction to *Yardbird Lives*, claims that Charlie Parker's formidable creativity and eclecticism inspired his and Al Young's editorial philosophies (Reed and Young, 1978:20).

[*14. Con dolce maniera. Contacting Reed and asking him to clarify his Chet Baker reference would not stand the reader in any better stead. This would have to be repeated for every word in the book, and it would assume (1) that the functioning of FLP is dependent on Reed's intentions and (2) that his intentions are locatable, retrievable, and transmittable. The fact is, if one knew all the referents Reed had in mind when he wrote FLP, one would have the mind—be a simulacrum or perfect replica—of Reed the reader; there would be no need for his book.*]

Second, free jazz posits "the liberation of melody from preset chord changes and fixed tempo" (Lyons, 374). Bebop signaled the triumph of improvisation based on an eighth-note pulse and the chord sequence of a standard popular song; free jazz signaled the abandonment of fixed pulse and chord sequences in favor of improvisation based upon melodic feeling. In it the "right note" is "not the one possible within theoretical limits, but rather the one which sounds right to the individual" (377). Coleman claims, "It was when I found out I could make mistakes that I knew I was onto something" (qtd. in Williams, 1983:240).

[*15. Con dolore. By the same token (tokos = 1. offspring, 2. interest), if one allows a multiplicity of Chet Bakers to which "Chet Baker" might possibly refer, if one allows that signs are social constructions, then determining the target of FLP's satire or the sense of the novel becomes an ideological act in itself (Shell, 95). Reading ceases to be a question of correctness; it becomes, as Thomas Lewis notes, a question of "social power," part of the process by which references are fixed and disseminated (1985:40). Who owns "Chet Baker" (controls its circulation)? To no longer fight against the homophone means that one must imagine or coin a Reed(ing).*]

Applied to *FLP*, this aesthetic of freedom allows for a reading that views (actually hears) the novel as an improvisation. More concretely, this means that the novel's first two and one-half pages, a kind of compressed myth of HARRY SAM, an alternative portrait of America in the 1960s, constitute a keynote, tonal center, or melody upon which Reed improvises.

[16. *Con espressivo. Given referentiality, FLP becomes a complex weave of signifiers that ceaselessly signify. The reader follows threads (pulls at semes). "[T]he content of a single term," writes Eco, "becomes something similar to an encyclopedia" (1979:184–85). For instance, one could assume that the sign "Chet Baker" refers to a now-deceased trumpet player named Chet Baker (let us imagine that semiosis has ceased, "fixing" this musician at some instant in his career). But if this is an allowable assumption, then Chet Baker might, among a host of other possibilities, signify cool jazz; cool jazz, in turn, might signify political disengagement; political disengagement might inversely signify a black aesthetic that values engagement; this aesthetic might take us to Cecil Taylor and, then, back to Chet Baker. By tracing this "interpretantial chain" (instead of another), the reader has legislated "a state of affairs (actions, habits, laws, attitudes, behaviors, etc.) in the only way possible, that is, from a particular perspective" (Lewis, 1985:44).*

Reed, like any writer, banks on dividends afforded by an economy founded on symbolic exchange, but like most satirists, he seems as ambivalent about the possibilities afforded by such an economy as Marx was about the cultural effects of money. The metaphoric transfer that allows him to convert cultural units into symbols (an analog of the metamorphosis of commodities into money) also allows his readers to convert symbols into cultural units other than those the author might desire or even imagine. FLP, like the music Reed most values, can come to mean—that is, refer to or signify—absolutely anything. Once begun, the economy of symbolic exchange cannot be stopped or easily governed. Archilochus, the Greek satirist whose iambics drove Neobule and Lycambes to suicide, understood this well. After witnessing a solar eclipse, he wrote: "Henceforth is anything whatsoever to be believed or expected. Let not one of you marvel, nay, though he see the beasts of the field exchange pasture with the dolphins of the deep, and the roaring waves of the sea become dearer than the land to such as loved the hill" (qtd. in Shell, 55).]

Third, free jazz constantly searches for new song structures. The repertory of bebop, with certain notable exceptions, consisted largely of standard popular songs (the stuff of Tin Pan Alley) or, more properly, the chord changes to those songs. Thus, when Coleman and Taylor first "loosened up" jazz, there was an accompanying expansion of song structures suitable for jazz treatment. The result was that jazz music began to assimilate African, Indian, modernist European, and other "foreign" influences. By the same token, the variety exhibited by Reed's *oeuvre* also indicates a constant search for new, workable (and often subvertible) structures of discourse.

[*17. Con fuoco. Hence, to coin something of a tautology, if referentiality is not allowed (semiosis started), one cannot read, but if referentiality is not stopped, a text cannot, in truth, be read; it becomes a mass of overdetermined codes. To choose, then, exactly where to stop and start the text, what signifier to link with another, what reading to legitimate, what reading to deem counterfeit, that determines one's place relative to a particular aesthetic ideology. "[R]eference," says Lewis in his reading of Derrida's "White Mythology," "is a process that implements power because—to borrow Peirce's term—it is seen as 'legislating' a state of affairs" (1985:47). "What is at stake in the program of dissemination, then, is the exact possibility of consuming cultural products [reproducing reference] in an effectively different way," for different purposes (54). Heuretics (dissemination applied) would teach one to make rapsodies.*]

For example, consider the following passage from *FLP*. It describes the frieze that adorns the hood of Nancy [Cardinal] Spellman's Rolls-Royce. It presents Reed's version of the Christian or, as he calls it, the Nazarene apocalypse.

> It showed HARRY SAM the dictator and former Polish used-car salesman sitting on the great commode. In his lap sat a businessman, a Nazarene apprentice and a black slum child. These figures represented the Just. Standing on each side of the dictator were four washroom attendants. In their hands they had seven brushes, seven combs, seven towels, and seven bars of soap, a lock of Roy Rogers' hair and a Hershey bar. Above the figures float Lawrence Welk champagne bubbles. Below this scene tombstones have been rolled aside and the Nazarene faithful are seen rising in a mist with their hands reaching out to the figure sitting on the commode. (1967a:45–46)

This parody of a scene from the Book of Revelation, like all parody, like a parasite, feasts off (counterfeits) a found or received form. In this case, to use a phrase from *Mumbo Jumbo*, it opposes "2,000 years of probing classifying attempting to make an 'orderly' world" (1972:175). We shall return to this notion.

[*18. Con garbo. Mumbo Jumbo foregrounds this issue. In a*

previous novel, Yellow-Back Radio Broke Down, *Reed presented an alternative reading of the cleaning-up of old New Orleans: the foolish Wallflower Order's fumigation of the Place Congo in the 1890s.* In Mumbo Jumbo, *published in 1971, he creates another alternative history, one set in New York in the 1920s.*

What is important to notice is Reed's contradictory desire to demonstrate that "the social use of signs also involves social conflict *over the use of signs" and his labor to establish his own discourse as a language of truth (Lewis, 1985:40). By legitimating it as an oppositional alternative to "dominant" culture, he associates himself with that group of "critics of mass culture" which Collins identifies as diverse in aesthetic and ideological orientation but similar as to shared presuppositions:*

1. *That cultures can be conceived as having "centers" from which all cultural activity may be measured;*
2. *That all cultural production functions according to a unitary master system;*
3. *That within such systems binary oppositions must be made between authentic art (the "best that has been thought and said" in both classic and avant-garde versions) and mass culture;*
4. *That the former is diverse because it is produced by artists, but the latter remains undifferentiated because it is produced by machines and corporations;*
5. *That the audience for the former is also diverse because they are enlightened, but the audience for the latter is merely a mass, identical as the texts it consumes;*
6. *That the role of the cultural critic is essentially an evaluative one in which the criteria for authentic art must be defined and defended against the onslaught of mass culture, thereby emphasizing culture as a master system, a cohesive "whole" with appropriate and inappropriate representations. (8)]*

Fourth, free jazz extended the emotional palette of music to its logical extreme. It realized music's potential for expressing the entire gamut of human emotions. Its musicians, according to Baraka, "rely to a great extent on the closeness of vocal reference that has always been characteristic of Negro music. Players . . . literally scream and rant in imitation of the human voice, sounding many times like unfettered primitive shouters" (Jones, 1963:227). Thus, the free jazz aesthetic is not committed exclusively to the production of "beautiful" music. It frequently sounds like a person crying, talking, or laughing, and it occasionally sounds ugly, angry, or hostile. Taylor says:

> Anybody's music is made up of a lot of things that are not musical. . . . Hostility's a genuine emotion. Why shouldn't jazz have hostility in it? That should be the one thing that would make everybody in the United States dig it. Most people in the United States shield their hostility with smiles. Jazz musicians don't bother. (qtd. in Goldberg, 213, 217)

"I lose fans and friends too because I'm blunt," echoes Reed. "A heathen, basically, I have cultivated as many enemies as friends. . . . [T]hese people who go around loving everybody say I write out of hurt. I do. Sometimes, maybe. I'm a heathen. A one-man heathen horde. When it hurts I say so and when it feels good I say so, too" (1977:3–4).

[*19. Con grandezza. Vance Bourjaily summarizes* Mumbo Jumbo: *"The book presents jazz [or "jes' grew," as Reed calls it] as triggering recurrent outbreaks of liberation of the human spirit, coming to us through history from Africa and then from Haiti to New Orleans, always opposed and dreaded by the establishment" (45).*]

Some of *FLP* is written out of hurt, like the image of SAM eating children (a satire on U.S. involvement in Vietnam), some is written out of anger, like Nancy Spellman censoring non-Nazarene worldviews (Cardinal Spellman damning "Vodou"), and some is written out of a sense of playfulness ("dem terrible, man-eating Latin roots"), or as Reed puts it in *Mumbo Jumbo*: "The dazzling parodying punning mischievous pre-Joycean style-play of your Cakewalking your Calinda your Minstrelsy give-and-take of the ultra-absurd" (1971:174).

[*20. Con gravità.* Mumbo Jumbo *could be described as an attempt to represent "jes' grew," a term that we, amending Bourjaily's definition, might call, not jazz, but the spirit that animates jazz, the yeast that made the Jazz Age rise (23). Reed states as much at the beginning of the novel. He writes, "So Jes Grew is seeking its words. Its text. For what good is a liturgy without a text?" (9)*]

Fifth, free jazz attends to the creation of "sound structures." Recognizing that descriptions such as "difficult," "dense," or "intense" are, at best, relative, it is, nevertheless, safe to say that free jazz is difficult, dense, and intense. Even sympathetic critics are apt to write descriptions like the one that labeled John Coltrane's *Ascension* as "the most powerful human sound ever recorded," or *The Great Concert of Cecil Taylor* as "90 minutes of unrelieved intensity" (in Lyons, 380, 358).

This inclination to density finds its expression in *FLP* with Reed's tendency to overwhelm with verbal pyrotechnics. Throughout the novel, verbiage is heaped upon verbiage, resulting in the impression that Reed luxuriated in his ability to spin out words—to rap or to jive.

[*21. Con grazioso. A couple of pages earlier, though, he had declared: "You see, it's not 1 of those germs that break bleed suck gnaw or devour. It's nothing we can bring into focus or categorize; once we call it 1 thing it forms into something else" (Reed, 1971:7).*

Mumbo Jumbo is, therefore, something of a rapp. Reed, like Plato before him, doubts the adequacy of language to represent the architectonic principle of jes' grew, but he hopes to pass off his discourse as authentic, make the spirit of jazz visible. His discourse circulates within a culture lacking an "official" standard, but one in which several different forms of linguistic currency vie for "legitimacy and superiority" (Collins, 111).]

Sixth, free jazz "refunctions" the old music of New Orleans. It remotivates an old form—the music of Louis Armstrong and Jelly Roll Morton—"'produced' in answer to certain social needs" in order to make that old form serve new social needs (Rose, 4-5). More specifically, by de-emphasizing the role of soloists and by re-emphasizing collective improvisation, free jazz marks the development of a music that addresses contemporary problems (both social and formal) by investigating its own mythic past.

[*22. Con gusto. (1) Reed's fiction exhibits all the features of "rhapsody." (2) It demonstrates writing with the trope of "rapsody." Rhapsody signifies writing that supposes and consequently maintains the opposition genuine/counterfeit (the "referential fallacy"). Its homophone, rapsody, signifies writing that calls this and related oppositions into question. Rapsodic writing might represent one way to employ jazz as a model for writing theory, since it would use a trope conventionally used to represent jazz, not as a model but, in Gregory Ulmer's phrase, as a "relay, organized by speed, rather than the gravity of a monument" (1989a:170).*]

The term "refunction," a translation of Brecht's term "*Umfunktionierung*," accurately describes Reed's stated intention to treat "tradition as a contemporary function" (1977:64). Viewed from a specifically literary perspective, *FLP* refunctions the satiric tradition that begins with Archilochus and runs through Rabelais and Sterne for use in an urban, technological society. It revises *Candide*. *Yellow Back Radio* revamps the western. And as I have already mentioned, *Mumbo Jumbo* reworks the detective story. Viewed from a more idiomatic perspective, though, *FLP*, *Yellow Back Radio*, and *Mumbo Jumbo* refunction the linguistic materials of voodoo. By employing the discourse of Vodou or Vodoun (a word with Dahomean origins meaning "the unknown"), Reed remobilizes a system of signification that literally gives him a voice (9).

[*23. Con lancio. To prove that Reed's fiction shares the characteristics of rhapsody one would have to produce its characteristics (charakter, "upper die used by the coinmaker or impressed mark on the coin"—Shell, 64), then show how Reed's fiction translates them into discourse equivalents. The problem is, such a demonstration would tend to be as mechanical an exercise as showing that Reed's fiction manifests all the features of free jazz.*]

Incidentally, to bring this point full circle, one could also claim that both Reed and jazz appropriate and transvalue exactly the same source materials. Jazz also refunctions voodoo. As Reed and others have stated, Vodoun "is based upon the belief that the African 'gods,' or loas, are present in the Americas and often use men and women as their mediums." In the United States, however, Vodoun became known as "HooDoo," "a word which appeared in about the 1890s, when Marie Laveau, the First HooDoo Queen, held power in New Orleans." There, writes Reed, "one of the forms it [HooDoo] took was what we call 'Jazz'" (1977:10). "The HooDoo shrines and the jazz shrines are in the same neighborhood, suggesting a possible connection. The 'HooDoo' guidebook says that 'jazz' is based upon VooDoo ritual music" (28). "The instruments in the old [New Orleans] music substitute for the spirits who possess the human hosts in a ceremony" (65).

[*24. Con malinconia. Nevertheless, here are a few characteristics of rhapsody. They are taken from two essays: Pat Rogers's "Shaftesbury and the Aesthetics of Rhapsody" and Frederick Erickson's "Rhetoric, Anecdote, and Rhapsody: Coherence Strategies in a Conversation among Black American Adolescents" (Rogers, 1972:249–50; Erickson, 1984:87–90).*]

1. Contains passages of emotive, highly wrought, utterance.

2. If oral, then an interactional construction produced through a close engagement between performer and audience, often

through a dialogue of call and response. If written, then an overtly dialogical effect of polynarration. A tendency toward one of two extremes:
   a. Slickness: studied insincerity and manipulation that dazzles by brilliance and wit.
   b. Soul: apparently unstudied, heart-on-the-sleeve sincerity in self-disclosure or pathetic evocation, which moves the reader to empathy, pity, or moral outrage (87).
3. *Narrational or performance units often consist of episodes that build to a climax, after which a new episode begins at a lower level of intensity.*
4. *Sentence structure tends toward a staccato pattern.*
5. *Direct invocation and apostrophe is common.*
6. *Frequent repetitions: employs parallelism and listing devices.*
7. *Neologisms invented.*
8. *Argumentation by anecdotes.*
9. *Organization by topoi (commonplace topics that function as resources for solidarity between author and audience) stitched together.*
   a. Semantic connection—metaphorical hinge points—of similarity and contrast from one anecdote to the next.
   b. Connections of semantic and rhetorical function across sets of utterances. (97)
10. *The underlying point of prosographic narration is not stated explicitly and does not seem to have been a full-fledged proposition. Absence of framing devices.]*

   Seventh, free jazz emphasizes group improvisation. This stylistic innovation provided the means for refunctioning the music of old New Orleans and, as Baraka notices, "restored improvisation to its traditional role of invaluable significance" (Jones, 1963:225). In his liner notes to *Change of the Century*, Coleman puts it thus:

   Perhaps the most important new element in our music is our conception of *free* group improvisation. The idea of group improvisation, in itself, is not at all new; it played a big role in New Orleans' early bands. The big bands of the swing period changed all that. Today, still, the individual is either swallowed up in a group situation, or else he is out front soloing, with none of the other horns doing anything but calmly awaiting their turn for *their* solos. Even in some of the trios and quartets, which permit quite a bit of group improvisation, the final effect is one that is imposed beforehand by the arranger. One knows pretty much what to expect.

When our group plays, before we start out to play, we do not have any idea what the end result will be. Each player is free to contribute what he feels in the music at any given moment. (1960)

[25. *Con malizia. Suffice it to say, we could go on to notice how these characteristics of rhapsody operate within Reed's fiction. The purpose of such an exercise would be to valorize rhapsody (invert a "received" opposition). This is exactly what Rogers and Erickson do in their respective essays. Erickson concludes with the following statement:*

In conclusion, then, we have shown that the conversation of the black teenagers in the discussion presented, which at times appeared disconnected, illogical, and difficult to follow to the white American group leader . . . in fact evidences a most rigorous logic and a systematic coherence. . . . This analysis demonstrates that in this discourse style we are confronted not with a substandard variant of American middle class discourse but with a fully developed, internally coherent, and (in in-group communication) entirely effective rhetorical system. (151–52)]

Admittedly, this all important innovation cannot gain full expression in the context of solo performance, whether by a musician or novelist, but a knowledge of the primacy of group improvisation in free jazz should make one doubly aware: (1) of the essentially oral quality of Reed's fiction (it seems designed to be read aloud, performed), and (2) of Reed's heteroglot discourse (which often approximates a call-and-response effect). Both qualities are observable in this selection from *FLP*:

At the foot of this anfractuous path which leads to the summit of Sam's Island lies the incredible Black Bay. Couched in the embankment are four statues of RUTHERFORD BIRCHARD HAYES. White papers, busted microphones and other wastes leak from the lips of this bearded bedrock and end up in the bay fouling it so that no swimmer has ever emerged from its waters alive. Beneath the surface of this dreadful pool is a subterranean side show replete with freakish fish, clutchy and extrasensory plants. (And believe you me, dem plants is hongry. Eat anything dey kin wrap dey stems around!!) (1967a:2–3)

There are two easily identifiable narrative voices here, playing off each other. The voice that utters a word like "anfractuous" (one of those words with "terrible Latin roots") sets us up for an antiphonal voice that uses words such as "dem," "dey," and "hongry." Or, to choose another example, Bukka speaks in at least three voices that are in a constant state of dialogic tension: (1) the voice of the ingenue (the "square" who is always "the last one on the block to know"), (2) the voice of a "hip" Bukka, able when he wants to do "the whole crying-the-blues repertory" (26), and (3) the voice of the narrator—Reed's *persona* or the voice of a mature, post-apocalyptic Bukka. The point is, *FLP* exhibits what Mikhail Bakhtin would call "heteroglossia" or what Taylor might refer to as the written equivalent of collective improvisation.

[26. *Con molta espressione. Take my word for it. I could do this for Reed! I could play the open-minded, liberal formalist, demonstrate how at first glance his texts appear fragmented, the incoherent ravings of a black man mad at the whole death-dealing-white-world, but upon closer analysis reveal themselves (in all splendor) as fully developed, internally coherent rhetorical systems. I could show how his rhapsodies are as subject to analysis as any improvisation by Taylor and Shepp. I could wax rhapsodic.*]

Up until now, I have discussed the major structural elements of free jazz and the attendant expressions of those elements in Reed's work. We now turn to the sociopolitical implications of the free jazz aesthetic. In outline form, the music signifies the following: (1) a rejection of the "cool" aesthetic, (2) a rejection of Western ideas and values (specifically the "American way of life"), (3) a restoration of African American art to "its valid separation from, and anarchic disregard of, Western popular forms," and (4) a return to ancient and pre-Christian rituals (Jones, 1963:225). Naturally, these values overlap. They can be illustrated by recourse to virtually any African American art of the '60s. But the particular way they receive their expression, that is, the way they are encoded in free jazz and Reed's fiction, merits consideration.

[27. *Con moto. Fact is, any time a critic coins a thesis in the form "X is like Y" (a Reed is like a rhapsody), you can rest assured that evidence, whether convincing or not, will be produced. Trust me, I will always say that I have found exactly what I claim I was looking for.*]

Frank Kofsky writes of the change that occurred in jazz when the '40s became the '50s (when bop became cool) and, thus, describes the background from which free jazz would emerge in 1959. His portrait of cool jazz goes a long way toward accounting for Reed's antipathy for Chet Baker.

> The jazz style that began to emerge as bebop went under was entirely in keeping with the character of the early Cold War period. Even the name of the style itself—*cool*—reflected the change. . . . [I]t was the quintessence of individual *dis*-engagement. If you want to hear the difference, compare a solo by the father of bebop trumpet, Dizzy Gillespie, to one from the cool period by the then-idolized but now almost forgotten trumpeter Chet Baker. (31)

Consequently, when Reed satirizes Baker, who has been anything but forgotten, one of his targets is most likely *dis*-engagement: the myth that one can extricate oneself from politics. Cool jazz—which was ultimately a redaction of the basic materials of bop, a more or less conscious attempt to legitimate, "whiten," or "bleach out" an essentially black musical form—was, above all, a music of detachment. It, not bebop, correlates most readily with attitudes expressed in writings of the "Beat Generation."

> Both [cool jazz and beat writing] celebrated the virtues of passivity and withdrawal—we should today call it *dropping out*—over those of active engagement. To display emotion within either the cool or beat milieus was at once to brand oneself as hopelessly square. (32)

Therefore, to coin an analogy, cool was to the beats as free jazz was to Reed.

But Reed not only satirizes the stance of cool, he satirizes the whole Western-Christian-technological worldview represented by HARRY SAM; he wants to "humble Judeo-Christian culture" by creating disruptivist fiction. He writes, "I think that the Western novel is tied to Western epistemology, the way people in the West look at the world" (1977:133).

[28. *Con obbligato. In S/Z (a text that "counterfeits" the motions of formalism), Barthes works toward the realization of rapsodic writing. He observes, "The area of the (readerly) text is comparable at every point to a (classical) musical score," and a lit-*

tle later he declares that "the readerly text is a tonal *text (for which habit creates a reading process just as conditioned as our hearing)" (1974:28, 30).*

The unity of the readerly text, he maintains, "is basically dependent on two sequential codes: the revelation of truth and the coordination of the actions represented." For Barthes the hermeneutic (revelatory) code corresponds to melody: to "what sings, what flows smoothly, what moves by accidentals, arabesques, and controlled ritardandos through an intelligible progression." Like a melody, the hermeneutic enigma, which urges the reader to keep reading, is predicated on "suspended disclosure" or "delayed resolution," and like a fugue, the classic or readerly narrative contains "a subject, *subject to an* exposition, *a* development *(embodied in the retards, ambiguities, and diversions by which the discourse prolongs the mystery), a* stretto *(a tightened section where scraps of answers rapidly come and go), and a* conclusion." *The proairetic (action) code corresponds to harmony. It sustains the narrative by bringing "everything together" in "the cadence of familiar gestures" (29).]*

Accordingly, Reed opts for a literature—neo-HooDoo fiction and poetry—incommensurate with Western ideology. In addition to this, he interprets free jazz as anticlassical, oppositional music congruent with his own program.

[29. Con slancio. Barthes declares: "to unlearn the readerly would be the same as to unlearn the tonal" (30). We might add, apropos of S/Z, *interrupting the hermeneutic and proairetic codes is the discourse equivalent of interrupting (undoing) tonality. To drop these codes for the "organization of knowledge," writes Ulmer in his elaboration of heuretical methodology, requires "the writer to find an alternative for the logic of classical reasoning, and for the interest of problem solving" (1989a:50). Rapsody (writing with the symbolic code) provides such an alternative. If Balzac's* Sarrasine *is analogous to classical music, say, Mozart's* The Magic Flute, *then Barthes's* S/Z *is analogous to atonal music, say, Boulez's* Pli selon pli. *By interrupting the two codes, which syntagmatically unfold according to a "logico-temporal order," and emphasizing the semic, cultural, and symbolic codes—the paradigmatic codes that "establish permutable, reversible connections, outside the constraint of time"—Barthes produces, out of* Sarrasine, *a modern, that is to say, a nonvectorized, tabular text. He writes:*

The five codes mentioned, frequently heard simultaneously, in fact endow the text with a kind of plural quality (the text

*is actually polyphonic), but of the five codes, only three
establish permutable, reversible connections, outside the
constraint of time (the semic, cultural, and symbolic codes);
the other two impose their terms according to an irreversible
order (the hermeneutic and proairetic codes). The classic text,
therefore, is actually tabular (and not linear), but its tabular-
ity is vectorized, it follows a logico-temporal order. It is a
multivalent but incompletely reversible system. What blocks
its reversibility is just what limits the plural nature of the
classic text. These blocks have names: on the one hand, truth;
on the other, empiricism: against—or between—them, the
modern text comes into being. (1974:30)*

*If Barthes is correct, then the modern narrative, and Reed's fiction
is as good an example of this as any, could be conceptualized as a
classic narrative coming apart—unraveling—at the semes. A rapsody: between truth and empiricism, the modern text works the
signifiers of the classic text to show (1) how they are stitched
together (by reading) and (2) how they, to create a pun by using
Black English vernacular, always mean more than they semes.]*

He is not alone in this reading. Baraka, discussing the utiliza-
tion of European classical music by jazz musicians, declares:

Taylor and Coleman know the music of Anton Webern and
are responsible to it intellectually, as they would be to any
stimulating art form. But they are not responsible to it emotionally, as an extra-musical catalytic form. The emotional
significance of most Negro music has been its separation from
the emotional and philosophical attitudes of classical music.
(Jones, 1963:229–30)

This desire for separation is grounded upon an essentialist belief
that certain musical structures are inherently bound up in Western
ideology. Rejecting Webern is, therefore, tantamount to a symbolic
rejection of the ideology that produced and institutionalized him
(and, by implication, the entire Western musical tradition).

*[30. Con spirito. Terence Hawkes writes: "This art—an art of
signifiers, not signifieds, can be said to be truly modern, whether
its modernity manifests itself in jouissance or jazz (and leaving
aside the question of a philological or semantic connection
between the two terms)" (121).]*

When free jazz manifested an "anarchistic disregard of Western forms," it signaled a willful refusal to interpellate itself into mainstream culture. Most interestingly, its discourse took exactly the same posture toward "dominant" culture as Theodor Adorno's, when it championed serial music over standardized musical forms. By presenting itself as an explicitly oppositional alternative to what Collins refers to as the "Grand Hotel" ("'culture' . . . as a totalizable system that somehow orchestrates all cultural production and reception according to one master system"—xiii), free jazz became, in effect, a modernist critique of "mass culture." If bebop, paraphrasing a formula devised by pianist Thelonious Monk, was music "they couldn't steal because they couldn't play it," then free jazz was music they wouldn't steal because they wouldn't listen to it (Monk, in Shapiro and Hentoff, 341).

[31. *Con strepito. More specifically, the* rap*sodic text, like the* rapp, *the indeterminable coin, actually owes its existence to the scarcity of signifiers; it makes something of shared signification, the fact that there are fewer words than things.*]

Bebop waged war with HARRY SAM by attempting to seize the means of musical production, but as Archie Shepp acutely observes—when he says, "You own the music and we make it"—this tactic was ultimately misguided and politically ineffectual (Shepp, in Kofsky, 12). The only solution was to "own" the art one made (or to control readings of it), and to do that, one had to wage war with HARRY SAM not only on the level of production, but on the levels of distribution and consumption as well.

[31. *Con strepito. More specifically, the* rap*sodic text, like* rap—*a collage music constructed out of "samples" stolen, spirited, and transplanted from found recordings—actually owes its existence to the overabundance of signifiers; it makes something new of texts that have lost their currency.*]

On the level of production, free jazz and Reed battle SAM (Western ideology) by assuming what Susan McClary calls a "mystique of difficulty" (1989:65). They set up situations (for example, a concert or novel) that play the possibility of scandalizing a "square" audience—either through assaultive techniques or by laughing behind the backs of the naïve and getting through to—that is, communicating or communing with—a "hip" audience. All in all, it is a common strategy of the modern avant-garde. What makes Reed and free jazz interesting as textual practices, however, is their unwillingness to divorce formal concerns from social functions. As McClary notes "the prestige value" of twentieth-century avant-garde music "is inversely correlated with public response and comprehension" (60); Reed and free jazz have simply refused to follow this formula. At some expense to their prestige, they point toward another kind of (a postmodern?) avant-garde.

[*32. Con tenerezza. Still, I am somewhat uncomfortable with this formulation. Given all the evidence I have been able to gather, Reed, like Lucian, Rabelais, Sterne, Swift, Wyndham Lewis, and other crazy satirists, has a point he hopes to convey. He is not just rapping, "drifting on a read" (following the "logic" of the signifier). He wants to say something of social consequence. He expects that his words will be decoded "properly": escape the metamorphosing power of metaphor (rapsodic logic).*]

On the level of distribution and consumption, free jazz and Reed battle SAM by establishing networks for the dissemination of products with limited commercial appeal. These networks often parallel and hence, bypass the censorious capitalist circuit (Attali, 138–40). Lyons states that the precursors of these quasi-union groupings "were the brotherhoods and 'secret societies' of early New Orleans, which yielded the first era of musical collectivism" (384). The two major examples of such cooperatives in jazz are the Association for the Advancement of Creative Musicians (AACM), founded in Chicago in 1965, and the Jazz Composers' Orchestra Association (JCOA), first organized in New York in 1959 as the Jazz Composers' Guild (charter members were Bill Dixon, Cecil Taylor, Sun Ra, Paul Bley, Carla Bley, George Russell, and Archie Shepp), and later reorganized, by Carla Bley and Michael Mantler, as the JCOA (1966). Carla Bley describes her organization as a "Wildlife Preserve protecting . . . possibly extinct music" (Bley, in Primack, 11). A similar claim could be made for Yardbird Publishing company, a corporation founded by Reed in 1972, "to serve as an outlet for Afro-American writers and the growing number of Asian and Chicano poets" (Reed, 1977:113).

[*33. Con tutta forza. Wait a minute, though! Reed has a point. Well, so do I! It goes like this: rhapsody turns on the possibility of rapsody. For Reed's texts to function in the way he intended, they must be capable of functioning in ways he would never intend. Finally, the fact that Reed cannot control readings, delimit or monitor the circulation of his semes, makes reading (im)possible.*]

Thus, this literature and this music was and is wildly syncretistic, representing a weaving (but not, necessarily, a reconciliation) of multifarious strains. Both resist prescriptions that would dictate their movements. Reed makes this position explicit when he states his opposition to "the Axis," which he describes as "that tacit alignment between 'black nationalists,' 'black revolutionaries,' 'white radicals,' and 'white liberals' which views the Afro-American writer as a kind of recruiter for their rather dubious political programs" (72).

[*34. Con velocità. For* Mumbo Jumbo *to function as a text, it has to be able to function in the absence of both author and audience, addressor and addressees. Writing, whether on vinyl, paper, or any other medium, supposes absence. It is a "sampling sport," a textile industry. "A written sign," Derrida explains in "Signature Event Context," "is proffered in the absence of the addressee," and he adds: This absence is not an extension of "the field and powers of a locutionary or gestural communication," a presence merely distanced or delayed, since in order for the structure of writing to be constituted "this distance, division, delay,* différance *must be capable of being brought to a certain absolute degree of absence" (1982:315, 311). In other words,* Mumbo Jumbo *has to remain "legible despite the absolute disappearance of every determined addressee in general for it to function as writing, that is, for it to be legible. It must be repeatable—iterable—like a rapp. But, Thomas Lewis warns, we must not purchase "epistemological uncertainty precisely at the cost of obscuring the role of social power in the process of fixing and disseminating references" (1985:40).*]

Finally, then, Reed and free jazz collect and chronicle "cultural icons that were stolen, spirited, and transplanted from Africa to the Carib and the U.S." (Palmer, n.p.). Both return to ancient, pre-Christian sources, ultimately African in origin—but that found unique expression in the culture of old New Orleans—in order to refunction them—give them new currency. Taylor says:

> What any musician must do . . . is recognize the function that they have in a jazz group and to function out of it with the whole history of America which is theirs. That's what America is. All these people. And to know what to do with all these things, blend them and make them go on, that's what creating the new music is about. (Taylor, in Goldberg, 222–23)

[*35. Con vigore. Recalling Herman Melville (*The Confidence Man*) and P. T. Barnum, Reed writes: "This is the country where something is successful in direct proportion to how it's put over; how it's gamed" (1971:42).*]

༼ั༽

FOUR

Charivari:
Conjugal Riffs

Tropology: The Art of Noisemaking

*People over the world like distortion, it's one of the
things you have to start with.*
　　　　　　　　　—Jim Dickinson (in Smith, 22)

*She knew from sermons and editorials that it wasn't real
music—just colored folks' stuff: harmful, certainly;
embarrassing, of course; but not real, not serious.*
　　*Yet Alice Manfred swore she heard a complicated
anger in it; something hostile that disguised itself as
flourish and roaring seduction. But the part she hated
most was its appetite.*
　　　　　　　　　　　　　—Toni Morrison (59)

*His music seemed to be merely an excuse for the life he
led. It sounded just that weird and disordered.*
　　　　　　　　　　　　　—James Baldwin (194)

Toward the end of *The Raw and the Cooked*, in a chapter
titled "Divertissement on a Folk Theme," Claude Lévi-Strauss
abandons the Amazon River Basin and the myths of the Bororo and
Ge tribes for a brief excursion into the realm of general mythology
and folklore. To get this intellectual *dérive* going, he informs readers of an anthropological commonplace. Lévi-Strauss writes, "If one
were to ask an ethnologist *ex abrupto* in what circumstances unre-

stricted noise is prescribed by custom, it is very likely that he would immediately quote two instances: the traditional *charivari* of Europe, and the din with which a considerable number of so-called primitive (and also civilized) societies salute, or used to salute, eclipses of the sun or the moon" (1969:286).

Before summarizing Lévi-Strauss's theory of noise, I want to add an etymological and a historical note. *Charivari* literally means "hubbub" and is probably derived from the Late Latin word *carībaria*, "headache." According to Diderot and d'Alembert's *Encyclopédie*, it "conveys the derisive noise made at night with pans, cauldrons, basins, etc., in front of the houses of people who are marrying for the second or third time or are marrying someone of a very different age from themselves" (qtd. in Lévi-Strauss, 286). "Shivaree" is an American corruption of *charivari*.

> The term, most likely borrowed from French traders and settlers along the Mississippi River, was well established in the United States by 1805; an account dating from that year describes a shivaree in New Orleans: *"The house is mobbed by thousands of the people of the town, vociferating and shouting with loud acclaim . . . many [are] in disguises and masks; and all have some kind of discordant and noisy music, such as old kettles, and shovels, and tongs. . . . All civil authority and rule seems laid aside"* (John F. Watson). (*American Heritage Dictionary* [AHD], 3rd ed.)

In music *charivari* "signifies a deliberately distorted and noisy performance." A corresponding term in German is *Katzenmusik* (literally "cat music"), in Italian, *scampata* (Randel, 92).

Richard Terdiman, whose book, *Discourse/Counter-Discourse*, offers a detailed history and theory of oppositional writing in nineteenth-century France, explains the significance of *Le Charivari*. Founded by Charles Philipon in 1832, it holds the distinction of being the first newspaper to employ lithography and reproduce images—often caricatures of prominent political figures—in its pages. More importantly, *Le Charivari* institutionalized "counter-discourse" as an intrusive, alternative commodity. It "sustained uninterrupted daily publication (even including Sundays) for sixty years" (Terdiman, 151–52). During this time, the newspaper labored not only to systematically ridicule "the bourgeois," but to "represent the world *differently*"; it sought to detect, map, and, then, subvert the naturalized codes that (1) regulated understanding of the social world and (2) promoted the vested interests of power. At stake in its struggle for the meaning and the control of cultural codes were the paradigms of social representation themselves (149–50). *Le Charivari* serves to remind us that the question of noise always concerns who—or what group—will be allowed to function as a *parasite*: that is, allowed to inhabit another (like a microbe or demon "that takes without giving and weakens without killing"), play the role of guest (exchange "talk, praise, and flattery for food"), or make noise. In French *parasite* means "the static in a system or the interference in a channel" (Serres, x). Additionally, in English the words "noise" and "nausea" are doublets, "that is, words borrowed in different forms from the same word." *Nausea* was taken directly from the Latin, from the word that literally meant seasickness; *noise* came into English through the Old French word *nois*, which meant "sound, din, uproar, quarrel" and was derived from the Latin *nausea* (*AHD*).

We return to Lévi-Strauss. After defining *charivari*, he asks: What do the two customary manifestations of noise have in common and what do people hope to achieve by them? He speculates and comes up with an easy answer. In one case, a sociological "monster" figuratively devours an innocent body; in the other, a cosmological monster devours the sun or moon (1969:287). Dining prompts dinning. The *charivari* punishes a reprehensible union on earth; noise at the time of an eclipse seeks to ward off a dangerous conjunction in the sky. Both rituals employ noise as a counter-discourse to drive off or expel a parasite; noise interrupts communication (communion or intercourse) between bodies—terrestrial and celestial.

But is it not true, writes Lévi-Strauss, that not conjunction but disruption of an enduring order is the phenomenon common to these two events? On a cosmological level, the normal alternation of the sun and the moon, day and night, light and darkness, heat and cold has been interrupted; on a sociological level, the convention of men and women—"who are in a relation of mutual suitability in regard to civil status, age, wealth, etc."—has been broken (288). The din at a marriage or at an eclipse, therefore, punishes "not just a simple conjunction . . . but something much more complex which consists, on the one hand, of the *breaking* of the syntagmatic sequence, and on the other, of the *intrusion* of a foreign element into this same sequence—an element that *appropriates*, or tries to appropriate, one term of the sequence, thus bringing about a distortion." The function of noise-making rituals is to draw attention to another type of noise, to expose "an anomaly in the unfolding of a syntagmatic sequence" (289). *Charivari* marks *jouissance*. "'Bliss' and 'noise,'" Simon Reynolds argues, "are the same thing"; they rupture/disrupt "the signifying system that holds (a) culture together" (13). When an old, wealthy widower marries a young woman, a shivaree converts social noise at one level—produced by the misalliance—into information at another level, so that the system—in this case, a community—will not be disorganized by its own noise. William Paulson schematizes this transaction:

> At a given level of the system there is transmission of information and generation of noise. The next level acts as an observer of the preceding one, and for this observer, the ambiguity resulting from noise in the first transmission of information becomes a source of new information, of added organizational complexity. (48)

"In a certain sense," writes Michel Serres, "the next level functions as a rectifier, in particular, as a rectifier of noise. What was once an obstacle to all messages is reversed and added to the information" (Serres, in Paulson, 1988:48). The *charivari*, therefore, represents the homeopathic use of noise: one sort of noise converted into another as a means to some sort of control. The following passage from James Baldwin's "Sonny's Blues" illustrates this point perfectly:

> "When she was singing before," said Sonny, abruptly, "her voice reminded me for a minute of what heroin feels like sometimes—when it's in your veins. It makes you feel sort of warm and cool at the same time. And distant. And—and sure." He sipped his beer, very deliberately not looking at me. I watched his face. "It makes you feel—in control. Sometimes you've got to have that feeling." (198)

Sonny's twin desires—his jones for bebop and heroin—are isomorphic, structurally indistinguishable. They are both interventions, varieties of *charivari*: damage control, means of managing the dialectic of freedom and control, pleasure and pain. To be presumptive and specific, drugs enable Sonny (or they enabled his idol, Charlie Parker) to play his body as thoroughly as he plays piano (or vice versa, to play piano as one's body). They are more or less effective means of mastering both environment and self—and losing environment and self. To be oversimple about this vexed topic, this is why drugs and music are regularly associated and, in turn, this is why the musician is an iconic and perpetual outsider (Becker). Music and drugs simultaneously serve two seemingly opposite purposes: that of noise buffer and noise intensifier. The musician is himself a kind of drug, injected into or ingested by the cultural body.

Consider also that the structure of the "abnormal unions" described by Lévi-Strauss are homologous to Freud's explanation of displacement in dream work and to Lacan's account of the construction of subjectivity ("where a sense of self displaces the recognition of the social construction of identity"—Saper, 1991:34). They are also homologous to Eisenstein's revolutionary theory of film editing: montage as the visualization of dialectics laying bare the sociopolitical context of production. But while the phenomena described by Lévi-Strauss are social, those described by Freud and Lacan psychological, and Eisenstein's an artistic-political phenomenon, all can be graphed as dramatizations of transference: writing out the trope of metaphor. All require an appropriation that breaks an ideal continuity in order to receive expression. The anthropologist, psychoanalyst, revolutionary filmmaker, and, I should add, the literary theorist are noise detectors. And they are noisemakers: interrupters that transform one message (system or order) into another.

Noise is knowledge. More precisely, it is structurally indistinguishable from information. Let me explain. Since noise, by definition, includes "any signal received that was not transmitted by the source, or anything that makes the intended signal harder to decode accurately," it is differentiated from information only through a contradictory operation (Fiske, 8). One must establish the signal transmitted *before* it becomes a signal received; noise is an effect of imputed intent.

Listening: Shivaree for C90

Noises were crotchets without stems.
> —John Cage (30)

If music is a language communicating moods and feelings, then noise is like an eruption within the material out of which language is shaped.
> —Simon Reynolds (60)

Before federal agents resorted to battering the walls of the Branch Davidian compound in Waco, Texas, they barraged it with high-volume music. Writing in *The New York Times*, shortly before standoff became conflagration, Jon Pareles reported that the government had established a "harrowing" playlist for the cultists: "Nancy Sinatra's 'These Boots Are Made for Walkin','' a Mitch Miller chorus singing Christmas carols, an Andy Williams album and the low, sonorous chants of Tibetan monks." A "cryptic assortment," wrote Pareles, it "seems to assume that nothing could be more devastating than a combination of tacky white-bread pop and exotic ritual" (IV, 2).

"What kind of noise annoys a bunkered cult leader?" asks the journalist and music critic. The answer? "It may not matter as long as it gets a rise out of the Government's quarry." Music in this type of situation is deployed *phatically*. It's Drano for auditory-political canals, intended to ream out clogged channels of communication. Pareles quotes Robert Louden, hostage negotiator and associate director of the Criminal Justice Center at the John Jay College of Criminal Justice: "The idea is not so much to drive them from their lair as it is to reaffirm the communication process."

But what kind of communication might be evoked by the recordings of Mitch Miller, Nancy Sinatra, or Tibetan monks played in heavy rotation? Would they prompt Robert Louden to reaffirm the communication process? Or, for that matter, how did they affect David Koresh? My suggestion? At the next showdown, government agents ought to upgrade their playlist and try an all-jazz format. They should compile a ninety–minute cassette tape featuring the following twelve tone-rows. Broadcast this dozen dozens of times; it will make Jericho's walls come tumbling down.

Then again, readers might want to create and give a listen to this proposed tape. Like those described in other chapters, it suggests a specific way to materialize a trope of jazz. This tape's raison d'être is noise, but it is far from monolithically cacophonous. No screamfest, it is calculated to display a variety of sonic textures, jazz-as-noise in all its guises. Some people might find it absolutely noxious. (For example, Pam, my wife, despises it. She believes that anyone who blithely claims, "Oh, I love jazz!" should have to suffer through this "music" at least once.) Others might take to it like Brer Rabbit tossed in a briar patch. In any event, this musical mix is guaranteed to give cowboys and Indians something substantive to discuss before talk turns to treaties and contracts.

Side I

01. Hal Russell (1992) "Buddhi," *Hal's Bells*, ECM.   4:13

    Bells, real ones, though the title also alludes to an album by Albert Ayler.

02. Sun Ra Arkestra (1963) "Moon Dance," *Cosmic Tones for Mental Therapy/Art Forms of Dimensions Tomorrow*, Evidence.   6:33

    By reinjecting tawdriness into the jazz mainstream, Ra suggested that creativity equals a healthy disrespect for tradition. This crazy-cool proto-beat-box track has only an occasional hint of apocalypse.

03. John Zorn (1988) "Feet Music," *Spy vs. Spy*, Elektra Musician.   4:45

    Two saxophonists, two drummers, and a bassist abandon all pretense to subtlety as they pound out the Ornette Coleman songbook—hardcore style.

04. Ronald Shannon Jackson (released 1990) "What's Not Said," *Red Warrior*, Axiom.   4:15

    Heavy-metal jazz: screaming guitars buoyed by tribal drumming.

05. Miles Davis (1975) "Prelude (Part Two)," *Agharta*, Columbia.   6:33

    Fusion without the logic of narrative—that is, no clear-cut beginning, middle, or end—it undulates like an organism.

06. Albert Ayler (1966) "Spirits," *Lörrach/Paris 1966*, hat ART.   3:10

    The sound of a tenor saxophonist (and his band) hotly pursued by demons and God Almighty.

07. Peter Brötzmann (1968) "Machine Gun (Second Take)," *Machine Gun*, FMP.   14:57

    Well yes, it sounds exactly like you'd think, except when the band kicks into an assaultive variety of rhythm and blues.

Total playing time 44:26

Side II

01. John Coltrane (1967) "Venus," *Interstellar Space,*
    Impulse!   8:28

    Reminiscent of television footage in which astronauts
    wave at the camera—just before blastoff.

02. Sonny Sharrock (1991) "Promises Kept," *Ask the Ages,*
    Axiom.   9:43

    Sharrock invented noise guitar years before it became
    de rigueur in rock. Joining him, on this late date, are
    saxophonist Pharoah Sanders and drummer Elvin Jones.

03. Art Ensemble of Chicago (1984) "The Third Decade,"
    The Third Decade, ECM.   8:19

    A snapshot of America's premier griot society, this is
    also the first recording on which the quintet used syn-
    thesizers. Mainstream jazz for those who consider neo-
    bop as anachronistic as Dixieland.

04. Ornette Coleman (1960) "First Take," *Free Jazz,*
    Atlantic.   17:03

    When the guys at Iko's—the record store I frequent—
    grow weary of customers, they spin this free-wheeling
    classic.

05. Cecil Taylor (1989) "Sirenes," *In Florescence,* A&M.   :48

    Less a musical selection—it's too short—than an aural
    snapshot of the most relentlessly inventive pianist
    alive.

Total playing time 44:21

Archeology: Can Jazz Find Marital Bliss?

Women were a dime a dozen, but where could you find
a good New Orleans jazz band? . . . If you could catch a
couple of cats that just met each other talking about cer-
tain musicians they know or humming a riff or two to
each other, before you could call a preacher they'd be
practically married.
    —Milton "Mezz" Mezzrow (24, 61)

Bring the Noise

Pete Kelly's Blues (1955) is a disguised western set in the Jazz Age. Much of its action revolves around the film's two principal female characters. They represent distinct threats to the autonomy of the protagonist, a cornet-playing outlaw hero motivated by what Robert Ray labels "an ideological anxiety about civilized life" (1985:60). Ivy Conrad, a slumming heiress played by Janet Leigh, embodies the lure of domestication. She tempts Pete Kelly (Jack Webb) to settle down and abandon the guys in his "trad" jazz band. Rose Hopkins, a battered, dipsomaniac singer played by Peggy Lee, embodies another sort of lure: commercialization. But she's no temptress. Rather, like the Billie Holiday of jazz legend, Rose is a hip tragedienne. Her aesthetic superiority is the putative result— the strange fruit—of being victimized. And a sort of bruised hipness prohibits Rose from vamping her way into the all-male enclave of "real" jazz. Instead, her abusive manager, a gangster (Edmond O'Brien), forces an entry. He "asks" Pete Kelly to give his client an audition. Realizing that this "offer" of a woman is both a demand and a temptation to sell out—to dilute his music like speakeasy gin—Pete demurs: *"It's jazz. The people here, they come for the noise."* He does not want a singer of any sort; she would destroy the integrity of his "trad" music.

I shall not analyze how this film manages these women, except to say that Rose goes insane and Ivy becomes Pete Kelly's devoted fan. Instead, I want to take *Pete Kelly's Blues* as a tutor text from which we can extrapolate a basic lesson. Within the world of jazz—as in the diegesis of all disguised westerns—women are represented as sociological monsters. They threaten to disrupt an enduring order—to alienate the jazzman from his music and his band—and to bring about a reprehensible harmony (through marriage and civilization). Two related points follow directly from this observation. First, jazz is always conceptualized as something of an institution dedicated to the advancement of noise.

sCReeeEEECHHHHHH SCREEEECCCCHHHH

goes a line from Sonia Sanchez's "a/coltrane/poem," and it serves notice that jazz enters discourse through the trope of *charivari*. It is, as Langston Hughes states with affection, "a blare from hell" (Hughes, in Albert, 12). Second, all jazzographies are fundamentally love stories. Some dramatize the conflict arising from the interruption of an enduring order: the normal but oftentimes stormy romance of musician and music. Others simply describe the enduring order. Ivy acknowledges the woman's place in this story when she says, "You don't want to get married, Pete, unless you find a girl who looks like a cornet. I'm short three valves. I might as well pack up and move someplace else."

The Object of Affection

As we have seen, Schuller identifies jazzography as a site where love labored: where "well-meaning amateur criticism" was "allowed to pass for scholarship and serious analysis" (vii). We should not be surprised. "[I]n ordinary criticism," writes Gregory Ulmer, "the critic (unconsciously) . . . relates to the object of study as to a love-object" (1980:66). He identifies with it; he assigns it a vocabulary by projecting or transferring his own image-system onto his object of affection.

What amateur jazzography loved in jazz was its own image, and what this culture saw reflected in amateur jazzography was ultimately itself. This is why amateur criticism "was allowed to pass for scholarship and serious analysis." It actively and self-reflexively participated in reinforcing (even in determining) what Louis Althusser calls the ideological formations by which a culture recognizes itself (1971:218–19). By accurately mirroring back cultural perceptions of jazz, amateur criticism (unconsciously) zoomed in on the very set of images, the mixed metaphors, that this culture routinely used to define itself. This, finally, is MacDonald Smith Moore's central point in *Yankee Blues*, a book we have already examined: Jazzography sold jazz to America by showing America itself in jazz. After all, the United States was a *satura*, a melting pot. It was a nation of proud outsiders, not quite ready to forfeit its isolated position: content to play obbligatos on the world stage but passionate, even rhapsodic and noisy, about its role in spreading democracy. How could it fail to embrace a music that embodied all of its best attributes?

Contrary to what Schuller maintains, then, the relative acceptability of amateur criticism was not attributable to the "humble, socially 'unacceptable' origin of jazz" or "to the widely held notion that a music improvised by self-taught, often musically illiterate musicians did not warrant genuine musicological research." Rather, amateur criticism accommodated its audience by framing its discourse in culturally receivable terms. For example, it accepted the meanings of words such as "amateur," "humble," "unacceptable," "self-taught," and "illiterate" as self-explanatory and uncontestable. It constructed itself out of the binary oppositions that enabled musicology and ethnomusicology: that is to say, the key naturalized metaphors that enabled Western ideology to maintain hegemony. Its complicity in reinforcing these metaphors-erected-into-concepts (philosophemes) ensured that its descriptions of jazz would be countenanced by the culture at large and by "genuine musicology." This is really why amateur criticism gained acceptance. "Success," Barthes says, "requires a complicity of institutions" (1985:130).

Why amateur criticism about jazz was *not* equated with "genuine musicology" is another, more interesting matter. Granted, the two were ineluctably different, and in that regard there is no reason they should have been equated. But their differences are worth sketching out because they stand to teach us a lesson about writing within the realm of cultural studies.

One way to initiate this lesson is to employ Lévi-Strauss's structuralist account of the *charivari* as a tool for conceptualization (hermeneutics). Once again, we shall observe that a trope structuring our image of jazz also structures cultural perceptions of jazzography. Here, in this section of archeology, I shall show that the *charivari* is a tool useful for *writing about* jazz and the relationship of jazzography and musicology. In subsequent sections, I conduct an experiment. Taking fiction by LeRoi Jones (Amiri Baraka) and theory by Gregory Ulmer as paradigms, I demonstrate the possibility of *writing with* the *charivari*, using it as a tool for invention (heuretics).

Convergence of the Twain

If we took the trope of *charivari* and projected it as film narrative, *New York, New York* (1977) might result. A revisionist musical directed by Martin Scorsese, it dramatizes a modern version of the myth of illicit conjunction. As such, it is diligently and consistently unlikable, presenting viewers with no sympathetic characters. This movie doesn't withhold pleasure. It actively generates displeasure (noise or nausea), and it takes upon itself the role of interrupting agent (noisemaker or parasite): the very role that, within the movie's story, Scorsese and scriptwriter Earl Mac Rauch assigned to the jazzman.

To a medley of songs that includes the movie's theme and

George Geshwin's "The Man I Love," the credits run: art-deco letters over a cut-out Manhattan skyline. Then, with a blast of noise, the movie proper begins. It's VJ Day, 1945. We arc in New York City, the Tommy Dorsey Orchestra is playing some palatial ballroom—the celebration is being broadcast over radio station WNEW—and Jimmy Doyle (Robert DeNiro) is roaming the margins of the dance floor, looking for a woman. Cinematic codes lead us to believe that, when he spots her, we too will recognize her. She will be a star.

Our expectations are fulfilled when a shot, from Jimmy's point-of-view, enables us to see Francine Evans (Liza Minnelli) sitting alone at a table. Jimmy walks up to her and, immediately, starts making sexual advances. He is repeatedly rebuffed. This couple is as different as we expect them to be: even more different than characters played by Fred Astaire and Ginger Rogers. Jimmy—a wolf straight out of a Tex Avery cartoon—is all behop nerves and *noir* dissonance. Francine—though obviously not as sweet as Doris Day—secms every bit as hip as Anita O'Day. The two are, in short, a formidable match, but they leave the dance alone.

Convention, however, dictates that Jimmy and Francine will later run into each other. They do so the next day. Again, in this second scene of the movie, they do not hit it off, but through a series of comic maneuvers, which I shall not detail, they end up sharing a cab. Jimmy, his saxophone stowed in the front seat, is headed toward an audition at, what turns out to be, a tiny Brooklyn club. In transit, he presumes to give Francine his philosophy of life.

JIMMY: Listen, I want to ask you something. You want to know what interests me the most, Francis? One is music. Number two is money. And number three is . . . [makes the sound of kissing while leaning on Francine's shoulder].
FRANCINE: I got it. Uh huh. I got it.
JIMMY: What's the matter?
FRANCINE: I don't want it. They're always in that order?
JIMMY: Sure, they're always in that order. Unless, you happen to come across someone who grooves you, and you want to groove with—say you. And if things work out, and you start acting a little more intelligent, then possibly—then I will make number three number one, number one number three, and number two. Now wait. Wait, I'm getting confused. You put it where ah . . .
FRANCINE: You put it where number three is.

JIMMY: Francis, let me start all over again. Let me get this. Number
    three would be number one.
FRANCINE: Number two would be number two.
JIMMY: Exactly. And when you have that, you have what you call a
    major chord.
FRANCINE: What is a major chord?
JIMMY: A major chord is when everything in your life works out per-
    fectly, when you have everything you could ever possibly
    want. Everything. You have the woman you want. You have
    the music you want. And you have enough money to live
    comfortably. And that's a major chord.

The film now cuts to the audition. Jimmy plays a tune that jumps
way too much for the terminally square clubowner; it looks like he
has blown his chance at landing a paying gig. But then Francine
starts snapping her fingers, and singing, "You brought a new kind of
love to me." She prompts Jimmy to play obbligati over her melody
line. He complies. The two sound great together, and they are
offered a job as a boy-girl act.

    Exposition now complete, we think we recognize this story. It
suggests a form Robert Ray calls the Hollywood "reconciliatory
pattern": a *thematic paradigm* where incompatible values—or
competing myths—are reduced to melodrama and resolved "sim-
plistically (by refusing to acknowledge that a choice is necessary),
sentimentally (by blurring the differences between the two sides),
or by laughing the whole thing off" (1985:67). If we are correct, *New
York, New York* represents a stylized, almost liturgical version of
the MGM musical (which was itself a stylized, almost liturgical
embodiment of Hollywood's basic story line). Jimmy plays tenor
sax in the legato style of Lester Young and disciples: Paul
Quinichette, Zoot Sims, Flip Phillips, and Georgie Auld (this latter
musician recorded the songs DeNiro mimes for the movie). Within
the semiotics of jazz this can mean only one thing. Jimmy's got
eyes for bebop. When swing loses its popularity—television comes
in, people stay home, and clubs close—he might weather the
changes, but, more likely, he will develop a "habit" and need reha-
bilitation. Francine, on the other hand, is golden—a canary or pop
singer who is, in no uncertain terms, a cinematic citation of Judy
Garland. She, the star-is-born system assures us, will undoubtedly
survive the demise of the big bands. She might go through a phase
where she drinks too much, but she will achieve immense fame.
Both characters will share (and the audience will endure) a big,

splashy production number toward the end of the movie.

But in this movie reconciliation never really occurs. Moments of conjunction are evoked to be immediately disrupted. To illustrate this point, I need only summarize the remainder of the film's plot. The successful audition at the Brooklyn nightclub comes to nothing. Francine immediately runs out on Jimmy when her agent, Tony Harwell (Lionel Stander), finds her a job singing with Frankie Harte's Big Band. (Harte, by the way, is played by saxophonist Georgie Auld.) Jimmy pursues Francine and catches up with her at a gig. The band is playing a dance, and in the middle of its performance, Jimmy ushers Francine outside. He says, "I love you. I mean I dig you." Jimmy joins the band, and the couple is soon married. When the road-weary Harte retires, Jimmy assumes leadership of the band. And it does well—until Francine becomes pregnant and returns to New York. Then, things quickly fall apart. After leading the band for a short time, Jimmy also returns to New York, but he and Francine are distant. They live together but pursue separate careers. Jimmy plays the Harlem Club by night; Francine records jingles and demos by day and, eventually, gets a contract with Decca Records. Their marriage dissolves. Jimmy leaves Francine on the morning their son is born, not even staying long enough to see the child. But Francine doesn't recover. That's too weak a word. She triumphs. She goes on to great commercial success as a recording artist and film star. Surprisingly, Jimmy also succeeds. He opens a club, The Major Chord, and scores a hit with "New York, New York," a song he had written for Francine. It is all they share. In the movie's final scene—the splashy production number—Francine sings her version of the song. Jimmy sits alone in the audience. After the show, he walks backstage, congratulates his ex-wife, and suggests that they get together later that evening. They don't, and the movie ends.

On the one hand, *New York, New York* disrupts an enduring order, the Hollywood thematic pattern. It calls attention to the unnatural unions regularly perpetrated by Hollywood musicals: to that powerful group of myths that reconcile opposing value systems through romantic love. It does this, most obviously, by refusing reconciliation, but also by parading its own artificiality. Like any number of "corrected" genre movies, *New York, New York* inhabits the form that it corrects. It consistently looks like a musical trying very hard to look like a musical. Filmed completely on sets, it gives us, not one location shot of New York City, but Hollywood's image of New York City (which, one might add, contributed greatly to New York's image of itself, which in turn contributed to Hollywood's image of New York, which . . . and so on and so on).

On the other hand, *New York, New York* doesn't demythologize so much as it remythologizes. It stands as an intrusive countermyth, abandoning the popular myths of Hollywood in order to embrace a subcultural myth of jazz. In this story—which we could call the "irreconciliatory pattern"—Jimmy and Francine's relationship represents an illicit conjunction. It is fated to fail: Jazz and pop don't mix. But while Jimmy and Francine are mutually ill-suited for one another, it is Jimmy who plays the role of noise; he is the agent of interruption. He breaks the primary bond—a syntagm or major chord—that links jazzman and jazz in order to intrude into the world of popular music. Once there, he immediately tries to appropriate Francine—a key term of the pop syntagm—and, thus, brings about a distortion. The movie exposes the couple as an anomaly; it shivers them asunder and restores Jimmy-the-jazzman to his normal mythic state. He lives on the margins; he's a *chasse beaux*.

Jazz Signs Its Name

Alan Merriam and Fradley Garner mention the term "*chasse beaux*" as they catalog theories about the word "jazz" (380). But whether or not "jazz" actually found in "*chasse beaux*" the linguistic germ from which it grew doesn't concern me. Rather, I want to point out that the term rates etymological plausibility because it fits or is homologous with cultural perceptions about jazz. It combines images of love, style, and marginality into one generative trope that signifies a desire to clear up the mystery of jazz's paternity and to explain its "socially 'unacceptable'" origins.

The story of the *chasse beaux* can be traced back to 1830s New Orleans. There, according to Merriam and Garner, it "was a popular French expression denoting a dandy, or a hip Gallic Don Juan." Transformed through a macaronic pun, it became first a title—Mr. Jazzbo, winner of the Cake Walk—then a common noun, "jazzbo." Later, "in vaudeville and on the circus lot," "jazzbo" came to mean "the same as 'hokum,' or low comedy verging on vulgarity," and the phrase "put in jaz" meant to "add low comedy, go to high speed and accelerate the comedy spark" (380). Additionally, a folk figure named Jasbo (who is always something of a *chasse beaux*), appears in a group of tales, mythic explanations actually, that locate the origin of the word "jazz" in "the change or corruption of personal names" (373). One such story—the earliest on record—appeared in the *Music Trade Review* on June 14, 1919:

> Chicago, Ill., June 9. Roger Graham, Chicago music publisher, has his own pet theory of the origin of jazz music and firmly believes it to be the true one. Five years ago, in Sam Hare's Schiller Cafe on Thirty-first Street, "Jasbo" Brown and five other alleged musicians, members of what might have been called, with the aid of imagination, an orchestra, dispensed "melody" largely for the benefit of Sam Hare's patrons.
>
> Jasbo doubled with the piccolo and cornet. When he was sober Jasbo played orthodox music, but wrapped around three or four glasses of gin Jasbo had a way of making his piccolo produce strains of the wildest, most barbaric abandon. Strange to say, though, Mr. Hare's patrons, if they could help it, never allowed Jasbo to maintain sobriety while on the job. They liked the thrilling sensation of the piccolo's lawless strains, and when Jasbo put a tomato can on the end of his cornet it seemed as if the music with its strange, quivering pulsations came from another world.
>
> Patrons offered Jasbo more and more gin. First it was the query "More, Jasbo?" directed at the darky's thirst; then the insistence, "More, Jasbo!" directed at the darky's music, and then just plain "more jazz!" (in Merriam and Garner, 374)

Alternate versions of this hilariously implausible account substitute James (or its abbreviation, Jas.), Jasper, Jack, Jess, Razz, or Chaz (from Charles) for the name Jasbo Brown, but they all retain the basic structural characteristics of the tale—namely a movement from the proper name to the common noun—leading Merriam and Garner to the rather dubious conclusion that all versions derive from "a single source, probably the 1919 issue of *Music Trade Review*" (379). Still, we would probably agree that the importance of the Jasbo story doesn't lie in its explanatory or hermeneutic power. It has little. Rather, the story offers a compelling demonstration of heuretics. It is undeniably inventive. In fact, I suspect that its creator had grammatological leanings; he knew how to employ jazz as a strategy for writing.

If one had the capacities of Borges's Pierre Menard and the patience of Beckett's Vladimir and Estragon, he or she could generate the discourse of jazz simply by playing in the gap that links and separates Jasbo and *chasse beaux*. That is to say, had we but world enough, and time, we could construct the entire corpus of jazzology simply by ringing changes on the name Jasbo. Such a signature experiment, to recall the two-step outline employed in chapter 2, would begin by breaking down Jasbo into a set of common nouns. These words would then establish keys, imply routes or possibilities for improvisation. For example, from *chasse beaux*, we can extrapolate (1) an interest in the musical concept of *swing* (the rhythms of copulation), (2) the elevation of personal or idiomatic *style* over conventional notions of propriety, and (3) the marginal person's ambivalence toward what Nietzsche called "gregarity of society" (qtd. in Barthes, 1985:335). In step two, we would improvise on—play out the signifying possibilities of—these concepts (being careful to show that "play" and "improvisation" are themselves terms derivable from *chasse beaux*), and we would elaborate a list of predicates that, forming a grid or matrix, could be employed as an "overlay" to mark off and organize the entire field of jazz music.

But, one might ask, what is the point, the reason for even visualizing such an experiment? I want readers to see that the Jasbo story constitutes what Derrida would call a *signature event*. When jazz signs itself, it writes, it is written by, *Jasbo*. Thus far, we have seen how this figure operates in folklore. Jasbo is a liminal figure: a dandy or trickster. And we have seen how he appears in cinema: Pete Kelly and Jimmy Doyle are eternal outsiders. Next, we shall examine the role Jasbo plays in jazzology.

The Language of Jazzology

Nowhere is formalism more firmly entrenched than in the field of music studies, and nowhere in music studies is formalism less contested than in the field of jazz studies. The most cursory glance at the stated goals of jazzologists reveals an alliance with methods borrowed from science. For example, Winthrop Sargeant states a desire "to analyze jazz as a distinct musical idiom, to trace its origins and influences, to take apart its anatomy and to describe those features that distinguish it from other varieties of music" (ix–x). Max Harrison, author of the jazz entry in *The New Grove Dictionary of Music and Musicians*, advocates informed objectivity, decrying listeners who are "much affected by inessentials such as the personality or reputation of a performer"; he insists that jazz "would be worthless if it bore much relation to its popular image"

(8). And Gary Giddins singles out Martin Williams as the ideal jazzologist: "a born pedagogue who seemed obsessed with locating masterpieces, pinpointing their significance, and demonstrating precisely what made them tick. He wrote in an unadorned style, authoritative and concise, with a minimum of local color and personal asides; yet his every sentence resonated with earnestness" (1983: 36).

Giddins's encomium should prompt readers to place Williams historically. He, like Harrison, was a child of the New Critics. Indeed, Williams's masterwork, *The Jazz Tradition* (1970, 1983), finds an analog in Cleanth Brooks and Robert Penn Warren's *The Well Wrought Urn* (1947). Sargeant's *Jazz: A History* is to jazz studies what Ezra Pound's *ABC of Reading* is to poetry studies. That is to say, all three of these jazzologists treat jazz recordings as autonomous works of art rewarding close analysis.

This structuralist-formalist approach to the study of jazz, to which virtually all postwar jazzologists pledge some allegiance, is enormously compelling. It has effectively transformed jazz discourse into something like an emerging discipline. Take, for example, Larry Gushee's analysis of Duke Ellington's "Ko-Ko"—one of twenty-eight explications found in the liner notes to *Duke Ellington 1940* (Smithsonian, n.d.). I have chosen it because it is brief and because it demonstrates structuralist-formalist analysis at its absolute best. Gushee effectively communicates relatively complex information to a general audience. He begins with a schematic "over-all plan," a formula indicating the structure of the piece. Its capital letters indicate *I*ntroduction, the main harmonic points of division (including variations), and the *T*ag; numbers indicate measures.

Ko-Ko

$$I_8 \; A_{12} \; B_{24} \; A'_{12} \; A''_{12} \; B'_8 \; A'''_{12} \; T[I_8 + _4]$$

It's odd that two quite distinct major landmarks in jazz—this along with Charlie Parker's reworking of *Cherokee*—should have the same title. Here the emotional vein exploited is that of primitivism and savagery, and it does not surprise to learn (via Barry Ulanov) that *Ko-Ko* is an excerpt from a projected opera on an African theme, *Boola*. The work is mostly minor blues, but that says nothing about the symmetry of form . . . or the climactic plan. After the first chorus mixing Tizol [on trombone] with the reeds, the second is a gangly 24 measures

consisting to my ears of an initial four bars and seemingly end-
less extensions for Nanton [on trumpet] and the brass. Matters
are brought to a preliminary peak in A', with the saxes in G-
flat major against the basic E-flat minor and Duke splattering
chords and runs all over the keyboard. A" retreats to convention, and then is followed with a compressed restatement of
the alternating harmonies of B, and finally the climactic fourth
blues chorus with a concentration of dissonant brass writing
such as had never been heard in any "dance" band. (n.p.)

The widespread acceptance of this sort of analysis offers testimony
to its value. Imagine how impoverished literary studies would be
without close readings of texts. Then again, imagine literary studies completely dominated by structuralist-formalist analysis—
where scholarly labor was nothing but a synonym for *explication
du texte*. (As John Lennon sang, "It isn't very hard to do.") Jazz
studies, I suspect, longs to become such a discipline. Maybe that's
a good thing. It could be that structuralism-formalism is a necessary stage in the cognitive development of any discipline. But even
then, jazzology ought to be wary. Musicology, its parent or tutor
discipline, looks suspiciously like a case of arrested development.
And this is not solely an outsider's perspective. Susan McClary,
who is herself an exceptional musicologist, proves my generalization by citing still other exceptions:

> There is, to be fair, a tiny cadre of American musicologists
> that has persistently advocated and practiced music criticism
> for the last thirty years. They include most prominently
> Edward T. Cone, Joseph Kerman, Leonard B. Meyer, Charles
> Rosen, Maynard Solomon, and Leo Treitler. Over the years,
> these critics have been a salutary presence in an otherwise
> arid discipline, for their work focuses on the music itself and
> attempts to deal with meaning as it is produced in various
> moments of music history. Their detailed, insightful interpre-
> tations of music compositions have demonstrated over and
> over again how to write about music with tremendous lucid-
> ity and integrity—in a field otherwise noteworthy for its
> absence and suspicion of intellectual activity. (1991:173)

"What I would call serious music criticism," wrote Joseph Kerman
in 1985, "does not exist as a discipline on par with musicology and
music theory on the one hand, or literary and art criticism on the

other" (17). Thanks to notable work by Krin Gabbard, Bernard Gendron, Scott Deveaux, Robert Walser, Ron Radano, John Corbett, Christopher Harlos, Eric Lott, Jed Rasula, and others, Kerman's assessment describes jazz studies less accurately than it did ten years ago. Still, it's fair to wonder, Why are jazzologists so generally committed to analysis, to following the lead of musicologists? Why, notwithstanding some notable exceptions, is there a relative absence of academic jazz criticism?

Perhaps jazzologists are drawn to analysis for pragmatic reasons. The language of structuralist-formalist analysis is especially sufficient for explicating the typically short, recorded compositions of jazz (in much the same way that Russian formalism seemed tailor-made for analyzing folk tales). Nonetheless, any unexamined attraction belies certain anxieties. First, the desire to ground discourse about music upon a foundation of objectivity, to link it with scientific observation and mathematics, while as old as Pythagoras, manifests an uneasiness with the conventional cultural perception of music as the most ephemeral art. More succinctly, it indicates insecurity. Structuralist-formalist jazzologists are uneasy about the status of jazz and jazz studies (and if they are academics without tenure or freelance journalists, they have their own status to worry about). Hoping to validate their object of study, as well as the discourse system that represents that object, these critics have embraced scientific methodology. This is the conjunction that informs jazz studies.

With it comes a problem. The rule of *charivari* teaches us to suspect that the conjunction of jazz and scientific methodology is made possible only by disjunction. But of what sort? Musicology doesn't provide us with the slightest clue (unless we take our lead from the exceptional scholars listed above). Poststructuralist critical theory, however, offers a ready answer: a shivaree that could teach jazzology a vital lesson. It goes like this: Knowledge (conjunction: combining some ideas) is always created by ignorance (disjunction: suppressing other ideas). Or as Paul de Man put it: Blindness causes insight. The substantial knowledge effects generated by musical analysis are obtained by ignoring or by concealing "a whole world of mediating presuppositions of an economic, social, aesthetic and political order" that intervenes between it and its object of study (Hawkes, 154). According to poststructuralist logic, then, the problem of jazzology isn't how to arrive at a more perfect knowledge that forever banishes not knowing by ignoring absolutely nothing. And it's certainly not how to be more rigorously analytical. Rather, the problem comes down to addressing a few questions. Is analytical knowledge, the conjunction of jazz and science, worth the kinds of ignorance that it costs? And if it isn't, what kinds of knowledge are worth pursuing? What kinds of ignorance (disjunctions) might we safely—or profitably—live with?

To summarize the consequences of music studies built on scientific methodology, I offer, first, an observation, then, an illustration. While the classical canon is arguably an effect of cultural politics, the analytical discourse of classical music (itself an apparatus of cultural politics) has served to disguise or normalize the complex system of inclusions and exclusions that make the canon possible; its primary task has been to make musical history feel like an evolution, not like revolutionary struggle. On the other hand, the discourse of jazz, both professional and amateur, has faced a dilemma. It has been called upon to serve a function similar to that of its classical counterpart: build an institution by creating and defending the *jazz tradition*: a canon and a history. Analysis is sufficient for this task. And it has been called upon to expose the reasons for the marginal status of jazz: lay bare the institutional-political basis for music making. Analysis is an impediment to this task.

Jazzologists have neatly solved this double call by adopting the role of *chasse beaux*. They routinely clamor about "unnatural" alignments—the conjunction of jazz and racism, jazz and the culture industry, or jazz and standard notation comprise three suitably diverse examples—while cheerfully bedding down with analysis and abandoning self-reflexive examination (that is, the very sort of introspection that jazzology prizes in jazz musicians). To illustrate what I mean, let me conclude with an anecdote.

Back in the late 1980s, Martin Williams gave me a short manuscript. It began with the following scenario (strangely reminiscent of an already described scene from *Jailhouse Rock*): Williams is at a cocktail party, when a woman, beaming enthusiasm, rushes up to him and launches into a litany of praise for New Age pianist George Winston. She gushes something on the order of, "Isn't he marvelous!" Williams, amused, asks her if she knows how to play piano. She admits that she doesn't, and he declares that he doesn't either. "Can you touch type?" he asks. She says, "Yes." "Well then," he says, "give me an hour, and I'll teach you to play like George Winston."

Actually, now that I think about it, Williams may have written "two hours" or he may have written "forty-five minutes." I'm bad with quantities, but I vividly remember my feelings. I was terribly disappointed with the article.

I had met Williams at a conference in Atlanta; we hit it off immediately. He knew that I was copyediting manuscripts for *Jazziz*. And I told him—it was the truth—that I made absolutely no editorial decisions about what was or wasn't published in the magazine. That was the job of Michael Fagien, the publisher. I remember being relieved when he gave me no grief about the magazine's focus on "pop-jazz," and I was flattered when he entrusted me with a manuscript.

As I read it, back in my hotel room, I realized that Michael would never publish it. And I didn't want him to. It made Williams look mean, petty, vengeful: patriarchal in the worst sort of way. I returned home to Gainesville, Florida, where I was living at the time, and dutifully showed Michael the manuscript. I can't remember what he said. That's not a matter of repression. It's something like perfect communication. Michael and I didn't exactly share an aesthetic, but we were close friends. I had anticipated his decision. *Jazziz* wouldn't publish Martin Williams's essay on George Winston.

An ingenue in poststructuralist clothing, I volunteered to phone Williams and explain "the magazine's" decision. But instead of trotting out the editorial policy of *Jazziz*, I decided to quiz Williams on the logic of his anti–New Age stance. This was a mistake. We talked for about thirty minutes. Paradigms clashed. "Look," I reasoned, "you championed Ornette Coleman in the face of critics who declared that he blew sax with all the finesse and facility of a second-grader. Can't you see that New Age music shares at least one feature with the avant-garde. It has reacted against the complexity of jazz? It affirms an aesthetic that includes simplicity. Furthermore, who are you to deny another person's pleasure? Can't you see how your so-called analysis shapes taste, shapes the 'jazz tradition'?"

Williams responded, in a word, as a modernist. He declared that the "jazz tradition" existed independently of him, that some pleasures were more shallow than others, that New Age music was less simple than simplistic, and that the music of Ornette Coleman—"Had I really listened as closely as I had claimed"—was deceivingly complex. Ornette's critics had been mistaken.

I blithely pressed on, but deference had evaporated, and my arguments came down to a zealous attempt to convert Williams to poststructuralism. Jazz writing, I maintained, was unwilling to concede that analysis and criticism were thoroughly entangled and, furthermore, that so-called objective analysis was just a form, an institutionally sanctioned form, of criticism. Objectivity, after all, is nothing but a mask worn by taste; sometimes it hides hatred, most often it hides love.

Williams, of course, bought none of this. I'm sure he regarded it as postmodernist blather and wrote me off as a lost cause, a symptom of the sorry state of jazz writing. We never spoke to one another again. He died in 1992.

Part of me claims that, in this anecdote, I'm doing nothing but trying to get the last word in an argument that ended years ago. Writing becomes a way to mourn: rewrite or reopen the tomb of history. Another more confident part of me knows differently. Within the realm of writing, within the realm of jazz, there is no final word. What disappointed me most about Williams wasn't his negative opinion of George Winston—I was indifferent about that— but his opinion of his opinion. Before we argued, I had always regarded Williams's writing as the first step in a project that could show musicology what jazzology might look like after structuralism/formalism. I admired the way Williams always failed to mask his love of jazz: the way his most studied observations seemed motivated by ardor. I wished that he had read Roland Barthes. After we argued, I realized that Williams did not share my view of his writing. He regarded it as a final step in the popularization of structuralist/formalist analysis. I still think he was wrong.

Paradigm: A Lesson from Jones's "The Screamers" and Ulmer's *CATTt*

> *Militant memories: For months, years after his passing Double would appear through my sleep to bump a lesser dream, still bopping with the armed resistance of his dedication to "jazz"—which he said was "two, say three broad crooked jumps off to the side of the mainstream straight and narrow, out to where sound becomes sight, as it should be!"*
> —Xam Wilson Cartiér (8)

> *It was that last cymbal crash that did it.*
> —Thomas Pynchon (1984:85)

The story told by LeRoi Jones's "The Screamers" is simple. A frenzied nightclub audience, led by a honking tenor saxophonist, dances its way onto the streets of Newark, staging a symbolic coup d'état. When "America's responsible immigrants" arrive with "paddy wagons and cruisers," the carnival ends (1990:267). On one level, through the interpretive lens of structuralism, this tale is little more than a revolutionary pipe dream. It refunctions the legend of the Pied Piper, casting as hero a Big Jay McNeeley imitator. The honk of his saxophone—jazz incarnated as noise—becomes a means of focusing our attention on "an anomaly in the unfolding of a syntagmatic sequence." A political monster (or leviathan) has broken a "natural" order and appropriated what, by rights, belongs to others. Hence, the people and their streets are in a state of disjunction. On another level, "The Screamers" provides us with a myth for writing with the trope of *charivari*. It audaciously suggests that "the honk"—a "repeated rhythmic figure, a screamed riff, pushed in its insistence past music"—can function as "a basis for thought" (264). Lévi-Strauss's theory of *charivari* is shown as useful for more than hermeneutics, and Jones's story is shown as more than merely susceptible to structural analysis. "The Screamers" performs a myth of noisemaking; it is *about* jazz as *charivari*: that is, as parasitic (of mass culture), marginal (with respect to the marketplace), and oppositional (antagonistic toward classical, bourgeois verities). Moreover, it demonstrates one way of writing *with* the trope of *charivari*: allegory. A few sentences ago, when I declared that "The Screamers" pairs jazz with a *dream of revolution*, I was not reaching for an easy interpretation. The story demands that we read it allegorically. Describing the night revelers' march to the streets, Jones writes:

> We screamed and screamed at the clear image of ourselves as we should always be. Ecstatic, completed, involved in a secret communal expression. It would be the form of the sweetest revolution, to hucklebuck into the fallen capital, and let the oppressors lindy hop out. (267)

Allegory, Jones rightly understands, is an appropriative reading practice, the textual analog of (unsuitable) marriages and eclipses, and the noise that salutes them. "The allegorist," writes Craig Owens, "does not invent images but confiscates them. He lays claim to the culturally significant, poses as its interpreter. And in his hands the image becomes something other (*allos* = other + *agoreuei* = to speak)" (69). Like the jazz musician or the heuretic theorist, he gleefully distorts "standards."

Or notice that allegories are texts dreaming or, conversely, that dreams allegorize unconscious desires. This insight is, of course, foundational for hermeneutics and psychoanalysis, both cryptographic sciences. The founding insight for heuretics is Gregory Ulmer's observation that (1) every method, every theory, "must itself be represented in some form or genre" and (2) that "[t]he popularity of any genre is relative to its appropriateness for 'representing the public concerns' of its moment" (1994:9, 87). Invention advances according to the "law" of the idiom: "thinking begins not from the generalized classifications of subject formation, but from the specific experiences historically situated." We think through stories—that is, by means of particular experiences—even when our thinking is directed against the institutions that formed us (Ulmer, 1989a:viii). In a sense stories are caught; they spread much like diseases. Knowledge has an epidemiologic.

Heuretics exploits this insight. Comparing "The Manifesto of Surrealism" (André Breton) with various classics on method—most notably by Plato, Ramus, and Descartes—Ulmer observes that these texts share a common set of elements: *contrast* (opposing a new method to an old one), *analogy* (figuration as a tactic of displacement), *theory* (repetition and literalization of the newly proposed method), *target* (proposed area for application of the new method), and *tale* (a dramatization of the new method). Thus, heuretics may be understood as a heuristic (*CATTt*) used to invent theory (methods), and Ulmer's *CATT*, a morphology of theory analogous to V. I. Propp's morphology of the folktale, turns out to be adequate for both analyzing and making a theory of method (Ulmer, 1994:8). It isn't, however, especially exciting. (Then again, excitement isn't everything. Some of the avant-garde's most interesting results have been generated by some of its most rigorous and boring methods: for example, recall that Cage's signature experiment—writing *through* books by constructing "mesostics" on the author's name—yielded both poetry and music.) Excitement, if that's what we're looking for, lies in the *tale* that conveys theory. It often dramatizes what it recommends. For example, as Ulmer notes, "Plato's dialogues represented his premise that learning must be face-to-face conversation. His discourse on method [*Phaedrus*] did what it said (was a showing as well as a telling)" (8).

This elemental observation has tremendous implications for heuretics. It suggests that a complete theory (a fully developed *CATT*) "could be generated by choosing the tale first and then imagining the learning experience appropriate to it" (9). What

Ulmer does in *Heuretics* is put his own tale to work. He interrogates his mystory as an alternative to ratio-analytical problem solving; he decomposes it into a "method for cyberwriting" (139). This is finally what distinguishes heuretics from contemporary reinvestigations of autobiography. Instead of *topography*, revisiting the places or *topos* of one's story, heuretics proposes *chorography*. Between being and becoming, *chora*—a word developed by Plato in *Timaeus* and defined by Francis Cornford as "space" or "receptacle"—is maddeningly resistant to interpretation (63). Still, through a route we shall not retrace, Ulmer finds a powerful simile for *chora* in the jazz term *riff*. He states: "The project is to learn to write with patterns that function more like music than like concepts" (91). Eureka! Thus, Ulmer identifies writing *with* jazz as a variety of *chorography*.

Schuller accounts for the emergence of the riff. It came about when "the repeated refrain structure of the blues" combined with the call-and-response patterns of gospel sermons (more sung than orated) and "found its way into the marching jazz of New Orleans."

> From there it infiltrated the entire spectrum of jazz from the improvised solo to the arranged ensemble. . . . The riff became an integral structural device in the strongly rocking jazz of the Southwest, centering in Kansas City and fanning out from there through the Benny Moten band, and later through Count Basie, to become eventually an overworked cliché of the Swing Era. (28–29)

Riff writing is another name for chorographic writing, which is, in turn, another name for writing with the trope of *charivari*. It is recommended for two reasons. First, because it "suggests the possibility of a method that is never practiced the same way twice," it is conducive to discovery (Ulmer, 1994:75). Riffing—*charivaric* or chorographic writing—treats what were once topics as points of relay. (This is why jazz musicians often speak of themselves as receivers and improvisation as a matter of transmission.) The stories or tales of chorographers don't beg for interpretation so much as they demand to be played; they function in a manner analogous to pots and pans at a shivaree or chords in a bebop tune. Second, writing *with* jazz, by whatever designation, encourages exploration of a still emerging paradigm. As mentioned before, jazz didn't emerge in an oral culture (America is not mythic Africa; jazzmen are not griots). And except as a reaction, jazz is not a response to print technology, since African Americans were routinely denied access to the benefits of published music. Jazz is, in fact, a response to and an effect of electronic culture (radio and records). As surely as cinema, it invented strategies for navigating electronic space. Louis Armstrong isn't a late arriving epic poet; hc's an early arriving cyberwriter. He has lessons to teach us about what is to come.

Assignment: Jazzing the Popular Dimension

> Here is all the true orator will ask, for here is a convertible audience & here are no stiff conventions that prescribe a method, a style, a limited quotation of books, & an exact respect to certain books, persons, or opinions. No, here everything is admissible, philosophy, ethics, divinity, criticism, poetry, humor, fun, mimicry, anecdotes, jokes, ventriloquism. All the breadth & versatility of the most liberal conversation <the most> high↑est↓ <the most> low↑est↓ <the most> personal <the most> local topics, all are permitted, and all may be combined in one speech; it is a panharmonicon,—every note on the longest gamut, from the explosion of cannon, to the tinkle of a guitar. . . . Here he may lay himself out utterly, large, enormous, prodigal, on the subject of the hour. Here he may dare to hope for ecstasy & eloquence.
> —Ralph Waldo Emerson (265)

The general task here is to rethink research in the Western tradition (which metaphorizes knowledge as frontier) for an electronic apparatus. The specific task is no less ambitious. It is to show how one might write *with* the trope of *charivari* as an alternative to writing jazzology.

To initiate this project (and do notice that the discourse of this assignment is unavoidably haunted by the very dead metaphors it would exorcise), choose an icon or "mythic image" that for you represents jazz. It should haunt you like a phantom limb; you should love it. Construed broadly, this icon might be a photograph, a poem, a fragment of music or text, a still or scene from a movie, but it could also be another sort of material object (a readymade). Whatever you select, make sure that it is something toward which you feel strong affection. Next, as a heuretic experiment, fashion a text that plays (or traces your play with) your iconic, mythic representation of jazz.

Interpretation isn't the goal here. Don't read your icon as classical musicians "read" scores. And if you decide to interrogate your affection, remember that such interrogation is a means, not a goal. Rather, treat your representing image of jazz as a text. Employ it as jazz musicians employ "riffs": as series of relays, patterns to follow and shape.

The key words in successfully completing this experiment in writing *with* the trope of *charivari* are *breaking* (a syntagmatic sequence), *intruding* (no illusions of dramatic distance), and *appropriating* (willed distortion). Assume interpellation. Start with the realization that you have been seduced and seized by a "popular" representation of jazz. You don't put it to work. And don't let it pimp you. Instead, you return its affection. (If there's going to be a shivaree marking this union, let readers provide it.) You let your icon guide you, reorient your writing toward its secrets, its method. Why? Because this is a way popular culture can teach theory how to write within electronic culture.

Experiment: The Tenor's Vehicle: *Way out West*

> *A prominent white educator was studying the culture of the Hopi, a desert-dwelling Native American tribe of the Southwest. He found it strange that almost all Hopi music was about water and asked one of the musicians why. He explained that so much of their music was about water because that was what they had the least of. And then he told the white man, "Most of your music is about love."*
>
> —Mose Allison (4)

> *Photographs looked as if they were replicas when in fact they were metaphors; they appeared to be records of actuality when they were frequently allegories; they seemed to display a few simple truths when, as often as not, they were paradoxes.*
>
> —Michael Lesy (7)

Cadenza (Reprise)

By now everyone should know the anecdote about Louis Armstrong and the socialite. If you don't, you probably never will.

Confessions of a Columnist

For some time, I've reviewed jazz recordings for Tower Records's magazine, *Pulse!*. In March 1990, my column began:

> Sonny Rollins's tone is something like the sonic equivalent of my wife's Newfoundland dog. It's burly, warm and smart. Nobody, but nobody, sounds like the Saxophone Colossus. He remains one of jazz's great originals, a prodigiously gifted improviser. (1990a:74)

I continued in this vein, singling out Rollins's then-current album, *Falling in Love with Jazz*, for special praise, rehearsing its particular virtues.

Like all descriptions of music or, for that matter, like all descriptions of art, mine relies on tautology and simile. I call *Falling in Love with Jazz* "a paradigm of what great jazz can be" (a tautology), but qualify my approval by admitting that it "lacks the intensity of, say, *G-Man* [an earlier recording], or the sheer visceral punch of Rollins live" (a simile). I, thereby, fall back on what Roland Barthes calls "a vast commonplace of literature" and, in effect, declare that this record is a repetition of the "previously played," the "already written." Barthes writes: "Beauty cannot assert itself save in the form of a citation"; deprived of "anterior codes," it "would be mute" (1974:33–34). The critic's task, then, is to store up signs—reference codes—for the sake of predicating beauty, bringing it into language.

As a record reviewer, I've done that. I've cultivated a set of ideological biases (or, more generously, I've accepted an aesthetic shared by fellow reviewers) and acquired an institutionally sanctioned discourse; I've processed so much music that I can tell whether a disc is "good" after listening for a few minutes. More honestly, I can normally determine whether I'll like a recording by merely glancing at its cover. I'm prejudiced by names, typography, and graphics. I listen, the first time through, in order to confirm or contradict what the album's jacket has already told me. After that, I listen either for pleasure or out of a sense of professional obligation. Finally, I predicate the musical work, translate it into a network of adjectives, into an epithet (Barthes, 1977b:179).

The goal of my work is the goal of all "normal" criticism or scholarship: "both a *mathesis* ['the closure of a homogeneous body of knowledge'] and a *mimesis*" (Barthes, 1985:238, 237). In exegesis the critic seeks to fashion, out of institutionally dictated predicates, an utterance that readers will decode as *literal*, as discourse transparently representing an object of study. He avoids sets of predicates that might be perceived as entirely predictable (redundant or conventional) or completely ineffable (entropic or unmotivated) and, thereby, constructs a work that will pass as at once original (a genesis) and definitive (an apocalypse).

Image-Music-Text

There is, however, another way to write. "The scholar's choice," Barthes declares, "is finally between two *styles*: the plain (*écrivance*—'clarity, suppression of images, respect for the laws of reasoning') or the rhetorical (*écriture*—writing or 'the play of the signifier')" (qtd. in Ulmer, 1980:65). The *plain style*, "the regular discourse of research" or language used literally, produces a "Work." If its claims are evident, this Work is received as "science"; if its claims are considered "secret, ultimate, something to be sought out," then it "falls under the scope of a hermeneutics, of an interpretation (Marxist, psychoanalytic, thematic, etc.)" (Barthes, 1977b:158). The *rhetorical style*, "writing" or language used figuratively, produces "Text" ("a *mise en scène* . . . not of content but of the detours, twists, in short the bliss of the symbolic") (Barthes, 1985:238).

How is this done? What could it mean to write rhetorically? Barthes answers this question when he likens writing and the "scarcely differentiated activity" of reading-as-production to *playing*—the generation of perpetual signifiers. He elaborates:

> "Playing" must be understood here in all its polysemy: the text itself *plays* (like a door, like a machine with "play") and the reader plays twice over, playing the Text as one plays a game, looking for a practice which re-produces it, but, in order that that practice not be reduced to a passive, inner *mimesis* (the Text is precisely that which resists such a reduction), also playing the Text in the musical sense of the term. The history of music (as a practice, not as an "art") does indeed parallel that of the Text fairly closely: there was a period when practicing amateurs were numerous (at least within the confines of a certain class) and "playing" and "listening" formed a scarcely differentiated activity. (1977b:162)

Writing as *"playing* with the text" or reading as co-authorship does not struggle against adjectival tyranny ("diverting the adjective you find on the tip of the tongue towards some substantive or verbal periphrasis") (180). Neither does it seek to retrieve a hidden Work, give it "expression." Rather, in refusing mimesis and interpretation, except as effects, it changes the object of study itself, altering our "perception or intellection" of the way the object presents itself to discourse (Perloff, 117). Text allows and, therefore, demands that readers map and remap: brand and rebrand. Works give rise to commentary (plod the dusty trails of criticism); Texts prompt affabulation (wander an open range of associations). They proceed parasitically, "alongside of" or "aside from."

In the following paragraphs I want to collapse "reading" (writing as interpretation) and "writing" (writing as invention), treat them as "scarcely differentiated" activities; I want to model a *third form* of writing that cuts across or combines the stylistic categories described by Barthes:

> neither a text of vanity, nor a text of lucidity, but a text with uncertain quotation marks, with floating parentheses (never to close the parenthesis is very specifically: *to drift*). (1977a:106)

Because it projects the rhetorical style onto the plain style, the metaphorical axis of language onto its metonymic dimension, my *drifting read*, a hybrid Work/Text, might be regarded as a reinvestigation of allegory (Owens, 72). Autobiographical, journalistic, and anecdotal materials—the novelistic—are "played out" in order to evoke (and, then, to resist reduction to) the critical and theoretical— the essayistic. Its reliance on what Craig Saper dubs "rigorous unsystematized thinking" should also prompt readers to identify this type of writing with experiments of Florida School theorists such as Gregory Ulmer, Robert Ray, and Saper himself (1988:393). Simply put, it is applied grammatology—heuretics: oriented toward the pleasures of theory, the development and popularization of a poststructuralist writing practice. Without abandoning the philosophical critique of literature (identified with the Yale School and deconstruction) or the critique of culture and institutions (identified with the University of Birmingham Centre for Contemporary Cultural Studies and the Center for 20th Century Studies at the University of Wisconsin), it aims to employ popular culture (the entertainment industry) as a source of and means to invention and innovation.

Amateur de musique

For a long time, from the eighth to the eleventh grade, I was an amateur musician. I played B-flat clarinet in school bands. Nowadays, my instrument sits unused in a bedroom closet, and I listen to recordings made by professionals (among clarinetists, I dote on Barney Bigard, Pee Wee Russell, Artie Shaw, Jimmy Giuffre, and Don Byron). Playing music has become for me a matter of consumption, not production (my condition parallels that of readers who have delegated literary work to specialists: critics, theorists, and authors—Barthes, 1974:4). And what to play has become a problem. Because record companies send me many new releases, I own hundreds of discs. I readily admit, however, that my collection reflects not so much what I like (though I like what I collect), but what I hope to find the time one day to "really" enjoy. Nevertheless, to a certain degree my situation—a *simulation* of unlimited resources—is not unique. It is replicated whenever anyone has unrestricted access to libraries, archives, galleries, the inventory of a store, and data bases.

Record reviews channel my listening. Writing them provides a means of managing overchoice: an effect of mechanical reproduction and the commodification of music (the reduction of "playing" to "listening"). But they also, contradictorily, exacerbate, or at least make more than theoretical, information overload. With the writing of reviews come more recordings, more choices. Thus we should observe that the top-ten or desert-island list, a staple of journalistic criticism, signifies the end of choice, of commodity fetishism. It is eschatological, predicated on an apocalyptic fantasy that allows writers to imagine themselves surviving some beneficent catastrophe that has winnowed the positively essential from the merely engaging, thus granting a release from the burden of actually attending to what they have hoarded (while at the same time holding forth the promise of a fresh beginning).

That off my chest, here is a list: My Top-Ten Record Covers. These images, closely entwined with sounds I love, enthrall me without my knowing exactly why ("such ignorance is the very nature of fascination"—Barthes, 1977a:3).

1. *Way out West*—Sonny Rollins (Contemporary, 1957); designer, Guidi/Tri Arts; photographer, William Claxton.
2. *Murmur*—R.E.M. (I.R.S., 1983); designer, Ann Kinney, Carl Grasso, and Sandra Lee Phipps; photographer, Sandra Lee Phipps.

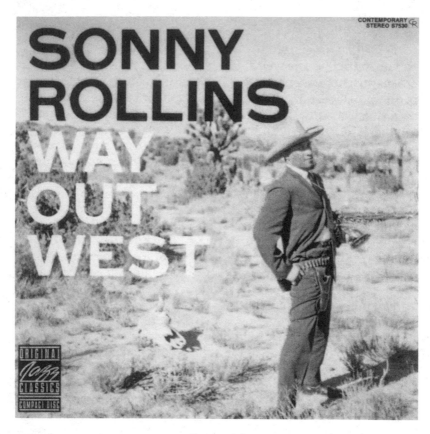

FIGURE 4.1

Sonny Rollins to Gary Giddings: "Don't ever shrink from the belief that you have to prove yourself every minute, because you do" (qtd. in Balliett, 1991:58). (*Way out West*, courtesy of Contemporary Records, 1957)

3. *Sweetheart of the Rodeo*—The Byrds (Columbia, 1968); designer, Geller and Butler Advertising; illustration, Jo Mora, 1933.
4. *Porgy and Bess*—Miles Davis (Columbia, 1958); photographer, Roy de Carava.
5. *Elvis Presley* (RCA, 1956); designer, Colonel Tom Parker; photographer: Popsie [William S. Randolph].
6. *London Calling*—The Clash (Epic, 1979); designer, Ray Lowry; photographer, Pennie Smith.
7. *The Basement Tapes*—Bob Dylan and The Band (Columbia, 1975); designer, Bob Cato; photographer, Reid Miles.

8. *This is Mecolodics*—The Universal Congress of (SST, 1988); designer, Jason Kahn; photographer, Martin Lyon.
9. *Dancing in Your Head*—Ornette Coleman (A&M, 1977); designer, Dorothy Baer.
10. *Underground*—Thelonious Monk (Columbia, 1969); designer, John Berg and Dick Mantel; photographer, Horn/Griner.

Just as writing is traditionally conceived as supplementary to speech (see Derrida's discussion of Rousseau's *Confessions* in *Of Grammatology*), so too a sartorially motivated nomenclature determines that jackets, covers, and sleeves supplement records (see Jonathan Swift's discussion of jackets in *A Tale of a Tub*). Record wrappers *add* to that which is present (are, therefore, accessories appended to music), and they *replace* that which is not present (that is, the musician's image) (Johnson, xiii). They can be read, writes John Corbett, as an "attempt to reconstitute the image of the disembodied voice," "to stitch the cut that separates seeing from hearing in the contemporary listening scenario" (1994:39). "Yet it can be shown that this project of reappropriation is inherently self-subverting" (Johnson, xi). Insofar as they imply absence ("lack of the visual, endemic to recorded sound"), album jackets, covers, and sleeves point toward a *desire* for presence, not toward some lost but recuperable plenitude. They mark a fundamental and originary lack: one that initiates the desire from which all recording technologies spring, "the erotic spark that drives the music industry motor" (Corbett, 37, 40).

The Rustle of Language

After deciding to write about two photographs that became front covers to Sonny Rollins's *Way out West* (1957)—I submitted to the urge that drives the endeavors of all specialists. Like Flaubert's characters Bouvard and Pecuchet, I sought to arm myself with knowledge; I borrowed lots of books from the library (stacked on the floor of my bedroom, they reminded me of Monument Valley). For example, on the subject of cowboys, I thumbed through the following:

- Edward Douglas Branch, *The Cowboy and His Interpreters*
- Mark H. Brown and W. R. Felton, *Before Barbed Wire*
- Jenni Calder, *There Must Be a Lone Ranger*
- Edward Everett Dale, *Cow Country*

- David Dary, *Cowboy Culture: A Saga of Five Centuries*
- Philip Durham and Everett L. Jones, *The Negro Cowboys*
- Emerson Hough, *The Story of the Cowboy*
- William MacLeod Raine, *Cattle, Cowboys and Rangers*
- William W. Savage, *The Cowboy Hero: His Image in American History & Culture*
- Richard W. Slatta, *Cowboys of the Americas*
- Lonn Taylor and Ingrid Maar, *The American Cowboy*
- Jane Tompkins, *West of Everything: The Inner Life of Westerns*
- Will Wright, *Sixguns and Society: A Structural Study of the Western*

Thumbed though them, mind you. I did not peruse. As Marianna Torgovnick notes: "No one who gets around to writing a book, or even an essay, ever reads everything that has been written about its subject" (27). Besides, I'm not only bored by but suspicious of works that lay bare myths constructing the West. Demythologizing is most often an excuse for aggression. The traditional critical essay, observes Jane Tompkins, reproduces the western's confrontational structure. As an imagined arena in which truth is not yet established (an intellectual frontier), it legitimates conflict as an epistemology, much as its analog romanticizes violence as a solution to moral and social dilemmas. In traditional scholarship the hero-scholar provoked by what he considers an insult, retaliates, "proving his moral superiority" (585–86).

But what if, as Tompkins recommends, we heed the voice of Amy (Grace Kelly) in *High Noon*? Just before Will (Gary Cooper) shoots it out with Frank Miller's gang, she exclaims: "I don't care who's right or who's wrong. There has to be some better way to live!" In other words, what could an alternative to the traditional critical essay look like? Or as Gregory Ulmer puts it, how might one drop the struggle for truth (expressed by the scholar's affection for classical reasoning and problem solving) as the means of organizing knowledge? (1989a:50).

Sax and Violence

In 1846, Adolphe Sax, son of the largest wind-instrument producer in Europe, took out a patent on a family of instruments he called saxophones. Music critic Mike Zwerin writes: the saxophone combined "the speed of woodwinds with the carrying power of brass" and was intended "to replace clarinets, oboes, and bassoons in military bands." In fact, it accomplished this aim after Sax won a "battle of the bands held on Paris's Champs de Mars," thus securing numerous orders for the instrument from the government of King Louis-Philippe. "The Revolution of 1848, however, intervened and official support dried up. Sax went bankrupt."

In the course of his life Sax "declared three bankruptcies, and jealous competitors made three attempts to kill him. On occasion his premises were trashed, furniture wrecked, and expensive tools stolen. One hapless employee, on an unusually late call to Sax, was stabbed through the heart. As the victim and Sax were of a similar build, an inquest concluded that the inventor had been the intended target." All told, Sax took out forty-six patents; one, significantly, was for the "'Saxocannon,' a monster mortar that could fire a shot of 550 tons" (Zwerin, 102–4).

Cock-and-Bull Story

This textualist parable from Texas speaks of the most frequently visited commonplace of semiotics: the arbitrariness and the iterability of the sign. The story goes that in 1847, Samuel A. Maverick, a lawyer living on the San Antonio River, acquired four hundred head of cattle as settlement for a debt. Unwilling to forsake his legal practice, he entrusted the beasts to one of his slaves. "The Negro," write Philip Durham and Everett Jones, "neglected to do much branding, and the cattle roamed free, growing and multiplying on the open Texas range." In 1856, Maverick sold his land, cattle, and brand to A. Toutant Beauregard, a rancher with ambition. He, in turn, "sent . . . men riding over several counties, searching for Maverick's cattle." Whenever they found an animal unbranded, they claimed it as Maverick's: that is, as their own (14–15).

1. Rollins's improvisations on *Way out West*—aberrant readings of "I'm an Old Cowhand" and "Wagon Wheels"—and his appropriation of the iconography of the American West for the album's cover—his "rewriting" of the image of buffalo soldier—are comparable to the textualist practice Gregory Ulmer identifies as a "new mimesis." This "representation without reference" or mavericking by other means—practiced most notably by Barthes, Derrida, Gilles Deleuze, and Félix Guattari—amounts to a perversion of the Western construct of *properness*: property and propriety (Ulmer, 1983:91–92). Poststructuralists respond to "State philosophy" (Western metaphysics) as Beauregard's cowboys responded to

unbranded cattle and as jazz musicians respond to the products of Tin Pan Alley (that is, to "standards").

2. ABC introduced *Maverick*, a television series that parodied every convention of the western, in 1957, the very year that Contemporary Records released *Way out West*. It was at this "exact moment," writes Robert Ray, that "mythological self-consciousness began to appear prominently in American popular culture" (1985:256–57). In the summer of 1994, *Maverick* was remade as a movie, and, of course, the White House was occupied by a saxophonist.

3. Malcolm McLaren, the provocateur who packaged the Sex Pistols, describes rap's scratch or "Do-It-Yourself" process on the record cover of "Buffalo Girls" (1982).

> Two manual decks and a rhythm box are all you need. Get a bunch of good rhythm records, choose your favorite parts and groove along with the rhythm machine. Use your hands, scratch the record by repeating the grooves you dig so much. Fade one record into another and keep that rhythm box going. Now start talking and singing over the record with the microphone. Now you're making your own music out of other people's records. That's what scratching is. (Qtd. in Taylor, 14)

McLaren, of course, did not invent scratching. He merely heard a good idea (the "dubbing" practiced by New York and Jamaican disk jockeys) and appropriated it. "He's very clever," said Boy George, "but he takes the credit for everything, including the things he never touched" (qtd. in Taylor, 12).

4. In this age of mechanical reproduction, we do well if we learn to maverick. Listening to "The Surrey with the Fringe on Top" (Rollins), *Duck Rock* (McLaren), and *Paul's Boutique* (the Beastie Boys), reading "Limited Inc a b c . . ." (Derrida), *S/Z* (Barthes), "Derrida at the Little Bighorn" (Ulmer), and *Flaubert's Parrot* (Julian Barnes), or looking at readymades by Marcel Duchamp or Sherrie Levine is to witness an exploitation of *copyright*, a concept that "now means the right to copy anything" (Ulmer, 1983:96). These texts celebrate the demise of the print medium, and they anticipate the advent of hypertext. Walter Benjamin writes: "Quotations in my works are like robbers by the roadside who make an armed attack and relieve an idler of his convictions" (qtd. in Arendt, 38). Robert Coover: "We are always astonished to discover how much of the reading and

writing experience occurs in the interstices and trajectories *between* text fragments" (24). In one of his notebooks, Leonardo da Vinci wrote:

> Seeing that I cannot choose any subject of great utility or pleasure, because my predecessors have already taken as their own all useful and necessary themes, I will do like one who, because of his poverty, is the last to arrive at the fair, and not being able otherwise to provide himself, chooses all the things which others have already looked over and not taken, but refused as being of little value. With these despised and rejected wares—the leavings of many buyers—I will load my modest pack, and therewith take my course, distributing, not indeed amid the great cities, but among the mean hamlets, and taking such reward as befits the things I offer. (1)

5. Laurie Anderson is from the Midwest. I'm from the South. But we both learned to maverick in the same place. In conversation with Nicholas Zurbrugg, Anderson explains:

> I grew up in the Bible Belt and spent a lot of my childhood listening to these stories, at Bible school, Bible camp, Sunday school and so on. And these stories were completely amazing. Outrageous stories! About parting oceans and talking snakes. And people really seemed to believe these stories. And I'm talking about adults. Adults who mainly just did the most mundane things imaginable (mowing their lawns, throwing potluck parties). They all believed in these wild stories. And they would sit around and discuss them in the most matter of fact way.

"So that was a kind of local surrealism," Zurbrugg declares. Anderson replies: "No, no, that was the local truth. Surrealism is an art term. We weren't artists." In the Jarrett family we discussed the Bible at the dinner table. That's where I discovered and practiced hermeneutics. Amidst our equivalent of loaves and fishes, I learned that people—made in the image of God, stamped with His brand, but rustled by Satan—were being rounded up by Jesus (the "express image" of the Father). The seminar tables of grad school, always devoid of food, lowered the stakes (and raised the rigor) of the family tableau. Zurbrugg asks Anderson: "How did you move from Bible Belt storytelling? When did you go through the art barrier, as it were?" She answers:

I haven't. I try to tell the truth as I see it. I'm just telling the same mixture of midwestern Bible stories that I always have. They're a mixture of the most mundane things with a fabulous twist on them. It's only what I learned in Bible school. How Bible school related to public schools is what I'm interested in. Always have been. (137)

Conversation with a Colossus

Having lost interest in telephone interviews with good and great musicians, I wanted to commune with the godhead. I contacted Milestone Records and asked Terri Hinte, director of publicity, if she could hook me up with Rollins: a saxophonist *Rolling Stone* magazine dubbed "one of the most inventive improvisers in the history of music"—"the last remaining titan" (Spencer 148). Months passed but, as always, Terri came though. Rollins and I talked for nearly an hour. *Cadence* published the interview (after *Interview* rejected it); that is, *Cadence* published everything except the following exchange, which I held back and, as part of a tiny feature, submitted to *Jazziz* (1990b:21). It became the germ from which this experiment grew.

JARRETT: My favorite record cover of all time is the one to *Way out West*. Was it your idea?

ROLLINS: The one on *Way out West*—it happened a long time ago. I'm pretty sure that it was my idea: the hat and the gun belt and all that stuff.

JARRETT: So how was it received? Was that a kick for your friends?

ROLLINS: It was very striking, very unusual. It was a big kick at the time. In fact recently I ran into a guy—there's a young tenor player in England called Courtney Pine. He came up to me and told me a story. He said that he didn't know what he wanted to do. He was just a kid, and when he saw this album—*Way out West*—he realized that he wanted to be a musician. So it's kind of nice when something like that happens. It was an unusual thing at the time, but I thought it went well with playing unusual songs for a jazz album. I thought that the whole thing was really right.

JARRETT: It's incredibly funny, ironic, anticipating one of the best jokes in *Blazing Saddles*. I look at it and laugh and then think, "This isn't funny. It's true. There were plenty of black cowboys."

ROLLINS: Exactly.

JARRETT: And jazz is metaphorically associated with myths of the American West: the musician as outlaw hero; the music as a movement or push outward. The cover says that. It works on many, many different levels.

ROLLINS: That's right. I've never thought of it in those words, but that's quite true. When I was a boy, I had seen these all-black films. There was a fellow who used to sing with Duke Ellington's Band, Herb Jeffries. He was in an all-black western. I remember that. I've forgotten whether it was *Rhythm on the Range* or *Bronze Buckaroo*, but that made an impression on me. And of course, as we all know, there were black cowboys. All of these things were in my mind.

Swinging Cowboys

Some estimates state that at least one fourth of the working cowboys in the late nineteenth century were African Americans; one fourth of the Hollywood films made between 1910 and the late '50s were westerns. Still, writes J. Hoberman, "the demographics of the western remained overwhelmingly white up until the eve of the genre's demise," when confidence in its "ethos of limitless growth and personal freedom" ebbed "in response to the struggle for civil rights at home and the question of imperial ambition abroad" (1991:53).

Herb Jeffries played the leading role in *Bronze Buckaroo* (1938, directed by R. C. Kahn). He also starred in *Harlem Rides the Range* (1939, directed by Sam Newfield). Rollins (born September 7, 1930) was eight or nine when he saw one or both of these films. I was born in 1953, the year Paramount released *Shane*; twenty years later Herb Jeffries appeared in Barry Shear's *Jarrett* (1973).

The Voice of the Camera

When I spoke with William Claxton in January 1990, he was working for *Motor Trend* magazine and living in Beverly Hills, California, but back in the mid-'50s, when he shot available-light photographs that made Art Pepper, Gerry Mulligan, Shorty Rogers, and Chet Baker icons of West Coast cool, he worked for Contemporary Records. At that time, stimulated by the rise of the long-playing record, jazz was enjoying a period of renewed prosperity, and Lester Koenig's new company was doing well. Contemporary was "the first jazz label to introduce 45rpm singles, stereo and attain

FIGURE 4.2
John Wayne (1969): "They tell me everything isn't black and white. Well, I say why the hell not?" (qtd. in Hoberman, 49). (*Way out West Plus*, courtesy of Contemporary Records, 1957)

national distribution" (Carr et al., 113). But prosperity brought its own set of artistic challenges. The speed with which photographers and graphic artists had to generate ideas matched the fast tempos of bebop.

The photo session for *Way out West* developed out of a conversation between musician and photographer. Rollins, Claxton recalls, "liked western things" and wanted to do something that would complement the material he was recording, plus commemorate his first trip to the West Coast. Claxton agreed but suggested that Rollins maintain the jazzman's air of urbanity. "I told him to keep his Brooks Brothers suit and skinny black tie."

Claxton says, "I knew the desert pretty well, so I knew exactly where to get the right kind of Joshua trees and cactus in the background. I went to a prop house and rented a steer's head—a skeleton—because I couldn't depend on finding one out there. And we put a holster on him.

"I picked him up. He was a terrific guy to be with, very nice, and we just drove out to the high desert, near Mojave. I had shot pictures there before. I put the skull out in the sand, and he put one foot up on it. He had this long, thin body. He looked great. He just posed beautifully. And he had great fun doing it. We laughed a lot."

Before he photographed Mel Brooks and Carl Reiner, at a sitting that yielded the cover to the comedians' first record album, Claxton showed them his recently completed work for *Way out West*. Brooks liked what he saw and, perhaps, remembered the image of Rollins as cowboy when he directed his western. "The ultimate desecration," Hoberman called *Blazing Saddles* (1974). It was also the highest grossing western before *Dances with Wolves*, capping "the assorted anti-, post-, spaghetti, revisionist, psychedelic, black, and burlesque westerns of the early '70s" (Hoberman, 52). *Blazing Saddles* boasted an African American actor, Cleavon Little, as the sheriff of Rock Ridge, and in one memorable gag, predicated on the audience mistaking diegetic for nondiegetic music, Brooks filmed the Count Basie Orchestra playing jazz—in the desert.

Joshing in the Mojave

Comedy, Aristotle claims in the *Poetics* (ch. 4), arose in the "outlying districts" as "those who led the phallic songs (that even now are still customary in many of our cities) . . . improvised" (Golden, 8).

Theory of Album Covers

Record covers mirror back our perceptions of particular types of music, perceptions that are to a great extent visually and not musically determined (the modern age, notes Heidegger, grasps the *real* as picture), perceptions that are shaped by past experiences with other texts representing aural "texts" (Heidegger, 131). Covers not only represent—encode in visual form—the myths associated with music, they contribute to the construction of those myths. They are part of the process that imbues music with meaning, giving it both a face and a voice.

Easily dismissable as a period piece, an egregious example of West Coast kitsch, the cover to *Way out West* is, in fact, a tightly packed bundle of highly charged metaphors. It's the jazz equivalent of Botticelli's *Primavera*. Think of it as a dream image, a case of transference or projection (*metapherein* means "to transfer"). It establishes a correspondence between two remote images. It speaks of modern jazz—conventionally understood as the ceaseless exploration of uncharted musical territory by social and artistic outsiders—and of the West. With it, the jazzman becomes Shane; jazz becomes California. Rollins, Claxton, and their audience gain symbolic knowledge of jazz (it enters language) by identifying the music with traditional mythological categories perpetuated by film, literature, theater, painting, television, and other media.

Claxton and Contemporary Records portrayed Rollins as outlaw hero (much as Andy Warhol would later portray Elvis Presley) and, in so doing, they anticipated an image that the counterculture would appropriate and refunction in less than ten years. At that time, through what Robert Christgau calls a "barstool-macho equation of gunslinger and guitarschlonger," the musician as outlaw was apotheosized, and his image, formerly signifying values approved by a few mavericks ("bohemians"), became an icon recognized by all and embraced by many (120). He stood for "freedom from restraint, a preference for intuition as the source of conduct, a distrust of the law, a prolonging of adolescence, and a bias against technology, bureaucracies, and urban life" (Ray, 1985:255). The radical left of the 1960s, notes Ray, was obsessed with the iconography of the American West.

> Clothes (jeans, boots, buckskins) and hairstyles (long and unkempt, moustaches) derived from daguerreotypes of nineteenth-century gunfighters; and pop music returned repeatedly to frontier images: The Buffalo Springfield's "Broken Arrow," The Grateful Dead's "Casey Jones," The Band's "Across the Great Divide," James Taylor's "Sweet Baby James," Neil Young's "Cowgirl in the Sand," Creedence Clearwater Revival's "Proud Mary," The Byrds' *Sweetheart of the Rodeo*, and the Eagles' *Desperado*. (255–56)

Rock mythology had followed a trail blazed by jazz. The quest for a unique sound, a privileging of invention over interpretation, an infatuation with drugs, sex, and spirituality: Both musics glorified an ideology founded on individualism.

Fish out of Water

For a semester, I tutored Scott, a freshman at Penn State York, on his writing skills, but the work of remediation never kept us from talking about more engaging matters. One day, our conversation turned to fishing. Scott told me that he planned to major in wildlife management. I told him that I used to live in Atlanta, not far from Lake Lanier. In it a large-mouth bass was caught that, at one time, held the world record for size.

"Really?" he said. "I have a calendar in my bedroom that shows pictures of fish. It lists the size of a world-record catch, then tells where it was caught. Did you know that the world's largest pike was caught in Germany?"

I confessed that I didn't.

"Yeah," he said. "Sometimes I just look at that picture and think, 'Damn, how'd it get all the way over there?'"

Sometimes I look at Rollins—born in Harlem, the child of immigrants from the Virgin Islands—and wonder, "How'd he end up way out West?"

The Joshua Tree

In her analysis of the mythic significance of the West, Joan Didion describes both a physical and a social geography. She writes: "California is a place where boom mentality and a sense of Chekhovian loss meet in uneasy suspension; in which the mind is troubled by some buried but ineradicable suspicion that things had better work here, because that immense bleached sky, is where we run out of continent" (qtd. in Schrag, 171).

The Joshua tree (*Yucca brevifola*) was named by Mormon pioneers who fancied that it resembled the biblical Joshua "pointing the way with uplifted arms to the Promised Land" (*Encyclopedia Americana*). Their spiritual quest—for transcendent identity and a traceable genealogy—was (and is) directed by the metaphor of the *root-tree*: that is, by the arborescent model theorized extensively by Deleuze and Guattari. The image of the tree led Mormons to conceptualize the West as a garden (Eden or Gethsemane) and to erect a bureaucracy: making property the basis of government; negotiating land through litigation and marriages.

Mormons repressed knowledge of "the rhizomatic West, with its Indians without ancestry, its ever-receding limit, its shifting and displaced frontiers" (Deleuze and Guattari, 19). They could not shake arborescence; they were unwilling to abandon faith in roots and radicles: "classical" trees. To them, the Joshua tree did not look upside down, its limbs—strangely forked and spreading in all directions—signifying nothing so much as indeterminacy.

If Charlie Parker Were a Gunslinger

When I see an African American dressed as a cowboy . . .

- George Clinton riding two dolphins bareback,
- The Soul Clan—Ben E. King, Joe Tex, Don Convay, Wilson Pickett, Solomon Burke—sporting Stetsons,
- Jimi Hendrix wielding a sixgun (on the back cover to *Smash Hits*),
- Bo Diddley reaching for his guitar (the cover to *Bo Diddley Is a Gunslinger*),

I supply the signified: Outlaw with a bad case of irony. Does that make me a Mormon?

The Truth in Photography

After sitting down to write on a group of drawings by Valerio Adami, Jacques Derrida observed: "As for painting, any discourse on it, beside it or above, always strikes me as silly, both didactic and incantatory, programed, worked by the compulsion of mastery, be it poetical or philosophical" (1987:65). His statement—an echo of Elvis Costello's assessment of discourse about music—strikes a resonant chord in me. I am somewhat embarrassed by my "Theory of Album Covers." It assumes too little. If *Way out West* communicates perfectly well, if it speaks the truth about jazz, then I ought to shut up. And it assumes too much. If Claxton's photograph needs me—let's say that it speaks the truth, albeit in signs so oblique that only well-trained eyes can discern them—then what will keep my version of its truth from renewing, reproducing, and reintroducing the very obliqueness I hope to allay? (2).

What I am looking for is an alternative to silence and formalism, a way to break away from writing that aims to represent an object of study mimetically. I want to respond to John Leavey's question: If no referent, no transcendental signified regulates Text, how is writing to proceed, writing that in the classical sense is anchored by the referent? (74). More importantly, I want to stage my answer, show how one might go about "representing" an object of study without falling back on a system of truth "as adequation

FIGURE 4.3
Back cover of Parliament's *Motor-Booty Affair*
(courtesy of Casablanca Records, 1978)

or as unveiling" (Derrida, 1987:367). That is why I am interested in the cover to *Way out West*. It is, to borrow a phrase Barthes used to describe *A Night at the Opera*, "allegorical of many a textual problem" (1977b:194). It suggests another way to write criticism, one that Ulmer describes as "fully referential, but referential in the manner of 'narrative allegory' rather than of 'allegoresis.'"

"Allegoresis," the mode of commentary long practiced by traditional critics, "suspends" the surface of the text, applying a terminology of "verticalness, levels, hidden meaning, the hieratic difficulty of interpretation," whereas "narrative alle-

gory" (practiced by post-critics) explores the literal—*letteral*—
level of the language itself, in a horizontal investigation of the
polysemous meanings simultaneously available in the words
themselves—in etymologies and puns—and in the things the
words name. (Ulmer, 1983:94, citing Quilligan, 1979:30–33)

In short, allegory, unlike allegoresis, is not *hermeneutics* (puzzle
solving); it "does not restore an original meaning that may have
been lost or obscured" (Owens, 69). Instead, it is *heuretics*—invention. It dramatizes or enacts "letteral" truth, enlarging upon the
possibilities of linguistic transference (Ulmer, 1983:95).

The allegorist does not analyze so much as he invents. He concerns himself with recomposition—how to compose a "nonidentical, staggered, discrepant 'repetition'" of what is, in fact, already a
"repetition" (Derrida, 1987:30). This is what aligns him with the
jazz musician (an artist whose every note is a response to prior
texts). Both of their methods are *touristic*: expressed either positively, through the role of fan or amateur, or negatively, through the
role of satirist. The allegorist and jazzman, while on native soil,
behave as if they are foreigners. (At home they're tourists.) To various degrees indifferent to textual authority, they go places, see
things, and manipulate customs in ways that indigenous people
either couldn't or would not dare. The allegorist and jazzman
remake texts in the way that a tourist's video perversely interprets
a trip West, using bits and pieces of images and sounds—cultural
clichés—for personal pleasure and for problem-solving: for "rereading the self" (Ulmer, 1994:119).

"Mystory," as we have seen, is Ulmer's label for the contribution of one's personal style (or story) to problem-solving. We should
note that this neologism and other Florida School applications of
grammatological theory (heuretics) are founded on the notion that
the signifier *joshes*. It points the way with strangely forked arms. It
is comic,

> laughter being what, by a last reversal, releases demonstration
> from its demonstrative attribute. What liberates metaphor,
> symbol, emblem from poetic *mania*, what manifests its power
> of subversion, is the *preposterous*. (Barthes, 1977a:80–81)

Allegoresis—normal criticism—is serious, an extrapolation of the
simple form of the riddle; its features are examination and cate-
chism. Allegory or mystory is an extrapolation of the simple form

of the joke. By "'loosening intelligibility' through play" it attempts to model a type of writing that evades "the inhibitions and compulsions of reason and criticism" (Ulmer, 1989a:52–53). Or by way of analogy, normal criticism is to mystory as *Shane* is to *Blazing Saddles*.

The Tenor's Vehicle

Craig Saper anticipates an answer to the following question: How might the cover to *Way out West*—the convergence of jazz iconography and critical theory—assist us in displacing the emotion—melancholia—that necessarily accompanies writing shaped by the confrontational structure of the western? He states that the "swerve of affect from alienated thought to carnivalesque thinking occurs by exploiting the indirections of metaphors, images, and key words employed in theoretical explanations or meta-languages" (1988:375). Craig Owens recommended a similar tactic (though that is too confrontational a word) in his instructions for actualizing the allegorical potential of texts (74–75). He pointed out that allegory proceeds according to a "pictogrammatical" logic. In it "the image is a hieroglyph; an allegory is a rebus—writing composed of concrete images." It confuses "the verbal and the visual" (75).

Looking again at the cover of *Way out West* and capitalizing on this insight, we discover that a confusion of "the verbal and the visual," made manifest by the substitution of tenor saxophone for the obviously absent sixgun, yields what Ulmer calls a "research pun." "The humor, if there is any, results from the inappropriate and incongruous sets of associated ideas *jarring* each other" (Paulos, 61, emphasis added). The *tenor* that Rollins holds (*tenere* = to hold) in Claxton's photograph might recall Sax's invention (the saxophone or saxocannon), but it also winks at I. A. Richards's distinction between the "tenor" and "vehicle" of a metaphor (comparable to Saussure's distinction between "signified" and "signifier"). It allows us to seize the cover to *Way out West* as a pictogrammatical set of instructions, a tutor-text on how to make other texts. (Ulmer writes: "What the baroque or romantic allegorist conceived of as an emblem, the post-critic treats as a model"—1983:99.) We may read *Way out West* as an allegory of allegory—that is, as an allegory about metaphor. Or exploiting Claude Lévi-Strauss's theory of the *charivari*, we may observe that *Way out West* illustrates how to make *noise* and, in the process, generate what we might call "knowledge effects." The "unnatural union" of jazzman and desert—or of saxophone and cowboy—recommends that invention proceeds through mavericking. A conventional syntagm (cowboy and desert; jazzman and New York City) is interrupted and into this same sequence a "foreign" element intrudes: an element that appropriates one term of a sequence brings about a distortion (Lévi-Strauss, 1969:289ff).

Way out West teaches a textualist lesson: Tenors are vehicles. It models Derrida's main point in "White Mythology: Metaphor in the Text of Philosophy." Interpretation (hermeneutics) and Western metaphysics begin with the in(ter)vention of metaphor. Without it "we cannot imagine what it is to be someone else," writes Cynthia Ozick. "Metaphor is the reciprocal agent, the universalizing force: it makes possible the power to envision the stranger's heart" (67). "Metaphors," Hannah Arendt noted, "are the means by which the oneness of the world is poetically brought about" (14). Invention (heuretics), on the other hand, begins when the concept of metaphor dissolves, that is, when tenor and vehicle collapse or when, as in allegory, structure is projected as sequence. *One plays a tenor by causing a read to vibrate* between literal and figurative levels of language; one finds an alternative to a hermeneutics of truth by unsettling "what turns out to be *the* metaphysical distinction, between words [signifiers] and meanings [signifieds]" (Cooper, 26).

But we might ask with Jean Baudrillard: "[H]ow far can we go in the extermination of meaning, how far can we go in the non-referential desert form without cracking up and, of course, still keep alive the esoteric charm of disappearance?" (1988:63–64). His answer ("a fundamental rule"): "[A]im for the point of no return. This is the key" (10).

Coda

When I lived in Chattanooga, I occasionally spent Sunday afternoons at a downtown flea market. One day, while browsing around, I happened onto a whole table of combination locks. Interested in purchasing one, I asked a woman sitting behind the table if she had a list of the combinations, since I saw none attached to any of the locks I had examined.

"No," she said.

I asked, "Well, then, how do you get them open?"

She said, "You try it. Some people get it right off."

Works Cited

Aaron, Charles (1989). "Gettin' Paid." *The Village Voice Rock & Roll Quarterly*, October 31:22–23, 26.

Adams, Robert M., trans. and ed. (1975). Sir Thomas More, *Utopia*. New York: W. W. Norton.

Adorno, Theodor (1984). "Perennial Fashion." In *Prisms*. Trans. Helene Iswolsky. Bloomington: Indiana UP.

Adorno, Theodor, with the assistance of George Simpson (1941). "On Popular Music." *Studies in Philosophy and Social Science* 9:17–48.

Albert, Richard N., ed. (1990). *From Blues to Bop: A Collection of Jazz Fiction*. Baton Rouge: Louisiana State UP.

Allen, Woody (1975). "The Query." In *Side Effects*. New York: Random House.

Allison, Mose (1994). Interview with Joel Dorn. Liner notes to *Allison Wonderland: The Mose Allison Anthology*. Atlantic.

Althusser, Louis (1971). "Freud and Lacan." In *Lenin and Philosophy and Other Essays*. Trans. Ben Brewster. New York: Monthly Review Press.

Anderson, Laurie (1994). *Stories from the Nerve Bible: A Retrospective 1972–1992*. New York: Harper Perennial.

Apollonio, Umbro, ed. (1973). *Futurist Manifestos*. Trans. Robert Brain et al. Documents of Twentieth-Century Art. New York: Viking.

Arendt, Hannah (1968). "Introduction." In *Illuminations*. New York: Harcourt, Brace & World.

Arrowsmith, William (1959). "Introduction." In *The Satyricon*. New York: New American Library.

Attali, Jacques (1988). *Noise: The Political Economy of Music*. Trans. Brian Massumi. Minneapolis: U of Minnesota P.

Bailey, Derek (1992). *Improvisation: Its Nature and Practice in Music*. New York: Da Capo.

Baker, Dorothy (1938). *Young Man with a Horn*. New York: Houghton Mifflin.

Baker, Houston (1984). *Blues, Ideology, and Afro-American Literature: A Vernacular Theory*. Chicago: U of Chicago P.

Baldwin, James (1990). "Sonny's Blues." In *From Blues to Bop: A Collection of Jazz Fiction*. Ed. Richard N. Albert. Baton Rouge: Louisiana State UP.

Balliett, Whitney (1986). *American Musicians*. New York: Oxford UP.

—— (1991). "Jazz: Rollins Rampant." *The New Yorker*, July 29:58–59.

Barbour, Douglas (1993). *Michael Ondaatje*. New York: Twayne.

Barra, Allen (1989). "Concert for Human Rights, Us and Them." *The Village Voice*, March 14:72.

Barthelme, Donald (1981). "The King of Jazz." In *Sixty Stories*. New York: E. P. Dutton.

Barthes, Roland (1974). *S/Z: An Essay*. Trans. Richard Miller. New York: Hill and Wang.

—— (1977a). *Roland Barthes*. Trans. Richard Howard. New York: Hill and Wang.

—— (1977b). *Image-Music-Text*. Trans. Stephen Heath. New York: Hill and Wang.

—— (1985). *The Grain of the Voice: Interviews 1962–1980*. Trans. Linda Coverdale. New York: Hill and Wang.

—— (1986). *The Rustle of Language*. Trans. Richard Howard. New York: Hill and Wang.

Basie, William "Count" and Albert Murray (1987). *Good Morning Blues: The Autobiography of Count Basie*. New York: Random House.

Baudrillard, Jean (1983). *Simulations*. Trans. Paul Foss, Paul Patton and Philip Beitchman. New York: Semiotext(e).

—— (1988). *America*. Trans. Chris Turner. London: Verso.

Beastie Boys (1994). Personal interview. February 22.

Becker, Howard (1963). *The Outsiders: Studies in the Sociology of Deviance*. New York: The Free Press.

Begley, Adam (1992). "The Tempest around Stephen Greenblatt." *The New York Times Magazine*, March 28:32, 34, 36–38.

Benjamin, Walter (1977). *The Origin of German Tragic Drama*. Trans. John Osborne. London: NLB.

—— (1978). "One-Way Street." In *Reflections*. Trans. Edmund Jephcott. New York: Harvest/HBJ.

Beuttler, Bill (1985). "On the Beat." *Down Beat*, August: 21.

Bevington, David (1975). *Medieval Drama*. Boston: Houghton Mifflin.

Bloom, Harold (1973). *The Anxiety of Influence*. New York: Oxford UP.

Borges, Jorge Luis (1956, 1962). "Pierre Menard, Author of the Quixote." In *Labyrinths: Selected Stories & Other Writings*. Trans. Emecé Editores, S.A., Buenos Aires. New York: Grove Weidenfeld.

Boulez, Pierre (1986). *Orientations: Collected Writings*. Ed. Jean-Jacques Nattiez. Trans. Martin Cooper. Cambridge: Harvard UP.

Bourjaily, Vance (1987). "In and Out of Storyville: Jazz and Fiction." *The New York Times Book Review*, December 13:1, 44–45.

Breton, Marcela, ed. (1990). *Hot and Cool: Jazz Short Stories*. New York: Penguin.

Brown, Roger (1958). *Words and Things*. New York: The Free Press.

Brown, Sterling (1991). "Cabaret." In *The Collected Poems of Sterling A. Brown*. New York: HarperCollins.

Cable, George Washington (1957). *The Grandissimes*. New York: Hill and Wang.

Cage, John (1961). *Silence*. Middletown, Conn.: Wesleyan UP.

Carr, Roy, Brian Case, and Fred Dellar (1986). *The Hip: Hipsters, Jazz and the Beat Generation*. London: Faber and Faber.

Cartiér, Xam Wilson (1987). *Be-Bop, Re-Bop*. New York: Ballantine.

Christgau, Robert (1981). *Christgau's Record Guide: Rock Albums of the Seventies*. New Haven, Conn.: Ticknor and Fields.

Claxton, William (1990). Personal interview. January 21.

Coleman, Ornette (1960). Liner notes to *Change of the Century*. Atlantic.

—— (1987). Liner notes to *The Music of Ornette Coleman: Forms & Sounds*. Bluebird.

Collins, Jim (1989). *Uncommon Cultures: Popular Culture and Post-Modernism*. New York: Routledge.

Cooper, David E. (1986). *Metaphor*. Oxford: Basil Blackwell.

Coover, Robert (1992). "The End of Books." *The New York Times Book Review*, June 21:1, 23–25.

Corbett, John (1994). *Extended Play: Sounding Off from John Cage to Dr. Funkenstein*. Durham: Duke UP.

Cortázar, Julio (1966). *Hopscotch*. Trans. Gregory Rabassa. New York: Pantheon.

Deleuze, Gilles and Félix Guattari (1987). *A Thousand Plateaus: Capitalism & Schizophrenia*. Trans. Brian Massumi. Minneapolis: U of Minnesota P.

De Man, Paul (1971). *Blindness and Insight: Essays in the Rhetoric of Contemporary Criticism*. 2nd ed. Minneapolis: U of Minnesota P.

Derrida, Jacques (1976). *Of Grammatology*. Trans. Gayatri Chakravorty Spivak. Baltimore: Johns Hopkins UP.

—— (1981). *Dissemination*. Trans. Barbara Johnson. Chicago: U of Chicago P.

—— (1984). *Signsponge*. Trans. Richard Rand. New York: Columbia UP.

—— (1987). *The Truth in Painting*. Trans. Geoff Bennington and Ian McLeod. Chicago: U of Chicago P.

—— (1992). *Given Time: I. Counterfeit Money*. Trans. Peggy Kamuf. Chicago: U of Chicago P.

DeVeaux, Scott (1991). "Constructing the Jazz Tradition: Jazz Historiography." *Black American Literature Forum*, Fall:525–60.

Dodge, Roger Pryor (1939). "Consider the Critics." In *Jazzmen*. Ed. Frederic Ramsey Jr. and Charles Edward Smith. New York: Harcourt Brace.

Dull, S. R. (1968). *Southern Cooking*. New York: Grosset and Dunlap.

Durham, Philip and Everett L. Jones (1965). *The Negro Cowboys*. Lincoln: U of Nebraska P.

Eco, Umberto (1976). *A Theory of Semiotics*. Bloomington: Indiana UP.

—— (1979). *The Role of the Reader*. Bloomington: Indiana UP.

Eliot, T. S. (1975). "Tradition and the Individual Talent." *Selected Prose of T. S. Eliot*. Ed. Frank Kermode. New York: Harcourt, Brace, Jovanovich, and Farrar, Straus, & Giroux.

Ellington, Duke (1971). *Music Is My Mistress*. Garden City, N.Y.: Doubleday.

Ellison, Ralph (1947). *Invisible Man*. New York: New American Library.

—— (1964). "Hidden Name and Complex Fate." *Shadow and Act*. New York: Vintage.

Emerson, Ralph Waldo (1969). *Journals and Miscellaneous Notebooks. 7* (1838–42). Cambridge: Belknap P of Harvard UP.

Erickson, Frederick (1984). "Rhetoric, Anecdote, and Rhapsody: Coherence Strategies in a Conversation among Black American Adolescents." In *Coherence in Spoken and Written Discourse*. Ed. Deborah Tannen. Norwood, N.J.: Ablex.

Evans, Bill (1959). Liner notes to *Kind of Blue*. Columbia.

Feather, Leonard (1957). *The Book of Jazz: From Then Till Now*. New York: Dell.

Feinstein, Sascha and Yusef Komunyakaa (1991). *The Jazz Poetry Anthology*. Bloomington: Indiana UP.

Ferlinghetti, Lawrence (1958). *A Coney Island of the Mind*. New York: New Directions.

Fisher, Rudolph (1990). "Common Meter." *Hot and Cool: Jazz Short Stories*. Ed. Marcela Breton. New York: Penguin.

Fiske, John (1982). *Introduction to Communication Studies*. New York: Methuen.

Fitzgerald, F. Scott (1931). "Echoes of the Jazz Age." *The Crack-Up*. Ed. Edmund Wilson. New York: New Directions.

Flinn, Carol (1986). "The 'Problem' of Femininity in Theories of Film Music." *Screen* 27:56–72.

Frith, Simon (1981). *Sound Effects: Youth, Leisure, and the Politics of Rock 'n' Roll*. New York: Pantheon.

—— (1988). *Music for Pleasure: Essays in the Sociology of Pop*. New York: Routledge.

Gabbard, Krin (1992a). "The Quoter and His Culture." In *Jazz in Mind: Essays on the History and Meanings of Jazz*. Ed. Reginald T. Buckner and Steven Weiland. Detroit: Wayne State UP.

—— (1992b). "Signifyin(g) the Phallus: Mo' Better Blues and Representations of the Jazz Trumpet." *Cinema Journal* 32:43–62.

Gendron, Bernard (1989–90). "Jamming at Le Boeuf: Jazz and the Paris Avant-Garde." *Discourse* 12.1:3–27.

Giddins, Gary (1983). "Fathers and Son: A Jazz Genealogy." *The Village Voice*, August 2:1, 36–37.

Gioia, Ted (1988). *The Imperfect Art: Reflections on Jazz and Modern Culture*. New York: Oxford UP.

Goldberg, Joe (1968). *Jazz Masters of the Fifties*. New York: Collier-Macmillan.

Golden, Leon, trans., and O. B. Hardison Jr., commentary (1968). *Aristotle's Poetics: A Translation and Commentary for Students of Literature*. Englewood Cliffs, N.J.: Prentice Hall.

Goodwin, Andrew (1992). *Dancing in the Distraction Factory: Music Television and Popular Culture*. Minneapolis: U of Minnesota P.

Gresham, James Thomas (1972). "John Barth as Menippean Satirist." Ph.D. diss., Michigan State U.

Gridley, Mark C. (1985). *Jazz Styles: History and Analysis*. 2nd ed. Englewood Cliffs: Prentice Hall.

Grossberg, Lawrence (1992). *We Gotta Get Out of This Place: Popular Conservatism and Postmodern Culture*. New York: Routledge.

Gushee, Larry (n.d.). Liner notes to *Duke Ellington 1940*. The Smithsonian Collection.

Hammond, John (1977). *John Hammond on Record*. New York: Ridge.

—— (1987). "Random Notes on the Spirituals to Swing Recordings." Liner notes to *From Spirituals to Swing*. Vanguard Records.

Harris, Middleton, ed. (1974). *The Black Book*. New York: Random House.

Harrison, Max (1976). *A Jazz Retrospect*. Boston: Crescendo.

Hawkes, Terence (1977). *Structuralism and Semiotics*. Berkeley: U of California P.

Hebdige, Dick (1979). *Subculture the Meaning of Style*. London: Methuen.

Heidegger, Martin (1977). "The Age of the World Picture." In *The Question Concerning Technology*. Trans. William Lovitt. New York: Harper & Row.

Hentoff, Nat (1961). *The Jazz Life*. New York: Dial.

Highet, Gilbert (1962). *Anatomy of Satire*. Princeton, N.J.: Princeton UP.

Hoberman, J. (1991). "How the Western Was Lost." *The Village Voice*, August 27:49–53.

Hobsbawm, E. J. (1987). "The Jazz Comeback." *The New York Review of Books*, February 12:11–14.

Hollier, Denis (1986). *The Politics of Prose: Essay on Sartre*. Trans. Jeffrey Mehlman. Minneapolis: U of Minnesota P.

Holman, C. Hugh (1980). "Rhapsody." *A Handbook to Literature*. 4th ed. Indianapolis: Bobbs-Merrill.

Huggins, Nathan Irvin (1971). *Harlem Renaissance*. New York: Oxford UP.

Hurston, Zora Neale (1981). *The Sanctified Church*. Berkeley: Turtle Island.

Ice-T (1994). Interview with Terry Gross. *Fresh Air*. WHYY, May 16.

James, Henry (1934). Preface to *The Aspern Papers*. In *The Art of the Novel*. New York: Charles Scribner's Sons.

Jameson, Fredric (1981). *The Political Unconscious: Narrative as a Socially Symbolic Act*. Ithaca, N.Y.: Cornell UP.

Jarrett, Michael (1990a). "Jazz Greats Still in Transition: Sonny Rollins and Cecil Taylor." *Pulse!*, March:74.

——— (1990b). "Sonny Rollins—Tenorman amidst the Joshua Trees." *Jazziz*, April–May:21.

Johnson, Barbara (1981). "Translator's Introduction." Jacques Derrida. *Dissemination*. Chicago: U of Chicago P.

Jones, LeRoi (1963). *Blues People: Negro Music in White America*. New York: William Morrow.

——— (1990). "The Screamers." In *Hot and Cool: Jazz Short Stories*. Ed. Marcela Breton. New York: Penguin.

"Joshua Tree" (1984). *Encyclopedia Americana*.

Juvenal (1967). *The Sixteen Satires*. Trans. Peter Green. New York: Penguin Classics.

Kenner, Hugh (1968). *The Counterfeiters: An Historical Comedy*. Bloomington: Indiana UP.

Kennington, Donald and Danny L. Read (1980). *The Literature of Jazz: A Critical Guide*. 2nd ed. Chicago: American Library Association.

Kerman, Joseph (1985). *Contemplating Music: Challenges to Musicology*. Cambridge: Harvard UP.

Kerouac, Jack (1955). *On the Road*. New York: New American Library.

Kofsky, Frank (1970). *Black Nationalism and the Revolution in Music*. New York: Pathfinder.

Kostelanetz, Richard (1991). "STRINGFOUR." In *The Jazz Poetry Anthology*. Ed. Sascha Feinstein and Yusef Komunyakaa. Bloomington: Indiana UP.

Leavey, John, Jr. (1988). "Time Signatures: Post*.* Responsibilities." *Strategies* 1:64–81.

Leonardo da Vinci (1957). "Observations and Aphorisms." *Notebooks*. Trans. Edward MacCurdy. New York: Modern Library.

Lesy, Michael (1985). *Visible Light*. New York: Times Books.

Lévi-Strauss, Claude (1969). *The Raw and the Cooked: Introduction to a Science of Mythology: I*. Trans. John Weightman and Doreen Weightman. Chicago: U of Chicago P.

Lewis, C. S. (1964). *The Discarded Image: An Introduction to Medieval and Renaissance Literature*. London: Cambridge UP.

Lewis, Thomas (1985). "Reference and Dissemination: Althusser after Derrida." *Diacritics* 15:37–56.

Lindberg, Gary (1982). *The Confidence Man in American Literature*. New York: Oxford UP.

Livingstone, E. A., ed. (1977). *The Concise Oxford Dictionary of the Christian Church*. Oxford: Oxford UP.

Lyons, Len (1980). *The 101 Best Jazz Albums: A History of Jazz on Records*. New York: William Morrow.

Lyotard, Jean-François and Jean-Loup Thébaud (1985). *Just Gaming*. Trans. Wlad Godzich. Minneapolis: U of Minnesota P.

Mackey, Nathaniel (1986). *Bedouin Hornbook*. Baltimore: Johns Hopkins UP.

—— (1992). "Other: From Noun to Verb." *Representations* 39:51–70.

Mallarmé, Stéphane (1982). *Selected Poetry and Prose.* Trans. Mary Ann Caws. New York: New Directions.

Marcus, Greil (1989). *Lipstick Traces: A Secret History of the 20th Century.* Cambridge: Harvard UP.

Marx, Karl (1973). *Grundrisse.* Harmondsworth, U.K.: Penguin.

Matthews, William (1991). "Bmp Bmp." In *The Jazz Poetry Anthology.* Ed. Sascha Feinstein and Yusef Komunyakaa. Bloomington: Indiana UP.

McClary, Susan (1989). "Terminal Prestige: The Case of Avant-Garde Music Composition." *Cultural Critique* 12:57–81.

—— (1991). *Feminine Endings: Music, Gender, and Sexuality.* Minneapolis: U of Minnesota P.

McDonough, John (1992). Liner notes to *Original Dixieland Jazz Band: The 75th Anniversary.* Bluebird.

Merriam, Alan P. and Fradley H. Garner (1968). "Jazz—The Word." *Ethnomusicology* 12:373–96.

Mezzrow, Milton, with Bernard Wolfe (1946). *Really the Blues.* New York: Random House.

Milkowski, Bill (1983). "Eno." *Down Beat,* June:14–17, 57.

Moore, MacDonald Smith (1985). *Yankee Blues: Musical Culture and American Identity.* Bloomington: U of Indiana P.

More, Sir Thomas (1975). *Utopia.* Trans. Robert M. Adams. New York: W. W. Norton.

Morrison, Toni (1992). *Jazz.* New York: Knopf.

Morton, Brian (1988). "Percussion." *Wire,* April:12.

O'Meally, Robert G. (1980). *The Craft of Ralph Ellison.* Cambridge: Harvard UP.

Ondaatje, Michael (1976). *Coming through Slaughter.* New York: Penguin.

Ong, Walter J. (1982). *Orality and Literacy: The Technologizing of the Word.* New York: Methuen.

Owens, Craig (1980). "The Allegorical Impulse: Toward a Theory of Postmodernism." *October* 12:67–85.

Ozick, Cynthia (1986). "The Moral Necessity of Metaphor." *Harper's Magazine,* May:62–68.

Palmer, Don (1984). Liner notes to *Conjure: Music for the Texts of Ishmael Reed*. American Clavé.

Pareles, Jon (1993). "It's Got a Beat and You Can Surrender to It." *The New York Times*, March 28:D2.

Parkinson, Thomas, ed. (1961). *A Casebook on the Beat*. New York: Crowell.

Paulos, John Allen (1980). *Mathematics and Humor*. Chicago: U of Chicago P.

Paulson, William (1988). *The Noise of Culture: Literary Texts in a World of Information*. Ithaca, N.Y.: Cornell UP.

Perlman, Alan M. and Daniel Greenblatt (1981). "Miles Davis Meets Noam Chomsky: Some Observations on Jazz Improvisation and Language Structure." In *The Sign in Music and Literature*. Ed. Wendy Steiner. Austin: U of Texas P.

Perloff, Marjorie (1986). *The Futurist Moment: Avant-Garde, Avant Guerre, and the Language of Rupture*. Chicago: U of Chicago P.

Petronius (1959). *The Satyricon*. Trans. William Arrowsmith. New York: New American Library.

Pound, Ezra (1934). *ABC of Reading*. New York: New Directions.

Primack, Bret (1979). "Carla Bley." *Contemporary Keyboard*, February:9–11.

Pynchon, Thomas (1961). *V.* New York: Bantam.

—— (1984). "Entropy." In *Slow Learner: Early Stories*. Boston: Little, Brown.

Quilligan, Maureen (1979). *The Language of Allegory*. Ithaca, N.Y.: Cornell UP.

Ramsey, Frederic, Jr. and Charles Edward Smith, eds. (1939). *Jazzmen*. New York: Harcourt Brace.

Randel, Don Michael (1978). *Harvard Concise Dictionary of Music*. Cambridge: The Belknap P of Harvard UP.

Ray, Robert B. (1985). *A Certain Tendency of the Hollywood Cinema, 1930–1980*. Princeton, N.J.: Princeton UP.

—— (1988). "The Bordwell Regime and the Stakes of Knowledge," *Strategies* 1:142–81.

—— (1994). "The Signature Experiment Finds Andy Hardy." In *Deconstruction and the Visual Arts: Art, Media, Architecture*. Ed. Peter Brunette and David Wills. New York: Cambridge UP.

Reed, Ishmael (1967a). *The Free-Lance Pallbearers*. New York: Avon.

—— (1967b). "The Black Artist: Calling a Spade a Spade." *Arts Magazine*, 41:48–49.

—— (1969). *Yellow Back Radio Broke-Down*. Garden City, N.Y.: Doubleday.

—— (1971). *Mumbo Jumbo*. New York: Avon.

—— (1977). *Shrovetide in Old New Orleans*. New York: Doubleday.

—— and Al Young, eds. (1978). *Yardbird Lives*. New York: Grove.

Reynolds, Simon (1990). *Blissed Out: The Raptures of Rock*. London: Serpent's Tail.

Riesman, David (1950, 1990). "Listening to Popular Music." In *On Record: Rock, Pop, and the Written Word*. Ed. Simon Frith and Andrew Goodwin. New York: Pantheon.

Rogers, Pat (1972). "Shaftesbury and the Aesthetics of Rhapsody." *British Journal of Aesthetics* 12:244–57.

—— , ed. (1983). Notes on "On Poetry: A Rhapsody." In *Jonathan Swift: The Complete Poems*. New Haven, Conn.: Yale UP.

Rollins, Sonny (1990). Personal interview. January 2.

Ronell, Avital (1989). *The Telephone Book, Technology—Schizophrenia—Electric Speech*. Lincoln: U of Nebraska P.

Rose, Margaret (1979). *Parody*. London: Croom Helm.

Ross, Andrew (1989). *No Respect: Intellectuals & Popular Culture*. New York: Routledge.

Rousseau, Jean Jacques (1975, rpt. of 1779 ed.). *A Complete Dictionary of Music*. 2nd ed. Trans. William Waring. New York: AMS.

Said, Edward W. (1978). *Orientalism*. New York: Vintage.

Santoro, Gene (1994). *Dancing in Your Head*. New York: Oxford UP.

Saper, Craig, ed. (1988). "Introduction." *Instant Theory: Making Thinking Popular. Visible Language* 22:371–97.

—— (1991). "A Nervous Theory: The Troubling Gaze of Psychoanalysis in Media Studies." *Diacritics* 21.4:33–52.

Sargeant, Winthrop (1938). *Jazz: A History*. Originally *Jazz: Hot and Hybrid*. New York: McGraw-Hill.

Sartre, Jean-Paul (1964). *Nausea*. Trans. Lloyd Alexander. New York: New Directions.

Schrag, Peter (1973). *The End of the American Future*. New York: Simon & Schuster.

Schuller, Gunther (1968). *Early Jazz: Its Roots and Musical Development*. New York: Oxford UP.

Scorsese, Martin, dir. (1977). *New York, New York*. MGM/United Artists.

Settle, Elizabeth A. and Thomas A. Settle (1982). *Ishmael Reed: A Primary and Secondary Bibliography*. Boston: G. K. Hall.

Serres, Michel (1982). *The Parasite*. Trans. Lawrence R. Schehr. Baltimore: Johns Hopkins UP.

Shaik, Fatima (1987). *The Mayor of New Orleans: Just Talking Jazz*. Berkeley: Creative Arts.

Shapiro, Nat and Nat Hentoff, eds. (1966). *Hear Me Talkin' to Ya*. Reprint of 1955 ed. New York: Dover.

Shattuck, Roger (1955). *The Banquet Years: The Origins of the Avant Garde in France, 1885 to World War I*. New York: Vintage.

Shell, Marc (1978). *The Economy of Literature*. Baltimore: Johns Hopkins UP.

Skvorecky, Josef (1977). *The Bass Saxophone: Two Novelas*. New York: Washington Square.

Smith, R. J. (1992). "Dixie Fried: Jim Dickinson's Memphis Productions." *The Village Voice Rock & Roll Quarterly*, Summer:16–23.

Spencer, Scott (1990). "The Titan of Jazz." *Rolling Stone*, December 13–27:148–56, 230.

Stowe, David W. (1994). *Swing Changes: Big-Band Jazz in New Deal America*. Cambridge: Harvard UP.

Swift, Jonathan (1960). *Gulliver's Travels and Other Writings*. Ed. Louis A. Landa. Boston: Houghton Mifflin.

Taylor, Paul, ed. (1988). "The Impresario of Do-It-Yourself." *Impresario: Malcolm McLaren and the British New Wave*. Cambridge: MIT P.

Terdiman, Richard (1985). *Discourse/CounterDiscourse: The Theory and Practice of Symbolic Resistance in Nineteenth-Century France*. Ithaca, N.Y.: Cornell UP.

Thompson, Robert Farris (1983). *Flash of the Spirit: African and Afro-American Art and Philosophy.* New York: Vintage.

Tolson, Melvin B. (1991). "Mu." In *The Jazz Poetry Anthology.* Ed. Sascha Feinstein and Yusef Komunyakaa. Bloomington: Indiana UP.

Tompkins, Jane (1988). "Fighting Words: Unlearning to Write the Critical Essay." *Georgia Review* 42:585–90.

Torgovnick, Marianna (1990). "Experimental Critical Writing." *Profession* 90:25–27.

Ulmer, Gregory L. (1980). "The Discourse of the Imaginary." *Diacritics* 10:61–75.

―――― (1983). "The Object of Post-Criticism." *The Anti-Aesthetic: Essays on Postmodern Culture.* Ed. Hal Foster. Port Townsend, Wash.: Bay Press.

―――― (1985). *Applied Grammatology: Post(e)-Pedagogy from Jacques Derrida to Joseph Beuys.* Baltimore: Johns Hopkins UP.

―――― (1989a). *Teletheory: Grammatology in the Age of Video.* New York: Routledge.

―――― (1989b). "Mystory: The Law of Idiom in Applied Grammatology." *The Future of Literary Theory.* Ed. Ralph Cohen. New York: Routledge.

―――― (1991). "The Euretics of Alice's Valise." *Journal of Architectural Education* 45:3–10.

―――― (1994). *Heuretics: The Logic of Invention.* Baltimore: Johns Hopkins UP.

Van Rooy, C. A. (1965). *Studies in Classical Satire and Related Literary Theory.* Leiden, Netherlands: E. J. Brill.

Van Vechten, Carl (1926). *Nigger Heaven.* New York: Knopf.

Walton, Ortiz (1972). *Music: Black, White and Blue.* New York: William Morrow.

Webb, Jack, dir. (1955). *Pete Kelly's Blues.* Warner Brothers.

White, Hayden (1973). *Metahistory: The Historical Imagination in Nineteenth-Century Europe.* Baltimore: Johns Hopkins UP.

Williams, Martin (1960). Liner notes to *Free Jazz.* Ornette Coleman. Atlantic.

―――― (1983). *The Jazz Tradition.* Oxford: Oxford UP.

Zinsser, William (1984). *Willie and Dwike: An American Profile.* New York: Harper & Row.

Zorn, John (1987). Notes to *Spillane/Two-Lane Highway/Forbidden Fruit.* Elektra/Nonesuch.

Zwerin, Mike (1990). "Sax and the Man." *Elle,* February:102–4.

Index

A

Aaron, Charles, 105
Aberrant reading, 71; and tropes, 4–5, 15
Adorno, Theodor, 3, 65
Affection, object of, 167–68, 184
Agréments, 62–63
Akiyoshi, Toshiko, 28
Album covers. *See* Record covers
Allegoresis, 2–4
Allegory, 181–82, 188, 203–205
Allen, Woody, 10
Allison, Mose, 185
Anderson, Laurie, 91, 195–96
Ansermet, Ernst-Alexandre, 40
Anti-story stories, 51
Archilochus, 143
Armstrong, Louis, 1, 5, 6, 66; as African American, 13; as castra-phobe, 11–12; as cyberwriter, 184; as deconstructer, 9–10; as ethnomusicologist, 14; as feminist, 11; as hipster, 14; as home-spun philosopher, 10–11; as ironic historian, 10; as itinerant musician, 12–13; as Lacanian, 13; as Marxist, 13; as metaphysical poet, 8; as modernist, 8; as phenomenologist, 7; as Saussurean, 7–8; as structuralist, 8–9; as zen master, 7
Art Ensemble of Chicago, 165
Assignments. *See Charivari; Obbligato; Rhapsody; Satura*
Autobiography, 55, 90, 183
Ayler, Albert, 164

B

Bailey, Derek, 71
Baker, Chet, 133, 135, 143
Baker, Dorothy, 49
Baldwin, James, 1, 161
Basie, Count, 66
Baraka, Imamu Amiri, 154. *See also* Jones, LeRoi
Barra, Allen, 27
Barthes, Roland, 48, 51, 126, 186–87; and Semiotic codes, 17–18, 153–54